CROCK POT

Cookbook for Beginners

1500+

Days of Amazing Mouthwatering
Crock-Pot Recipes

Easy and Tasty Everyday Slow Cooker
Recipes with Simple to Follow Instructions
for Beginners, **from Breakfast to Dessert**

ALEC POOLE

TABLE OF CONTENTS

INTRODUCTION

A Crock-Pot is a contemporary kitchen appliance that is used for cooking food in a traditional manner. The Crock-Pot, on the other hand, is much more than a piece of kitchen equipment. It alters your attitude toward eating and, as a result, your lifestyle. Consider the following scenario. You wake up feeling rested and ready to take on the day! Everything is in order; your delicious and excellent morning breakfast is ready. Of course, you do not have to envision this wonderful morning anymore!

With your crock cooker, it is feasible! There is no need to stay around the pot, stir your food, change the temperature, or do anything else. You simply put all of your favorite ingredients in your Crock-Pot the night before and set up this great kitchen appliance. Furthermore, many people believe that the meals are more savory and fuller in flavor than anything prepared on the burner. Crock-Pots are ideal for anyone who prefers to keep things simple in both life and the kitchen.

The majority of common recipes can be prepared in a Crock-Pot. Because liquid does not evaporate as quickly in a Crock-Pot as it does on the stove, you should only use half of the liquid recommended for in the original recipe. Unless you are cooking beans, rice, or pasta that absorbs liquid, use only two cups of chicken stock if the recipe calls for four.

There are different tasty recipes in this book for every meal of your day with easy-to-follow instructions. Let's begin your trip with a new technique of cooking that produces delightful, scrumptious and simple food with this cookbook.

Chapter 1: Basics of Crock-Pot

Cooking dinner when you are a busy parent of four is difficult. You can start dinner earlier in the day with my Crock-Pot, rather than later in the evening when everybody is tired & cranky.

The majority of Crock-Pot dishes may be prepared in 30 minutes or less, with many requiring only 10 to 15 minutes of active preparation time. When it is time for dinner, all that is left to do is serve a delectable home-cooked meal. Crock-Pot recipes are a practical way to cook, whether you will be out of the house all day or just want to make your meal ahead of time. Crock-Pot recipes range from soups & stews to roasts, pasta meals, and casseroles, and are a convenient method to serve your family. The best part is that at the conclusion of a long day, you will have a warm meal ready to serve. Below are all of the Crock-Pot fundamentals, as well as tips and tactics We have picked up through the years of using my Crock-Pot dozens of times. These Crock-Pot instructions will help you prepare the greatest make-ahead meals possible.

Basics of the Crock-Pot

1.1 What is the Crock-Pot?

A Crock-Pot is an electric device that cook food slowly over a long period of time, usually between 4 and 8 hours. Food is placed inside a stoneware insert within the Crock-Pot base to utilize it. The heat is dispersed evenly throughout the cooking pot, from the bottom to the sides. Always cook with the cover on the Crock-Pot to keep the heat trapped inside the

Crock-Pot as it cooks your meal.

1.2 Sizes of Crockpot

We recommend a 5 or 6-quart Crock-Pot if you are cooking for a family. The majority of Crock-Pot recipes have been tested in a 5 or 6-quart pot. A tiny Crock-Pot, such as a 3 quart or 4-quart, may be great for cooking for one or two people. You can halve recipes & cook them inside a smaller Crock-Pot, but the cook time may need to be reduced slightly.

1.3 Surprising Advantages of Hands-free Cooking

Whether you already possess a Crock-Pot or are considering purchasing one, you should be aware of the benefits of this kitchen appliance. Many chefs consider them "irreplaceable" in many classic recipes prepared by our forefathers.

For the Average Modern Family, the Crock-Pot is Ideal.

People nowadays work more than 40 hours every week. So, who has two hours to stand over the stoves and prepare meals for the entire family? You can now create all of your meals quickly and easily. Prepare a beautiful family salad, prepare traditional meals, plan a large-group dinner party, and wow your children with delicious nutritious snacks! Many busy women work multiple jobs and may not have time to prepare desserts for their children. The good news is that practically all of your favorite desserts can be made in the Crock-Pot, and you can satisfy your sweet desire with delicious Crock-Pot recipes. As a result, after reading this cookbook, you will realize that you can prepare your favorite foods in a much easier manner.

Delicious Budget Friendly Meals

The Crock-Pot, like any other slow cooker, is inexpensive to use & the meals are less expensive to prepare. There are several less expensive cuts of meat that are difficult to chew when cooked in a traditional manner, such as in the oven or on the stovetop. Meat softens naturally and effectively when cooked in a Crock-Pot. You may cook great meals while staying within your budget by using bone-in chicken thighs, beef sirloin, bone-in pork chops, and other inexpensive cuts of meat.

You Can Cook Whenever You Want Throughout the Year

For obvious reasons, many people avoid cooking during the summer. It is hot outside, and you would rather be outside! Unlike a stove or an oven, the Crock-Pot does not heat up the entire kitchen. Simply combine all of the ingredients in a Crock-Pot, set the temperature, then go out and enjoy yourself! Your Crock-Pot will not only save you money, but it will also save you time and energy. You may also use the fantastic Crock-Pot to free up your entire kitchen (pots, oven, stove, and so on) for other forms of cooking.

Simple is Preferable

The Crock-Pot is reverting to a simpler and healthy lifestyle. Manufacturers have enhanced technology features to make Crock-Pots easier to use over the years. As a result, the Crock-Pot is designed to provide delicious meals with minimal effort. Sure, you will feed even the pickiest eaters, and they will finish their meals! You can bring your Crock-Pot camping with you and enjoy delectable fresh meals all day, every day.

You Can Leave Your Crock-Pot Alone.

One of the most significant advantages of the powerful Crock-Pot is this! You can grab your favorite items, put them in the Crock-Pot, and go to night if you want a beautiful and hot cooked supper for tomorrow morning. Furthermore, you can leave your Crock-Pot filled with your favorite cuisine and go wherever you like. When you and your family return home, there will be a delicious lunch waiting for you. Dinner, desserts, and snacks are all the same. If you are throwing a huge party, it can be a real task and cause a lot of stress. You do not have to be concerned since you have your Crock-Pot.

1.4 Tips for the Better Crock-Pot Meals

This cookbook will teach you how to cook in a variety of styles, including roasting, poaching, baking, stewing, and braising. These recipes have been carefully chosen and designed to offer you with all of the information you need to master slow cooking. Here are some frequently asked questions, along with some additional tips.

How can you make your food the correct thickness?

There is a tip that always works if your dinner is cooked but too watery. Set the Crock-Pot to high & simmer for 10 minutes with the lid on.

For every cup of undesired liquid, combine 2 teaspoons flour & 1/4 cup of cold water. Stir for another 2 to 3 minutes. If you do not have fresh tomatoes and the recipe calls for tomato juice, you can substitute tomato paste instead of the tomato juice to make a denser sauce.

Is it necessary to stir the ingredients while they are cooking?

No. Do not bother stirring. You can stir items if the recipe specifies it. Because the Crock-Pot employs indirect heat, there is no risk of your favorite meal being burned.

Is there any kind of planning ahead of time?

The Crock-Pot is quite simple to operate. In any case, toss everything into your Crock-Pot & start cooking. It is preferable if you can brown the meat before cooking it, but it is not required.

Onions, garlic, mushrooms, and some vegetables are all in this category. In any case, just stick to the recipe and you will not go wrong. Root vegetables will take longer to cook than other veggies, so put them towards the bottom of the Crock-Pot.

Slow cooking might cause vital nutrients to be lost in vegetables. To avoid this, lightly sauté the vegetables before slow simmering.

Is this a healthy cooking method?

Yes. Because you do not need to add any fat or oil in most circumstances, this is a low-fat cooking method. Of course, you should trim the fat off the flesh and remove the skin from the bird. The majority of Crock-Pot recipes include veggies, nuts, seeds, legumes, & high-fiber foods, ensuring that you and your family consume nutritious meals.

There are different recipes in this handbook, ranging from appetizers, quick meals, & old-fashioned breakfast to magnificent sweets. You will be able to make a variety of scrumptious meat and vegetarian meals. As you can see, the Crock-Pot is not just for soups and stews, as many people believe. Cooking slowly will provide you with far more joy than you can think. The Crock-Pot & this cookbook will introduce you to the joys of cooking at home and motivate you to cook more frequently!

RECIPES

Chapter 2:
Crock-Pot Breakfast Recipes

1. Amazing Spiced Omelet

(Preparation time: 10 minutes | Cooking time: 2 hours | Servings: 4)

Per serving: Calories 537, Total fat 39g, Protein 36g, Carbs 11g

Ingredients:

- 1 teaspoon of dried basil
- 6 eggs
- 1/4 teaspoon of chili powder
- 1 medium-sized red onion, chopped
- 1/2 cup of whole milk
- Chives for the garnish
- 1 teaspoon of sea salt
- 1 teaspoon of dried thyme
- 1/4 teaspoon of freshly ground black pepper
- 1 cup of Cheddar cheese, shredded
- 1 teaspoon of dried oregano
- Olives for the garnish
- 1 small head of cauliflower, broken into florets
- 1 minced garlic clove

Instructions:

- Oil the interior of your Crock-Pot lightly.
- Whisk the eggs, milk, & spices together inside a mixing dish or measuring cup. Mix everything together till it is completely smooth.
- In a Crock-Pot, combine cauliflower florets, onions, & garlic. Place the seasoned egg mixture on top.
- Cover and simmer for around 2 hours on high, or till the eggs are set. Cover with shredded cheese and set aside till the cheddar cheese has melted.
- Serve the omelet in slices with chives & olives on the side.

2. Breakfast Delight

(Preparation time: 10 minutes | Cooking time: 4 hours | Servings: 4)

Per serving: Calories 345, Total fat 13g, Protein 2g, Carbs 49g

Ingredients:

- 1 chopped celery stalk
- 2 tablespoons of canola oil
- 1/4 teaspoon of dried thyme
- 1 cup of chopped scallions
- 1 ½ cups of water
- 1 minced garlic clove
- 1/3 cup of Parmesan cheese
- 2 medium-sized carrots, thinly sliced
- 1 cup of rinsed quinoa
- A pinch of ground black pepper
- 2 cups of vegetable stock
- Salt to taste
- 1 tablespoon of fresh cilantro
- 1/4 teaspoon of dried dill weed

Instructions:

- Heat canola oil inside a medium-sized skillet on medium flame.
- Five minutes, or till the vegetables are just soft, sauté carrots, scallions, garlic, and celery. Place the vegetables inside the Crock-Pot.
- Toss in the quinoa, cilantro, vegetable stock, water, dried thyme, black pepper, dill weed, and season using salt & pepper to taste.

- Cook for around 4 hours on LOW with the lid on. Serve immediately with a sprinkling of Parmesan cheese on top.

3. Banana Pecan Oatmeal

(Preparation time: 10 minutes | Cooking time: 8 hours | Servings: 4)
Per serving: Calories 264, Total fat 10g, Protein 4g, Carbs 41g

Ingredients:

- 1 cup of steel-cut oats
- 2 cups of water
- 1/2 teaspoon of cinnamon
- 2 ripe bananas
- A pinch of salt
- 1/4 cup of coarsely chopped pecans
- Honey to taste
- 2 cups of soy milk
- 1 teaspoon of pure almond extract

Instructions:

- Fill your Crock-Pot halfway with the water.
- Place the bowl inside an oven-safe bowl (glass casserole dish works well here).
- Use a fork to mash the bananas or a blender to puree them. Place in an oven-safe bowl.
- Toss in the remaining ingredients inside the bowl.
- Cook on low for around 8 hours.
- Before serving, give it a good stir and top using your favorite toppings. Enjoy!

4. Breakfast Sausage and Sauerkraut Sandwiches

(Preparation time: 10 minutes | Cooking time: 8 hours | Servings: 6)
Per serving: Calories 677, Total fat 62g, Protein 25g, Carbs 28g

Ingredients:

- 1 cup of sauerkraut
- 1/2 cup of chicken broth

- 6 hot dog buns
- Mustard for the garnish
- 6 fresh sausages of choice
- 1 teaspoon of caraway seeds
- 1 medium-sized onion, chopped
- Catsup for the garnish
- 1 small-sized apple, peeled, cored & thinly sliced
- 1/2 teaspoon of ground black pepper
- Salt to taste

Instructions:

- Cook sausage inside a nonstick medium pan on medium flame; drain & set aside.
- Combine garlic, onions, parsley, sweet bell pepper, jalapeno pepper, and cilantro in a medium-sized mixing dish. To blend, stir everything together thoroughly.
- Layers should be alternated. Inside the Crock-Pot, place 1/3 of the hash browns, sausage, onion mixture, & cheese. Layers should be repeated twice in the same way.
- Inside a separate dish, whisk together the remaining ingredients. Pour the ingredients into the Crock-Pot & evenly distribute it.
- Cook on low for around 8 hours or overnight, covered. Serve warm & enjoy.

5. Bacon and Veggie Quiche

(Preparation time: 10 minutes | Cooking time: 5 hours | Servings: 6)
Per serving: Calories 171, Total fat 6g, Protein 18g, Carbs 10g

Ingredients:

- 1 chopped green bell pepper
- Disposable Crock-Pot liner
- 1 teaspoon of granulated garlic
- 2 cups of whole milk
- 4 slices of bacon
- 1 tablespoon of olive oil
- 1 chopped red bell pepper
- 1/4 teaspoon of cayenne pepper
- 2 cups of chopped mushrooms

- 1 teaspoon of fine sea salt
- 1 cup of spinach
- 1/2 cup of biscuit mix
- 1 ½ cups of Swiss cheese, shredded
- 8 large-sized eggs
- 1 tablespoon of fresh basil
- 1/4 teaspoon of ground black pepper

Instructions:

- Use a disposable Crock-Pot liner to line your Crock-Pot.
- Cook bacon slices till crisp in a saucepan; drain & crumble.
- Warm the olive oil in the same saucepan on medium-low flame. Cook till the bell pepper & mushrooms are soft. Combine the spinach and Swiss cheese in a mixing bowl.
- Combine milk, eggs, cayenne pepper, granulated garlic, basil, salt, and black pepper inside a mixing bowl. This should be added to the mushroom mix in the pot.
- After that, fold in the biscuit mix. Transfer the prepared mix to the Crock-Pot from the saucepan. Scatter the bacon crumbles over top.
- Cover using a lid and cook for around 5 hours on low flame. Allow to cool slightly before serving, then divide among serving dishes.

6. Cereal with Peanut Butter and Fruit

(Preparation time: 10 minutes | Cooking time: 8 hours | Servings: 6)
Per serving: Calories 262, Total fat 12g, Protein 9g, Carbs 33g

Ingredients:

- 1/2 cup of basmati rice
- Peanut butter for the garnish
- 1/2 cup of wheat berries
- 4 cups of water
- 1/4 cup of brown sugar
- 1 cup of Irish-style oats

- 1/4 teaspoon of ground cinnamon
- 1 cup of dried fruit of choice

Instructions:

- Inside a crockpot, combine oats, wheat berries, sugar, cinnamon, basmati rice, and water; stir to incorporate.
- Cook for approximately 8 hours.
- Serve by dividing the mixture among six serving bowls & garnishing with dried fruit & peanut butter.

7. Cheesy Spinach Quiche

(Preparation time: 10 minutes | Cooking time: 3 hours | Servings: 6)
Per serving: Calories 513, Total fat 48g, Protein 23g, Carbs 24g

Ingredients:

- 1/2 cup of sharp cheese, shredded
- 1/2 teaspoon of cayenne pepper
- Non-stick cooking spray
- 1 ½ cups of evaporated milk
- 4 eggs
- 1/2 teaspoon of black pepper
- 3/4 cup of baby spinach
- 1/4 cup of chopped green onion
- 2-3 cloves of garlic, minced
- 2 slices of whole-grain bread, cubed
- 1/2 teaspoon of sea salt

Instructions:

- Spray your Crock-Pot lightly using cooking spray.
- Combine the eggs, onion, cheese, spinach, garlic, salt, cayenne pepper, black pepper, & evaporated milk inside a medium-sized mixing bowl. Stir till all ingredients are properly combined.
- Arrange the bread cubes in the Crock-Pot's bottom. Over the bread cubes, pour the egg-cheese mixture.
- Cover using a lid and cook on high for around 3 hours. Warm the dish before serving.

8. Crockpot Banana Bread Quinoa

(Preparation time: 10 minutes | Cooking time: 6 hours | Servings: 6)
Per serving: Calories 229, Total fat 9g, Protein 4g, Carbs 35g

Ingredients:

- 1 cup of quinoa
- ½ teaspoon of vanilla extract
- 1 cup of water
- 1 ½ tablespoon of melted butter
- ½ cup of low-fat milk
- ½ cup of seasonal warm cinnamon sugar cookie, like coffee-mate
- 1 ½ ripe banana
- 3 tablespoons of brown sugar
- 2 tablespoons of chopped walnuts

Instructions:

- Mash the bananas inside a bowl & set them aside. Combine the walnuts and brown sugar inside a separate bowl. Inside a crockpot, combine the light cream, butter, quinoa, vanilla, milk, and water. Combine the mashed banana and mix till it is uniformly distributed. Toss the quinoa with the walnuts and brown sugar and whisk to combine.
- Cook for around 4 to 6 hours, till the quinoa is thoroughly cooked, adding liquid & sugar as needed and to taste. Serve immediately using banana slices as a garnish.

9. Crock-Pot Peach Oatmeal

(Preparation time: 10 minutes | Cooking time: 4 hours | Servings: 4)
Per serving: Calories 147, Total fat 2g, Protein 4g, Carbs 29g

Ingredients:

- 2 tablespoons of organic honey
- ½ teaspoon of cinnamon
- 1 cup of oats, dry
- ¼ teaspoon of salt

- 1 Del Monte diced, yellow cling peaches inside the light syrup
- 1 tablespoon of butter spread
- ½ cup of peanuts or walnuts, chopped
- 2 cups of milk
- 2 tablespoons of brown sugar

Instructions:

- Combine all of the ingredients inside a medium-sized mixing bowl. Coat your crockpot using nonstick cooking spray, then pour in the oatmeal mixture & cover with the lid.
- Cook for around 4 hours on low, or till the oatmeal is done. It is worth noting that you can cook the oats on high for around two hours or slow cook it overnight for around eight hours. The key is to make sure the oatmeal is mushy when you serve it. Drizzle milk over it to serve.

10. Crockpot Sausage Cheddar Casserole

(Preparation time: 10 minutes | Cooking time: 8 hours | Servings: 10)
Per serving: Calories 272, Total fat 16g, Protein 11g, Carbs 21g

Ingredients:

- ¼ teaspoon of garlic powder
- 12 eggs
- 6 finely chopped green onions
- 1 teaspoon of salt
- 12 ounces of shredded sharp cheddar cheese
- Additional pepper & salt to taste
- 16 ounces of cooked & crumbled breakfast sausages
- ¼ cup of milk
- 32 ounces of shredded frozen Hash Brown
- ½ teaspoon of pepper

Instructions:

- Using nonstick cooking spray, coat the interior of your Crock-Pot. Layer a third of Hash Browns on the bottom. Season them using salt and black pepper.

- Place a third of the cooked sausage on top, followed by a third of the green onions & cheddar cheese. Repeat the stacking procedure two more times, finishing with the cheese.
- Whisk the eggs inside a large-sized mixing bowl. Combine the garlic powder, pepper, and milk in a mixing bowl.
- Cook on low for around 6 to 8 hours, or till the edges brown, after pouring this over the ingredients in the crockpot. If you do have any leftovers, keep them refrigerated for no longer than four days.

11. Chocolate Chip French Toast

(Preparation time: 10 minutes | Cooking time: 4 hours | Servings: 6)
Per serving: Calories 190, Total fat 5g, Protein 7g, Carbs 32g

Ingredients:

- 3/4 cup of packed brown sugar
- 1 pound of French bread that has been cut into 1 inch cubes
- 1 teaspoon of vanilla
- 3 eggs
- 1 cup of semisweet chocolate chips
- 1-1/2 cups of milk
- 1 teaspoon of cinnamon

Instructions:

- Put the French bread cubes inside the bottom of a Crock-Pot that has been sprayed using a nonstick spray.
- Inside a large-sized mixing dish, whisk together the milk and eggs.
- Combine the sugar, cinnamon, & vanilla.
- Overnight in the refrigerator, spoon the egg mixture over the bread, cover, & chill.
- Cover & cook on low for around 4 hours, or till chocolate chunks are melted.

12. Cinnamon Apple Oatmeal

(Preparation time: 10 minutes | Cooking time: 7 hours | Servings: 6)
Per serving: Calories 217, Total fat 4g, Protein 8g, Carbs 38g

Ingredients:

- 2 peeled, cored & diced apples
- 1-1/2 cups of coconut milk
- 1 teaspoon of cinnamon
- 1 cup of Steel Cut oats
- 1-1/2 cups of water
- 2 tablespoons of brown sugar
- Chopped nuts for the garnish
- 1 tablespoon of coconut oil
- 1/4 teaspoon of salt

Instructions:

- Using a nonstick spray, coat a Crock-Pot.
- Stir in all of the ingredients.
- Cook on low for around 5 to 7 hours and high for around 3 hours, covered.
- Before serving, sprinkle with the nuts.

13. Country Sausage and Cauliflower Breakfast

(Preparation time: 10 minutes | Cooking time: 6 hours | Servings: 8)
Per serving: Calories 600, Total fat 60g, Protein 20g, Carbs 20g

Ingredients:

- 1 cup of condensed cream of potato soup
- 1 tablespoon of fresh basil
- 1 pound of sausage
- 1 cup of carrots, sliced
- Non-stick spray
- 1 cup of whole milk
- 1/2 teaspoon of ground black pepper
- 1 teaspoon of dry mustard
- 1 cup of cauliflower, broken into florets
- Salt to taste
- 1/2 cup of Cheddar cheese, shredded

- 1 (28-ounces) package of frozen hash browns, thawed

Instructions:

- Brown the sausage inside a cast-iron skillet and cut it into bite-sized bits.
- Using a non-stick spray, coat the interior of the Crock-Pot. Combine all ingredients, except for the Cheddar cheese & gently toss to combine.
- Cover using a lid & cook on low for around 6 hours. Top with a sprinkling of Cheddar cheese. Allow 30 minutes to sit before serving.

14. Cocoa Oatmeal with Bananas

(Preparation time: 10 minutes | Cooking time: 8 hours | Servings: 4)

Per serving: Calories 414, Total fat 15g, Protein 15g, Carbs 37g

Ingredients:

- 1/2 teaspoon of ground cinnamon
- 3 cups of water
- 1/2 teaspoon of pure vanilla extract
- 1 cup of milk
- 4 tablespoons of cocoa powder, unsweetened
- 1 cup of steel-cut oats
- Chopped pecans for garnish
- 1 mashed banana
- 1 sliced banana

Instructions:

- Inside a Crock-Pot, combine the milk and water.
- Steel-cut oats, chocolate powder, cinnamon, mashed banana, and vanilla are then added.
- Set your Crock-Pot on low and simmer for around 8 hours or overnight.
- Stir just before serving; divide amongst serving bowls; top with banana & pecans then serve.

15. Chili Mushroom Omelet

(Preparation time: 10 minutes | Cooking time: 4 hours | Servings: 4)

Per serving: Calories 363, Total fat 26g, Protein 24g, Carbs 6g

Ingredients:

- 1 chili pepper, minced
- 2 cloves of garlic, minced
- 1 tablespoon of fresh cilantro
- 1/4 teaspoon of cayenne pepper
- Non-stick cooking spray
- 8 eggs, beaten
- 1 sliced green onion
- 1/4 teaspoon of ground black pepper
- 2 cups of sliced mushrooms
- 1 teaspoon of salt
- 2 ripe tomatoes, sliced

Instructions:

- Put all of the ingredients inside your Crock-Pot.
- Cook on low for around 3 to 4 hours, covered.
- Cut into wedges & serve with sour cream & tomato ketchup while still warm.

16. Cheese Steak Sandwiches

(Preparation time: 10 minutes | Cooking time: 8 hours | Servings: 8)

Per serving: Calories 654, Total fat 28g, Protein 30g, Carbs 40g

Ingredients:

- 1 cup of beef stock

- 2 tablespoons of dry red wine
- 1 pound of thinly sliced round steak
- 1/4 teaspoon of ground black pepper
- 1 cup of onions, sliced
- 1 teaspoon of celery seeds
- 1 green bell pepper, sliced
- 1 cup of shredded mozzarella cheese
- 1 clove of minced garlic
- 1 tablespoon of Worcestershire sauce
- 1/2 teaspoon of salt
- 8 hamburger buns

Instructions:

- Inside a Crock-Pot, place the sausages. Place the caraway seeds, onion, sauerkraut, apple, salt, chicken broth, and black pepper.
- Cook on low for around 6 to 8 hours, covered. Make sandwiches with the buns and catsup and mustard on the side.

17. Country Smoked Sausages

(Preparation time: 10 minutes | Cooking time: 6 hours | Servings: 6)
Per serving: Calories 700, Total fat 60g, Protein 19g, Carbs 20g

Ingredients:

- 1 sliced yellow bell pepper
- 1 tablespoon of extra-virgin olive oil
- 4 crushed garlic cloves
- 1/2 teaspoon of ground black pepper
- 6 sliced green onions
- 1 (28-ounces) can of tomatoes, diced
- 1 sliced red bell pepper
- Mustard for the garnish
- 1 teaspoon of salt
- 2 pounds of smoked sausage
- 1/2 teaspoon of crushed red pepper flakes

Instructions:

- Heat olive oil inside a large-sized skillet on medium flame. Sauté garlic, onions, bell peppers, and sausages till the veggies are soft, and the sausages are lightly browned. Place inside the Crock-Pot.

- Toss in the tomatoes, along with the salt, black pepper, & red pepper flakes. Cook for around 6 hours on low. Serve with mustard of your choice.

18. Coconut Maple Granola

(Preparation time: 10 minutes | Cooking time: 3 hours | Servings: 6)
Per serving: Calories 181, Total fat 3g, Protein 3g, Carbs 37g

Ingredients:

- 2 tablespoons of chia seeds
- 1/4 cup of maple syrup
- 1 cup of coconut flakes
- 1 cup of slivered almonds
- 1 teaspoon of ground cinnamon
- 2 tablespoons of canola oil
- 1 cup of hulled sunflower seeds
- A pinch of salt
- 1 cup of chopped dried cherries
- 1/4 teaspoon of ground cloves
- 1 teaspoon of pure vanilla extract
- 3 cups of rolled oats

Instructions:

- Inside a Crock-Pot, combine cinnamon, maple syrup, canola oil, sunflower seeds, chia seeds, coconut flakes, salt, vanilla essence, and rolled oats.
- Cook for around 3 hours, stirring once in a while. Allow 15 minutes for the granola to cool before adding the almonds & dried cherries. Stir till all of the ingredients are properly combined.
- To cool completely, spread onto a baking sheet.

19. Cheesy Rosemary Bread

(Preparation time: 10 minutes | Cooking time: 2 hours | Servings: 8)
Per serving: Calories 138, Total fat 4g, Protein 4g, Carbs 21g

Ingredients:

- 1 cup of grated Parmesan cheese
- 1 medium-sized loaf of bread
- 6 tablespoons of butter, room temperature
- 1 tablespoon of fresh rosemary

Instructions:

- Mix together the Parmesan cheese, butter, and fresh rosemary till everything is completely combined.
- Make 8 slices from a loaf of bread. Spread the rosemary-cheese mixture on both sides of the bread slices.
- Wrap bread slices using aluminum foil to keep them warm.
- Place inside your Crock-Pot & simmer for around 2 hours on low flame. Allow cooling for around 5 minutes after removing the cover.

20. Caramel-Flavored Banana Bread

(Preparation time: 10 minutes | Cooking time: 2 hours | Servings: 8)
Per serving: Calories 312, Total fat 12g, Protein 4g, Carbs 49g

Ingredients:

- 2 medium-sized eggs
- 1 teaspoon of baking powder
- 4 tablespoons of butter, melted
- 1⁄4 teaspoon of salt
- 3⁄4 cup of brown sugar
- 1⁄4 cup of applesauce
- 1 tablespoon of water
- 1 ¾ cups of all-purpose flour
- 1 tablespoon of milk
- 3 ripe bananas, mashed
- 1⁄4 cup of almonds, coarsely chopped
- 1 teaspoon of baking soda

Instructions:

- Inside a mixing bowl, cream together the butter, milk, applesauce, eggs, water, and brown sugar until smooth and creamy. Combine the baking soda, mashed bananas, flour, baking powder, and salt. Add the almonds and mix well. Pour the batter into a loaf pan that is suited for it.
- Then, in your Crock-Pot, set this baking pan onto a rack. Cook for around 3 hours on high with the lid on, or till a toothpick (or knife) placed in the middle comes out clean.
- Remove the banana bread out from the loaf pan and set it aside to cool.

21. Creamy Oatmeal with Berries

(Preparation time: 10 minutes | Cooking time: 8 hours | Servings: 4)
Per serving: Calories 307, Total fat 10g, Protein 10g, Carbs 49g

Ingredients:

- 1 cup of coconut water
- 1 cup of oats
- 1 pinch of salt
- 1/2 teaspoon of allspice
- 1/4 cup of brown sugar
- 2 cups of water
- 1 pinch of grated nutmeg
- Berries of choice for garnish
- 1 pinch of ground cinnamon
- 1 cup of half-and-half cream

Instructions:

- Just before going to bed, combine all ingredients (excluding the berries) in your Crock-Pot.
- Set the Crock-Pot at low and leave it to cook all night.
- Serve heated with your favorite berries or a variety of fruit.

22. Cranberry Coconut Steel Cut Oatmeal

(Preparation time: 10 minutes | Cooking time: 6 hours | Servings: 8)
Per serving: Calories 208, Total fat 12g, Protein 10g, Carbs 41g

Ingredients:

- 2 cups of coconut water
- 1/2 teaspoon of ground cinnamon
- 2 cups of steel-cut oats
- 1/4 cup of snipped apricots
- 4 cups of water
- 1/2 cup of almonds, chopped
- 1/4 cup of dried cranberries
- 1 tablespoon of brown sugar
- Shredded coconut for the garnish
- 1/2 teaspoon of salt

Instructions:

- Combine oats, water, cinnamon, coconut water, almonds, sugar, & salt inside a Crock-Pot.
- Cook for around 6 hours on low flame with the lid on.
- Serve warm with cranberries, apricots, & coconut on top of each serving.

23. Deluxe Breakfast Beef Sandwiches

(Preparation time: 10 minutes | Cooking time: 3 hours | Servings: 12)
Per serving: Calories 199, Total fat 7g, Protein 24g, Carbs 10g

Ingredients:

- 1 cup of mushrooms, thinly sliced
- 2 pounds of lean ground beef
- 1 tablespoon of tomato catsup
- 1 chopped red bell pepper
- Salt and black pepper, to taste
- 1 chopped green bell pepper
- 1/2 cup of fried turkey bacon, crumbled
- 1 chopped yellow onion
- 1 cup of cubed processed cheese
- 2 minced cloves of garlic
- 12 sandwich buns, toasted
- 3/4 cup of tomato paste
- 2 tablespoons of dry red wine

Instructions:

- Cook the ground beef, bell peppers, and onion inside a large-sized skillet

on medium flame till the meat is browned and the onion is transparent. Transfer to a Crock-Pot.
- Cook on low flame for around 3 hours, adding the additional ingredients except for the sandwich bread.
- Serve on the sandwich buns with salad and mustard on the side.

24. Easy-to-make Date Granola

(Preparation time: 10 minutes | Cooking time: 3 hours | Servings: 6)
Per serving: Calories 417, Total fat 17g, Protein 8g, Carbs 63g

Ingredients:

- 1/4 teaspoon of grated nutmeg
- 1/4 cup of honey
- 1 teaspoon of vanilla extract
- 6 tablespoons of applesauce
- 3 cups of rolled oats
- 1/4 teaspoon of cardamom
- 1 cup of Medjool dates, pitted & chopped
- 1/4 teaspoon of ground cloves
- 1 tablespoon of hemp seeds
- 1 teaspoon of ground cinnamon
- 1 cup of walnuts, toasted & chopped
- A pinch of salt
- 1/2 teaspoon of maple extract

Instructions:

- Inside a Crock-Pot, combine honey, nutmeg, applesauce, cardamom, cloves, vanilla extract, cinnamon, salt, and maple extracts. Toss in the hemp seeds and toss to mix.
- Combine the rolled oats & walnuts. To blend, stir everything together.
- Cook on high for around 3 hours, slightly venting the cover. Stir once in a while. Allow cooling for a few minutes before adding the sliced dates.
- Place the granola on a baking sheet to cool completely before storing it in sealed containers.

25. Easy Cheesy Quinoa with Veggies

(Preparation time: 10 minutes | Cooking time: 3 hours | Servings: 4)

Per serving: Calories 280, Total fat 23g, Protein 7g, Carbs 34g

Ingredients:

- 1 cup of sliced button mushrooms
- 1 heaping tablespoon of fresh cilantro
- 2 tablespoons of melted margarine
- 1 cup of rinsed quinoa
- 1 medium-sized chopped onion
- 1 ½ cups of water
- 1 minced garlic clove
- A pinch of ground black pepper
- 1 sweet red bell pepper
- 1/3 cup of Parmesan cheese
- 2 cups of vegetable broth
- 1 heaping tablespoon of fresh parsley
- Salt to taste
- 1/4 teaspoon of crushed red pepper flakes

Instructions:

- Melt margarine inside a medium-sized skillet on medium flame.
- Inside a heated buttered skillet, sauté onions, mushrooms, garlic, and red bell pepper for around 6 minutes, or till just soft. Use a Crock-Pot instead.
- Turn the Crock-Pot on low and cook for roughly 3 hours, with the exception of the Parmesan cheese.
- Top with Parmesan cheese & serve immediately.

26. Easy Crockpot Breakfast Casserole

(Preparation time: 10 minutes | Cooking time: 6 hours | Servings: 8)

Per serving: Calories 206, Total fat 22g, Protein 18g, Carbs 7g

Ingredients:

- ½ cup of chopped onions
- ¼ cup of milk
- 1 or 2 chopped green or red peppers
- 1 pound of any breakfast meat of your choice, cooked
- 1 can of green chilies
- A dozen eggs
- 4 scrubbed, rinsed and diced to small cubes russet potatoes
- Grated cheese
- Salt & pepper to taste

Instructions:

- Use a nonstick cooking spray to coat the crockpot. Arrange the diced potatoes first, then a pinch of salt & pepper. Following that, layer the meat and veg. The green chilies come next, followed by the cheese. Repeat the layering process twice more, but do not add cheese to the second layer.
- Inside a medium-sized mixing bowl, whisk together the pepper, eggs, milk, and salt. Pour this combination over the crockpot's layers.

- Cook for around 5 to 6 hours on low. Drain any fluid from the top of the dish before serving and sprinkle using shredded cheese. Cook for a few minutes and then serve.

27. Eggs Florentine with Oyster Mushroom

(Preparation time: 10 minutes | Cooking time: 2 hours | Servings: 4)
Per serving: Calories 279, Total fat 23g, Protein 16g, Carbs 4g

Ingredients:

- 1 cup of Swiss chard
- Non-stick spray
- 1 peeled and diced small onion
- 1 cup of light cream
- 2 cups of shredded Monterey Jack cheese
- 1 cup of oyster mushroom, sliced
- 1/4 teaspoon of ground black pepper
- 2 to 3 crushed garlic cloves
- 5 large-sized eggs
- Salt to taste

Instructions:

- Use non-stick spray to coat the interior of the Crock-Pot. 1 cup of Monterey Jack cheese should be spread across the bottom of your Crock-Pot.
- The spinach should then be placed on top of the cheese.
- After that, layer the oyster mushroom on top. Garlic & onion should be placed on top of the mushroom layer.
- Combine the eggs and additional ingredients inside a measuring cup or mixing dish. Pour this combination over the Crock-Pot's layers.
- The remaining 1 cup of cheese should be sprinkled on top.
- Preheat your Crock-Pot at high, cover, and simmer for around 2 hours.

28. Family Mid-Winter Porridge

(Preparation time: 10 minutes | Cooking time: 9 hours | Servings: 8)
Per serving: 465, Total fat 15g, Protein 13g, Carbs 61g

Ingredients:

- 1 cup of raisins
- 7 cups of water
- 1/2 teaspoon of ginger
- 1/8 teaspoon of grated nutmeg
- 2 cups of steel-cut Irish oats
- 1 cup of dried cherries
- 1 teaspoon of lemon zest
- 1/2 vanilla bean
- 1 cup of dried cranberries
- 1 tablespoon of shredded coconut
- 1 teaspoon of allspice
- 1/4 cup of honey

Instructions:

- Inside a Crock-Pot, combine all ingredients & cook on low.
- Cook for around 8 to 9 hours or overnight.
- Stir the porridge the next day and divide it among eight serving dishes. If preferred, top with a dollop of the whipped cream & roasted nuts.

29. Herbed Chili Cornbread

(Preparation time: 10 minutes | Cooking time: 2 hours | Servings: 8)
Per serving: Calories 368, Total fat 15g, Protein 12g, Carbs 47g

Ingredients:

- 1 teaspoon of dried basil
- 3/4 cup of all-purpose flour
- 1 teaspoon of baking soda
- 1/2 teaspoon of dried oregano
- 1/4 cup of cornmeal
- 1 tablespoon of sugar
- 1 large-sized egg, beaten
- 1 teaspoon of baking powder
- 1 teaspoon of ground cumin

- 1/2 teaspoon of salt
- 1/4 poblano pepper, cooked and minced
- 1/2 cup of buttermilk
- 1/4 cup of whole kernel corn

Instructions:

- Inside a large-sized mixing bowl, combine the first 10 ingredients.
- Combine the buttermilk, poblano, and corn. To blend, stir everything together thoroughly.
- Place the dough inside a baking pan that has been greased & floured.
- Then, in your Crock-Pot, set this baking pan onto a rack. Cook for about 2 hours on high flame with the lid on.
- Allow for a 10-minute cooling period before serving.

30. Muesli with Coconut and Peanuts

(Preparation time: 10 minutes | Cooking time: 2 hours | Servings: 12)
Per serving: Calories 300, Total fat 14g, Protein 6g, Carbs 40g

Ingredients:

- 1 cup of wheat germ
- 4 cups of rolled oats
- 1 teaspoon of almond extract
- 4 cups of water
- 1/2 cup of brown sugar
- 1 teaspoon of allspice
- 1 cup of baking natural bran
- 1/4 teaspoon of turmeric
- Peanuts for the garnish
- 1/2 cup of shredded coconut, unsweetened
- 4 tablespoons of melted butter
- 2 tablespoons of pumpkin seeds

Instructions:

- Toss all of the ingredients into the Crock-Pot, except for the peanuts.
- Cover using a lid and cook for around 2 hours on high flame, stirring twice.

- Serve by dividing the mixture among 12 serving bowls and topping using chopped peanuts.

31. Mouth-Watering French Toast Casserole

(Preparation time: 10 minutes | Cooking time: 5 hours | Servings: 8)
Per serving: Calories 450, Total fat 9g, Protein 17g, Carbs 77g

Ingredients:

- 6 large-sized eggs
- 1 cup of half-and-half
- 2 bread loaves, cut into bite-sized cubes
- 1/4 teaspoon of ground cloves
- 3 tablespoons of melted butter
- 1 teaspoon of lemon zest
- 1 ½ cups of milk
- 1 cup of brown sugar
- 1 teaspoon of pure almond extract
- 2 cups of slivered almonds
- 1/4 teaspoon of grated nutmeg
- 1 teaspoon of ground cinnamon

Instructions:

- Use nonstick spray or melted butter to grease your Crock-Pot.
- Preheat oven at 225°F. Place the prepared bread cubes on a baking sheet and bake for around 30 minutes, or till completely dry.

- Inside the bottom of the Crock-Pot, place the bread cubes.
- Lemon zest, almond extract, eggs, milk, cloves, half-and-half, nutmeg, and cinnamon should all be combined. Inside the Crock-Pot, pour this mix over the bread cubes.
- Combine the butter, brown sugar, and almonds inside a separate small-sized bowl. In your Crock-Pot, mix everything together.
- Set the Crock-Pot on low, cover, & simmer for around 5 hours.
- If preferred, top with fruits & maple syrup.

32. Melt-In-Your-Mouth French Toast

(Preparation time: 10 minutes | Cooking time: 5 hours | Servings: 8)
Per serving: Calories 127, Total fat 3g, Protein 5g, Carbs 20g

Ingredients:

For the French Toast:

- 1 tablespoon of almond extract
- 1 cup of almonds, coarsely chopped
- 12-ounces of loaf bread of choice
- 3 eggs
- 1/4 teaspoon of turmeric powder
- 2 cups of whole milk
- 1/4 teaspoon of ground nutmeg
- 1/2 cup of brown sugar
- 2 bananas, sliced
- 1/4 teaspoon of allspice
- 1 teaspoon of ground cinnamon
- 3 tablespoons of melted unsalted butter

For the Sauce:

- 1/2 cup of butter
- 1 teaspoon of almond extract
- 1/2 cup of brown sugar
- 2 tablespoons of corn syrup
- 1/2 cup of half-and-half cream

Instructions:

- Preheat oven at 300°F. Use a disposable crockery liner to line a Crock-Pot.

- Arrange the bread cubes into a single layer inside a baking pan. Bake the bread for around 15 minutes, or till golden brown. Then, add the bread cubes to the Crock-Pot that has been prepared.
- Whisk together sugar, whole milk, eggs, turmeric, almond extract, nutmeg, allspice, and cinnamon inside a large-sized mixing dish. In the Crock-Pot, pour this spicy mixture over the bread cubes. To wet the bread cubes, press them down using a spoon.
- Toast the almonds inside a small-sized non-stick skillet for a few minutes. Combine toasted almonds and melted butter. Pour this mixture over the Crock-Pot's ingredients.
- Cook for roughly around 5 hours on low flame with the lid on. Remove the crockery liner from the French toast and set it aside.
- Prepare the sauce next. Cook the sauce ingredients inside a medium-sized pot over medium-high flame. Bring to the boil, then reduce to a low flame and simmer for another 3 minutes.
- The prepared sauce can be left at room temperature or refrigerated. Spoon the sauce over the French toast and serve with banana slices.

33. Nutty Banana Frittata

(Preparation time: 10 minutes | Cooking time: 6 hours | Servings: 6)
Per serving: Calories 344, Total fat 15g, Protein 8g, Carbs 46g

Ingredients:

- 1 cup of cream cheese
- 1 tablespoon of canola oil
- 10 large eggs
- 1 cup of half-and-half
- 1 loaf of bread, cut into cubes
- 2 ripe bananas
- A pinch of salt
- 1 cup of almonds, coarsely chopped
- 1/4 cup of maple syrup

Instructions:

- Canola oil should be used to grease the inside of the Crock-Pot.
- 1/2 of the bread cubes should be placed in the bottom of the Crock-Pot. After that, equally distribute half of the cream cheese.
- Place 1 banana slice on top of the cream cheese. After that, put half of the chopped almonds on top.
- One more time, repeat the layers.
- Whisk together the half-and-half, eggs, maple syrup, & salt inside a mixing dish or measuring cup; pour over the layers inside the Crock-Pot.

- Refrigerate for at least 12 hours before serving. After that, cover & cook for around 6 hours on low. If desired, top with a few additional bananas.

34. Nutella French Toast Casserole

(Preparation time: 10 minutes | Cooking time: 3 hours | Servings: 4)
Per serving: Calories 296, Total fat 13g, Protein 11g, Carbs 39g

Ingredients:

- 2 bananas, sliced
- 3 large eggs
- 1 teaspoon of vanilla extract
- ½ loaf of challah bread, cut into cubes
- 2 tablespoons of Nutella + extra for the topping
- ½ tablespoon of brown sugar
- 1 cup of vanilla-flavored almond milk
- ½ teaspoon of ground cinnamon
- A pinch of salt
- ½ tablespoon of unsalted butter

Instructions:

- Inside the Crock-Pot, place the bread cubes. In a dish, whisk together the eggs, salt, milk, cinnamon, vanilla, & Nutella, then pour over the bread cubes inside the Crock-Pot. Mix thoroughly. Cook at high for around 2 hours or low for around 4 hours, covered. If at all feasible, stir in the middle.
- In the meantime, heat a nonstick skillet on medium-high flame. Toss in the butter. When the butter has melted, add the banana & brown sugar and stir to combine. Cook till both sides of the bananas are light brown.
- To serve, spoon a small amount of Nutella mixture onto each serving plate. Place a few bananas on top of it. Serve with a dollop of Nutella on top.

35. Overnight Sausage Casserole

(Preparation time: 10 minutes | Cooking time: 8 hours | Servings: 10)
Per serving: Calories 356, Total fat 26g, Protein 21g, Carbs 8g

Ingredients:

- 1 thinly sliced sweet bell pepper
- 1 1/2 cups of shredded sharp cheese
- 1 jalapeño pepper
- 1/2 teaspoon of salt
- 1 ½ cups of spicy sausage
- 1/4 teaspoon of cayenne pepper
- 1 heaping tablespoon of fresh cilantro
- 1 chopped red onion
- 1 (30-ounces) package of hash brown potatoes, shredded and thawed
- 2 crushed garlic cloves
- 1 teaspoon of dry mustard
- 1/4 cup of fresh parsley
- 12 eggs
- 1/8 teaspoon of pepper
- 1 cup of milk
- 1 teaspoon of celery seeds

Instructions:

- Cook sausage inside a nonstick medium pan on medium flame; drain & set aside.
- Combine garlic, onions, parsley, sweet bell pepper, jalapeno pepper, and cilantro in a medium-sized mixing dish. To blend, stir everything together thoroughly.
- Layers should be alternated. Inside the Crock-Pot, place 1/3 of the hash browns, sausage, onion mixture, & cheese. Layers should be repeated twice in the same way.
- Inside a separate dish, whisk together the remaining ingredients. Pour the ingredients into the Crock-Pot & evenly distribute it.
- Cook on low for around 8 hours or overnight, covered. Serve warm & enjoy.

36. Overnight Western Omelet

(Preparation time: 10 minutes | Cooking time: 12 hours | Servings: 12)
Per serving: Calories 320, Total fat 24g, Protein 20g, Carbs 6g

Ingredients:

- 1 pound of sliced cooked ham
- 1 red bell pepper, seeded and diced
- 2 pounds of hash brown potatoes
- 1 teaspoon of sea salt
- 1 cup of spinach
- 2 cloves of minced garlic
- 1 yellow onion, diced
- 10 eggs
- 1/4 teaspoon of chili powder
- 1 cup of shredded Gouda cheese
- 1 ½ cup of milk
- 1/4 teaspoon of ground black pepper

Instructions:

- Spray your Crock-Pot lightly using nonstick cooking spray.
- In your crock cooker, alternate layers. Place 1/3 of the hash brown potatoes, 1/3 of the spinach, 1/3 of the cooked ham, 1/3 of the garlic, 1/3 of the onion, and 1/3 of the bell pepper on top of the spinach.
- Repeat layers two more times using shredded Gouda cheese on top.
- Combine the remaining ingredients inside a large-sized mixing bowl. Fill the Crock-Pot halfway with the mixture.
- Cover with a lid and cook for around 10 to 12 hours on low flame. Serve alongside bread & mustard.

37. Orange Poppy Seed Bread

(Preparation time: 10 minutes | Cooking time: 2 hours | Servings: 12)
Per serving: Calories 268, Total fat 16g, Protein 3g, Carbs 29g

Ingredients:

- 1 tablespoon of baking soda

- Non-stick cooking spray
- 1/2 cup of canola oil
- 1/4 cup of poppy seeds
- 2 cups of flour, all-purpose of choice
- 1 teaspoon of orange zest
- 1 tablespoon of honey
- 3/4 cup of brown sugar
- 1/2 cup of sour cream
- 1/2 teaspoon of kosher salt
- 1 teaspoon of vanilla extract
- 3 large-sized eggs
- 1/4 cup of whole milk
- 1/4 cup of fresh orange juice

Instructions:

- Using nonstick cooking spray, coat a Crock-Pot.
- Combine flour, poppy seeds, and baking soda inside a mixing dish and set aside.
- Combine honey, canola oil, orange juice, sugar, salt, eggs, orange zest, sour cream, whole milk, and 1 teaspoon of vanilla extract inside a separate bowl. Combine the orange juice and poppy seeds in a mixing bowl. Combine all ingredients in a Crock-Pot and set aside.
- Cook for roughly around 2 hours on high, covered.
- Allow it to cool completely before serving, then serve with fresh orange juice.

38. Pumpkin Blueberry Bread

(Preparation time: 10 minutes | Cooking time: 5 hours | Servings: 6)
Per serving: Calories 146, Total fat 5g, Protein 3g, Carbs 23g

Ingredients:

- 1 cup of half and half
- 1 teaspoon of salt
- 3 teaspoons of pumpkin pie spice
- 1 ½ cups of canned pumpkin
- 1 ½ cups of fresh blueberries
- 1 cup of pecans, chopped and toasted
- 4 cups of all-purpose flour

- Cooking spray
- 4 teaspoons of baking powder
- 1 cup of maple syrup
- 4 tablespoons of packed brown sugar
- ½ cup of cold butter, cubed
- Disposable Crock-Pot liner
- 4 tablespoons of melted butter
- 2 tablespoons of all-purpose flour for dusting

Instructions:

- Use a disposable liner to line your Crock-Pot. Set aside after spraying using cooking spray. Inside a mixing dish, combine the half-and-half, pumpkin, and brown sugar. Mix thoroughly and set aside. Combine baking powder, flour, pumpkin pie spice, and salt inside a separate large-sized mixing dish. Using a pastry blender, chop the butter into small pieces. Transfer the pumpkin combination into the flour mixture and stir till everything is thoroughly mixed.
- Toss the blueberries in a bowl using 2 tablespoons of flour. Toss the berries in with the flour mixture and toss thoroughly. Fold in half carefully. Fill the Crock-Pot halfway with the ingredients. Overtop it with maple syrup & melted butter. Pecans should be sprinkled on top. Cook at high for around 2 to 2 1/2 hours or low for around 4 to 5 hours, covered. When the bread is done, carefully remove the lid so that water droplets do not fall on the bread. Allow cooling. Remove from the pot, slice, & serve.

39. Philly Inspired Cheese Sandwich

(Preparation time: 10 minutes | Cooking time: 6 hours | Servings: 8)
Per serving: Calories 588, Total fat 23g, Protein 36g, Carbs 74g

Ingredients:

- 1/4 cup of Worcestershire sauce

- 2-1/2 pounds of boneless beef chuck pot roast
- 1 teaspoon of dried oregano
- 1 cup of peeled and chopped onion
- 1/2 teaspoon of dried thyme
- Slices of Provolone cheese
- 1/2 cup of beef broth
- 2 peeled and minced cloves of garlic
- 1 cup of pickled peppers
- 1/2 teaspoon of dried basil

Instructions:

- Remove the fat out from the pot roast before slicing it into thin slices. Inside a Crock-Pot that has been sprayed using nonstick spray, place the strips.
- Inside the Crock-Pot, combine the onion, Worcestershire sauce, beef broth, and all of the herbs. If using bell peppers, add them now as well. If you are using the pickled peppers, put them on the side for now.
- Cook on low for around 10 to 12 hours or high for around 5 to 6 hours, covered. To keep the meat from sticking together, stir it occasionally. If using, add the pickled peppers during the last 30 minutes of cooking.
- Broil the hoagie buns till they are golden brown. Remove them & top with the meat combination and a few slices of Provolone cheese. Return to the broiler till the cheese has melted, then serve.

40. Pumpkin-Almond Bread

(Preparation time: 10 minutes | Cooking time: 4 hours | Servings: 16)
Per serving: Calories 355, Total fat 16g, Protein 5g, Carbs 50g

Ingredients:

- 2 cups of all-purpose flour
- 1/4 teaspoon of grated nutmeg
- 1 cup of pumpkin, canned
- A pinch of salt

- 4 tablespoons of melted margarine
- 2 medium-sized eggs, beaten
- 1 teaspoon of baking soda
- 1/2 cup of granulated sugar
- 1/2 cup of milk
- 1 teaspoon of baking powder
- 1/2 cup of almonds, chopped and toasted
- 1 teaspoon of pumpkin pie spice

Instructions:

- Combine pumpkin, margarine, and sugar inside a large-sized mixing bowl till well combined; toss in milk and eggs.
- Combine flour, baking powder, pumpkin pie spice, baking soda, nutmeg, and salt; stir in chopped almonds.
- Fill a loaf pan halfway with the batter and place it inside the Crock-Pot. Cook for around 3 hours and 12 minutes on high. Place the pumpkin bread on a wire rack to cool. Enjoy with honey on top!

41. Restaurant Style Hash Browns

(Preparation time: 10 minutes | Cooking time: 8 hours | Servings: 10)
Per serving: Calories 334, Total fat 19g, Protein 5g, Carbs 37g

Ingredients:

- 1 minced jalapeño pepper
- 1 cup of Cheddar cheese
- 1 (32-ounces) bag of hash brown potatoes
- 1/2 teaspoon of ground black pepper
- 1 pound of cooked turkey bacon
- 12 eggs
- 3 cloves of crushed garlic
- 1 teaspoon of dried thyme
- 1 cup of spring onions, diced
- 1 cup of whole milk
- 1 teaspoon of salt

Instructions:

- Alternate the layers in your Crock-Pot as follows: 1/2 of hash browns, 1/2 of bacon, 1/2 of jalapeno peppers, 1/2 of garlic, 1/2 of onions, and 1/2 of cheese.

- Next, put 1/2 hash browns, 1/2 bacon, 1/2 jalapeno peppers, 1/2 garlic, 1/2 onions, 1/2 cheese in the following order.
- Combine milk, black pepper, egg, salt, and thyme inside a mixing bowl. Fill the Crock-Pot halfway with this mixture.
- Cook for around 8 hours on low or overnight.

42. Super Greens and Bacon Casserole

(Preparation time: 10 minutes | Cooking time: 2 hours | Servings: 6)
Per serving: Calories 297, Total fat 12g, Protein 22g, Carbs 28g

Ingredients:

- 1/2 cup of sliced bacon
- 1 cup of low-fat sharp cheese, shredded
- 1/2 teaspoon of kosher salt
- 1 cup of leafy greens (such as kale, spinach, Swiss chard)
- 1 cup of mushrooms, sliced
- 3 slices of bread, cubed
- 1 cup of vegetable broth
- 1/4 teaspoon of cayenne pepper
- 6 eggs
- 1 medium-sized onion
- 1/4 teaspoon of black pepper
- 1 cup of evaporated milk

Instructions:

- Half of the cheese should be spread onto the bottom of your Crock-Pot.
- Add a layer of leafy greens on top. After that, place half of the bacon on top.
- Place the bread cubes first, followed by the mushrooms.
- Add the leftover bacon and the remaining cheese to the top.
- Combine the remaining ingredients inside a measuring cup or mixing dish.
- Fill the Crock-Pot halfway with this mixture.
- Cook on a high heat setting for around 2 hours.

- Enjoy by dividing the mixture among six serving plates.

43. Sausage Mushroom Omelet Casserole

(Preparation time: 10 minutes | Cooking time: 3 hours | Servings: 4)

Per serving: Calories 503, Total fat 49g, Protein 33g, Carbs 7g

Ingredients:

- 1 cup of chopped scallions
- 1/2 teaspoon of dry mustard
- 1 pound of chicken breast sausage, sliced
- 1 cup of whole milk
- 1 cup of sliced mushrooms
- 1/2 cup of Swiss cheese, grated
- 1 teaspoon of sea salt
- 4 medium-sized eggs
- 1/4 teaspoon of ground black pepper
- 1/2 teaspoon of granulated garlic

Instructions:

- Inside a Crock-Pot, arrange the sausages.
- Then, on top of the sausages, scatter onions & mushrooms.
- Whisk together the eggs, milk, & spices inside a mixing dish.
- To combine the ingredients, whisk them together.
- Cook for around 3 hours on low flame.
- Then, on top of that, spread the cheese and let it melt.
- Serve with mayonnaise & mustard on the side.

44. Summer Granola with Seeds

(Preparation time: 10 minutes | Cooking time: 2 hours | Servings: 16)

Per serving: Calories 120, Total fat 7g, Protein 4g, Carbs 12g

Ingredients:

- 1 cup of sunflower kernels
- 6 cups of oats, old-fashioned
- 1/2 cup of canola oil
- 1 cup of pumpkin seeds
- 1/2 teaspoon of kosher salt
- 1/2 cup of chopped dried figs
- 2 tablespoons of orange juice
- 1 cup of chopped dried pineapple
- 1 cup of maple syrup

Instructions:

- Combine oats, sunflower kernels, pumpkin seeds, and salt inside a Crock-Pot.
- Inside a small mixing bowl, whisk together orange juice, oil, & maple syrup till well combined. Add this to the oat mixture and stir well. Cook for roughly around 2 hours, covered, on high flame, tossing every 20 minutes.
- Remove the granola from the flame and set it aside to cool. Stir in the dried figs & pineapple till everything is well combined.
- Place the prepared granola onto a baking sheet & evenly distribute it. Before storage, allow cooling fully.

45. Spiced Apple Bread Pudding

(Preparation time: 10 minutes | Cooking time: 3 hours | Servings: 8)

Per serving: Calories 123, Total fat 4g, Protein 4g, Carbs 18g

Ingredients:

- 3/4 cup of packed brown sugar
- 4 medium-sized apples, cored and chopped
- 1 teaspoon of ground cinnamon
- 3 cups of bread, cubed

- 1/2 teaspoon of ground cloves
- 3 large-sized eggs
- 2 (12 fluid ounces) cans of evaporated milk
- 1/4 teaspoon of allspice
- 1 teaspoon of nutmeg

Instructions:

- Inside a Crock-Pot, combine apples with bread cubes.
- Inside a mixing dish, whisk the eggs till they are foamy. Mix in the other ingredients till well combined.
- Inside the Crock-Pot, pour the prepared egg mix over the apples and bread.
- Cook for around 4 hours on high flame, or till custard forms.

46. Tropical Overnight Oatmeal

(Preparation time: 10 minutes | Cooking time: 8 hours | Servings: 8)
Per serving: Calories 434, Total fat 16g, Protein 8g, Carbs 57

Ingredients:

- 1 tablespoon of fresh orange juice
- 2 cups of steel-cut Irish oats
- 1/4 cup of dried mango
- 4 cups of water
- 2 tablespoons of coconut flakes
- 1 cup of apple juice
- 1/2 cup of dried pineapple
- A pinch of salt
- 1/2 cup of dried papaya
- 1/4 cup of maple syrup

Instructions:

- Inside your Crock-Pot, add all of the ingredients.
- Cover using a lid and set aside for around 7 to 8 hours or overnight.
- Garnish with a dab of whipped cream or milk. Enjoy!

47. Tater Tot Breakfast Casserole

(Preparation time: 10 minutes | Cooking time: 8 hours | Servings: 8)
Per serving: Calories 395, Total fat 29g, Protein 20g, Carbs 17g

Ingredients:

- 1 cup of green onions, chopped
- 3 tablespoons of all-purpose flour
- 1 (30-ounces) package of tater tots
- 1/4 teaspoon of cayenne pepper
- 1 cup of bacon
- 12 eggs
- 1 teaspoon of kosher salt
- 2 cups of sharp cheese, shredded
- 1 cup of whole milk
- 1/4 teaspoon of ground black pepper

Instructions:

- Put 1/3 of the tater tots, 1/3 of the bacon, 1/3 of the green onions, & 1/3 of the shredded cheeses inside a greased Crock-Pot. Rep these layers twice more, finishing with the cheese.
- Whisk together the other ingredients inside a large-sized mixing dish before adding to the Crock-Pot.
- Cook for around 6 to 8 hours on low, covered inside the Crock-Pot.

48. Vanilla Blueberry Quinoa

(Preparation time: 10 minutes | Cooking time: 6 hours | Servings: 6)
Per serving: Calories 381, Total fat 6g, Protein 14g, Carbs 69g

Ingredients:

- 2 cups of blueberries
- 4 cups of vanilla-flavored almond milk
- 1/3 cup of flax seeds
- 4 cups of water
- 1/4 teaspoon of grated nutmeg
- 2 cups of quinoa
- 1/3 cup of brown sugar
- 1/4 teaspoon of ground cinnamon

Instructions:

- Inside a Crock-Pot, combine all of the ingredients.
- Cook on low for around 8 hours or overnight, covered with a lid.

49. Winter Morning Sausage and Vegetables

(Preparation time: 10 minutes | Cooking time: 6 hours | Servings: 6)

Per serving: Calories 223, Total fat 11g, Protein 4g, Carbs 28g

Ingredients:

- 1 sweet green bell pepper
- Non-stick spray
- 1 cup of whole milk
- 1/2 teaspoon of black pepper
- 3/4 pound of highly-spiced sausage
- 1 large-sized onion
- 2 pounds of frozen hash browns, thawed
- 1/2 teaspoon of chili powder
- 1 sweet red bell pepper, chopped
- 1 cup of vegetable or beef broth
- Sea salt to taste
- 1/2 cup of Cheddar cheese, shredded

Instructions:

- Use non-stick spray to coat the inside of your Crock-Pot.
- Cook the sausage inside a medium-sized skillet for around 10 minutes, or till it is browned. Transfer to a Crock-Pot.
- Except for the Cheddar cheese, stir in the remaining ingredients.
- Cook for around 6 hours on low inside the Crock-Pot.
- Scatter On top, there is a layer of cheddar cheese. Serve warm and enjoy.

50. Yummy Spiced Pumpkin Frittata

(Preparation time: 10 minutes | Cooking time: 6 hours | Servings: 6)

Per serving: Calories 458, Total fat 28g, Protein 29g, Carbs 26g

Ingredients:

- 1 cup of cream cheese
- 8 eggs
- 1/4 teaspoon of grated cardamom
- 2 tablespoons of coconut oil, melted
- 1 teaspoon of pumpkin spice
- 2 bananas, sliced
- 1 loaf of bread, cut into small-sized cubes
- 1 cup of pumpkin, shredded
- 2 tablespoons of raw honey
- Powdered sugar for the garnish
- 1 cup of walnuts, coarsely chopped
- 1 cup of half-and-half
- 1/2 teaspoon of ground cinnamon
- 1/2 teaspoon of allspice

Instructions:

- Coconut oil should be used to coat the inside of your Crock-Pot.
- 1/2 of the bread should be placed inside the Crock-Pot. Place 1/2 of the cream cheese on top of it.
- After that, equally distribute 1/2 of the shredded pumpkin. 1 banana slice should be placed on top of the pumpkin. 1/2 of the chopped walnuts should be strewn over the bananas.
- One more time, repeat the layers.
- Beat the eggs with the remaining ingredients, except for the powdered sugar, inside a medium-sized mixing dish. Spread this mixture over the Crock-Pot's layers.
- Cook on a low flame setting for around 6 hours, covered. Serve your frittata dusted with the powdered sugar.

Chapter 3:
Crock-Pot Chicken Recipes

1. Artichoke Chicken and Rice

(Preparation time: 10 minutes | Cooking time: 6 hours | Servings: 6)

Per serving: Calories 450, Total fat 13g, Protein 67g, Carbs 34g

Ingredients:

- 1 teaspoon of paprika
- 1 to 1 1/2 pounds of chicken breasts halves
- 4 chopped green onions
- 1/4 cup of flour
- 1 can low-fat cream of celery soup
- 3 tablespoons of Parmesan cheese
- 1/2 teaspoon of coarsely ground pepper
- 2 tablespoons of olive oil
- 1 1/2 cups of converted rice
- 1 teaspoon of salt
- 1/4 cup of chopped red bell pepper or pimiento
- 4 ounces of mushrooms, sliced
- 1 can of artichokes, quartered and drained
- 1 1/2 cups of chicken broth

Instructions:

- Heat the olive oil inside a large skillet on medium flame.
- Combine flour, pepper, cheese, salt, and paprika.

- Chicken should be dredged in flour and then browned inside the hot oil.
- Place the chicken inside a crockpot. Sauté bell pepper, green onions, & mushrooms inside a heated skillet for around 2 minutes; add the chicken broth & soup, stirring well to blend; pour over chicken. Stir in the rice and artichokes, then cover and simmer on low for around 5 to 6 hours.

2. Asian-Style Chicken

(Preparation time: 10 minutes | Cooking time: 7 hours | Servings: 4)

Per serving: Calories 209, Total fat 11g, Protein 14g, Carbs 16g

Ingredients:

- 1/4 cup of Hoisin sauce
- 1 medium piece of fresh ginger root, about 2 inches, peeled & thinly sliced or grated
- 1/4 cup of plum sauce
- 3 lbs. of chicken thighs or leg quarters
- Juice of 1 whole fresh lime
- 1/4 cup of low sodium soy sauce
- 3 tablespoons of corn starch

Instructions:

- If desired, remove the skin off the bird. Inside a large-sized mixing bowl or food storage bag, whisk together the hoisin sauce, lime, plum sauce, soy sauce, ginger, and corn-starch. Place the chicken pieces and toss well to coat. Inside a Crock-Pot, combine the chicken and marinade.
- Cook for around 5 to 7 hours on LOW, till chicken is cooked and juices flow clear. Serve with steaming rice.
- Serve & enjoy.

3. Betty's Garlic Chicken with Cabbage

(Preparation time: 10 minutes | Cooking time: 6 hours | Servings: 4)

Per serving: Calories 184, Total fat 14g, Protein 15g, Carbs 26g

Ingredients:

- 1 head cabbage
- 1 whole chicken
- Salt and pepper to taste
- 1 medium onion chopped
- Pepper
- 3 to 8 garlic cloves
- 2 tablespoons of butter

Instructions:

- Place the chicken inside the Crock-Pot after seasoning it. Season using salt & pepper and add the onion and garlic cloves. Fill Crock-Pot 1/4 full with water, cover, and cook for around 4 to 5 hours on HIGH. The chicken should be falling off the bone tender.
- 1 head of green cabbage, core removed, chopped up during the last hour of cooking the chicken Place the cabbage inside a large-sized pot with just enough water to cover it, roughly around 1/2 to 1 cup.
- Add 2 tablespoons of butter & season with garlic, salt and pepper to taste. Cook for around 20 to 30 minutes, covered, on a medium-high flame, till tender; drain.
- Place some cabbage inside a bowl and top with the chicken and part of the chicken broth when the chicken and cabbage are done. Any of the seasonings, as well as the butter, can be changed.

4. Beverly's Creamy Broccoli Chicken

(Preparation time: 10 minutes | Cooking time: 8 hours | Servings: 8)
Per serving: Calories 470, Total fat 25g, Protein 36g, Carbs 23g

Ingredients:

- 1 bag (12 to 16 ounces) of frozen broccoli
- 1 can (approx. 10 1/2 ounces) of condensed Cream of Broccoli Soup
- 1 cup of milk
- 3 pounds of boneless chicken breasts
- Salt and black pepper

Instructions:

- Inside the Crock-Pot, place the chicken pieces. Cover with the frozen broccoli and serve with a dollop of cream of broccoli soup on the top. Season to taste with salt and pepper.
- Cook on LOW for around 6 to 8 hours or HIGH for around 3 to 4 hours, covered. (If boneless chicken breasts are cooked for too long, they may get dry.) Add the milk 45 minutes before the end of the cooking time, or 30 minutes if the cooking is on a high.
- Pour over rice & serve!

5. Buffalo Chicken Meatballs

(Preparation time: 30 minutes | Cooking time: 4 hours | Servings: 3)
Per serving: Calories 374, Total fat 11, Protein 18g, Carbs 21g

Ingredients:

- 7 ounces of lean chicken or turkey, ground
- 1 egg
- 1/8 teaspoon of pepper
- 2 tablespoons of coconut milk
- 1/4 cup of Parmesan cheese
- 1 slice of sandwich bread
- 1/8 teaspoon of cayenne pepper
- 1/2 teaspoon of salt, divided

For the Sauce:

- 1/8 teaspoon of cayenne pepper
- 1/4 cup of honey
- Dash of salt
- 1 clove of garlic, minced
- 1/4 teaspoon of black pepper
- 1 teaspoon of olive oil
- 1/2 teaspoon of paprika
- 1/2 cup of hot sauce
- 1/2 teaspoon of chili powder
- 1/2 (4 ounces) can of diced green chilies
- 1/2 small green onions, diced

Instructions:

- Preheat your oven at 450°F and prepare a baking sheet using aluminum foil.
- Then, inside a small-sized dish, soak the bread in milk. Combine the meat, egg, salt, & the soaked bread inside a separate bowl. To make a compact mixture, mix everything together thoroughly.
- To make the meatballs, take a tablespoon of meat & roll it between your palms, then place them on a baking sheet and bake for about 6 minutes.
- Heat the olive oil over a medium-low flame before adding the garlic and onions to produce the sauce. Sauté till the onions are transparent, about 5 minutes.
- Add the garlic, onions, and other ingredients. Whisk till the mixture is completely smooth.
- Fill the Crockpot with enough meatballs to fill the bottom, then pour in 1/2 of the sauce. Add the remaining meatballs and sauce to the pan.
- Cover and cook on low for around 2 to 4 hours, or till the balls are cooked through.

6. Chicken & Artichoke Casserole

(Preparation time: 10 minutes | Cooking time: 8 hours | Servings: 8)
Per serving: Calories 450, Total fat 13g, Protein 67g, Carbs 14g

Ingredients:

- 1 to 2 tablespoons of butter
- 1/4 pound of sliced mushrooms
- 3 to 4 pounds of chicken pieces
- 3 tablespoons of dry white wine
- Salt & pepper
- 1 tablespoon of cornstarch blended with 1 tablespoon of cold water
- 1/2 teaspoon of paprika
- 1 teaspoon of chicken bouillon granules, dissolved in 1/2 cup of hot water
- 1 can (15 ounces) of artichoke hearts, drained
- 1/2 teaspoon of dried tarragon

Instructions:

- Rinse the chicken & pat it dry. Season using paprika and salt, and black pepper. Brown the chicken inside a large-sized skillet with about 1/2 of the butter. Place inside a Crock-Pot. Inside a skillet, combine the broth with wine. To loosen brown bits, stir.
- Pour the sauce over the chicken and season with the tarragon.
- Cook on LOW for around 6 to 8 hours, covered. Sauté mushrooms in the remaining butter till soft and browned just before serving. Preheat the Crock-Pot on high.
- Stir in the cornstarch & water mixture once the sauce is heated and boiling. Cook till the sauce has thickened. Heat through the sautéed mushrooms & artichoke hearts.
- Serve & enjoy.

7. Chicken & Cornmeal Dumplings

(Preparation time: 10 minutes | Cooking time: 7 hours | Servings: 8)
Per serving: Calories 189, Total fat 7g, Protein 16g, Carbs 13g

Ingredients:

- 1/2 cup of chopped onion
- 2 cups of cubed and cooked chicken
- 1 (12 oz.) can of tomato juice (around 1 1/2 cups)
- 1 1/4 cups of packaged biscuit mix
- 2 cups of diced potatoes
- 1 teaspoon of chili powder
- 1 1/2 cups of chicken broth
- 2 tablespoons of finely chopped fresh parsley
- 1/2 cup of sliced celery
- 4 to 6 drops of Tabasco sauce
- 2/3 cup of milk
- 1/2 teaspoon of salt
- 1 1/2 to 2 cups of frozen cut green beans, thawed
- 1/3 cup of yellow cornmeal

- 1 cup of shredded Cheddar cheese

Instructions:

- Inside a Crock-Pot, combine the vegetable juice, potatoes, chicken broth, celery, salt, onion, chili powder, and hot pepper sauce. Cook on LOW for around 4 hours, covered. Heat on HIGH till bubbling, then add the thawed green beans & diced chicken. Combine cornmeal, biscuit mix, 1/2 cup of shredded cheese, & parsley or chives inside a mixing basin. Stir in the milk till it is just moistened. Cover & drop by tablespoons into the stew.
- Cook for an additional 2 hours & 30 minutes without raising the lid. 5 minutes before they are done, top the dumplings with remaining shredded cheese.

8. Chicken and Green Onion Curry

(Preparation time: 10 minutes | Cooking time: 7 hours | Servings: 8)

Per serving: Calories 472, Total fat 40g, Protein 27g, Carbs 14g

Ingredients:

- 1/2 teaspoon of ground cumin
- 1 thinly sliced medium onion
- Dash of ground cloves
- 1/2 cup of chicken broth
- 3 medium cloves of garlic, minced
- 1 tablespoon of fresh ginger root, grated
- 3 1/2 pounds of chicken pieces, skin removed
- Chopped fresh cilantro for the garnish
- 1 cinnamon stick
- 1 teaspoon of curry powder
- 1/2 teaspoon of crushed red pepper flakes
- 2 tablespoons of cornstarch, blended with 2 tablespoons of cold water
- 1/4 teaspoon of ground cardamom
- 1/2 teaspoon of ground turmeric
- 1/4 to 1/2 cup of green onions, with tops, sliced
- Salt

Instructions:

- Combine the thinly sliced onion, cumin, garlic, cinnamon, ginger, cloves, red pepper flakes, turmeric, and cardamom inside a Crock-Pot.
- Place the chicken pieces on top of the onion mixture. Over the chicken, pour the broth. Cover and simmer on LOW for around 6 to 7 hours, or till the chicken is extremely soft & juices run clear once pierced.
- Carefully transfer the chicken to a hot serving dish & keep it warm.
- If necessary, skim & discard fat from the cooking liquid; remove and discard the cinnamon stick.
- Combine cornstarch and cold water, then stir into the cooking liquid.
- Increase the heat setting on the cooker to high; cover & cook till the sauce thickens, stirring 2 or 3 times.
- Season using salt and pour the sauce over your chicken.
- Serve with cilantro & chopped green onions as garnish.

9. Chicken and Mushrooms

(Preparation time: 10 minutes | Cooking time: 3 hours | Servings: 6)

Per serving: Calories 398, Total fat 30g, Protein 28g, Carbs 4g

Ingredients:

- 2 teaspoons of chicken bouillon granules
- 1/2 cup of dry white wine
- 6 chicken breast halves, bone-in, skin removed
- 1 1/4 teaspoon of salt
- Minced fresh parsley
- 1/4 teaspoon of pepper
- 2/3 cup of evaporated milk
- 1/4 teaspoon of paprika
- 1/2 cup of sliced green onions

- Hot cooked rice
- 1 1/2 cups of sliced mushrooms
- 5 teaspoons of cornstarch

Instructions:

- Combine salt, pepper, & paprika inside a small-sized bowl. All of the ingredients should be rubbed into the chicken.
- Alternate layers of chicken, mushrooms, bouillon granules, and green onions inside a Crock-Pot. Pour the wine over the top. Stirring is not recommended.
- Cook for around 2 1/2 to 3 hours on HIGH or around 5 to 6 hours on LOW, or till chicken is cooked but not falling off the bone. If possible, baste one around midway through the cooking process.
- Using a slotted spoon, transfer the chicken and veggies to a dish.
- Keep warm by wrapping inside a foil.
- Combine together evaporated milk & cornstarch inside a small pot and whisk till smooth. Take 2 cups of cooking liquid and stir in gradually. Bring to the boil, constantly stirring on medium flame, for around 1 to 2 minutes, or till thickened.
- Spoon some of the sauce over the chicken and sprinkle with the parsley, if desired. Serve the rest of the sauce on the side.
- Serve with the steaming rice.

10. Chicken Breasts in Creamy Creole Sauce

(Preparation time: 10 minutes | Cooking time: 7 hours | Servings: 4)
Per serving: Calories 225, Total fat 5g, Protein 30g, Carbs 12g

Ingredients:

- 3 tablespoons of butter
- 1 to 2 tablespoons of tomato paste
- 1 bunch of green onions (6 to 8, with most of the green part)
- 1/4 to 1/2 cup of half and half or milk
- 2 slices of bacon
- 4 tablespoons of flour

- 1 teaspoon of Creole or Cajun seasoning
- 3/4 cup of chicken broth
- 4 boneless chicken breast halves

Instructions:

- Melt the butter inside a saucepan over a low flame. Cook & stir for around 2 minutes after adding the onions and bacon. Cook for 2 minutes more after adding the flour and stirring it in. Cook till the stock has thickened, then add the tomato paste. Inside a Crock-Pot, place the chicken breasts and the sauce mixture. Cook on low for around 6–7 hours, stirring once after 3 hours. Around 20 to 30 minutes before the end of the cooking time, stir in the milk. Serve over rice or pasta.
- Serve & enjoy.

11. Chicken Burritos

(Preparation time: 10 minutes | Cooking time: 2 hours | Servings: 6)
Per serving: Calories 219, Total fat 10g, Protein 11g, Carbs 20g

Ingredients:

- 6 flour tortillas
- 1/2 cup of minced onion
- 2 cups of chopped cooked chicken
- 1 can (16 ounces) of refried beans
- optional garnishes: diced avocados, sour cream, sliced green onions, shredded cheese, diced tomatoes, and sliced ripe olives
- 1 packet (1 ounce) of burrito seasoning mix
- 3 plum of tomatoes, diced
- Salsa, green or tomato, for the serving
- 8 ounces of shredded Cheddar Jack

Instructions:

- Toss the chopped chicken with the seasoning mix to coat it completely.
- Divide the refried beans evenly among the Six tortillas and spread them out. Season using salt & pepper, then top with shredded cheese, diced tomatoes, &

minced onions. Roll them up. Wrap each tortilla in foil and layer inside a crockpot. Cook for around 2 hours on HIGH, covered.
- Serve with the salsa and toppings of your choosing.

12. Chicken Cacciatore

(Preparation time: 10 minutes | Cooking time: 8 hours | Servings: 4)
Per serving: Calories 520, Total fat 28g, Protein 35g, Carbs 21g

Ingredients:

- 8 ounces of fresh sliced mushrooms
- 1 sliced thinly large onion
- 1/2 teaspoon of basil
- 2 cloves of garlic minced
- 1 1/2 pounds of skinless and boneless chicken breast halves
- 1/4 cup of dry white wine
- 1 teaspoon of oregano
- 2 (6 oz. each) cans of tomato paste
- 1/2 teaspoon of salt
- 1/4 cup of water
- 1/4 teaspoon of pepper
- 1 bay leaf

Instructions:

- Inside the bottom of the Crock-Pot, place sliced onion; top with the chicken breast halves. The remaining ingredients should be combined and stirred together.
- Spread the sauce all over the chicken.
- Cook on low for around 6 to 8 hours, or high for around 3 to 4 hours. Serve with hot cooked spaghetti or equivalent pasta as a sauce.

13. Chicken Chow Mein

(Preparation time: 10 minutes | Cooking time: 9 hours | Servings: 6)
Per serving: Calories 380, Total fat 7g, Protein 24g, Carbs 55g

Ingredients:

- 4 thinly sliced medium carrots
- 1 to 2 tablespoons of vegetable oil
- 1/3 cup of light soy sauce
- 1 cup of low sodium chicken broth
- 1 medium clove garlic, crushed
- 1/4 cup of cornstarch
- 1/4 teaspoon of crushed red pepper flakes
- 1 1/2 pounds of boneless chicken breasts, skin removed, cut into 1-inch cubes
- 1 can (8 ounces) of bean sprouts
- 6 to 8 green onions, sliced, including green
- 1 1/2 cups of sliced celery
- 1 tablespoon of granulated sugar
- 1/3 cup of water
- 1/4 teaspoon of ground ginger
- 1 can (8 ounces) of sliced water chestnuts

Instructions:

- Inside a skillet, heat the oil & brown the chicken, flipping to brown each side. Place the chicken pieces inside the Crock-Pot. With the exception of cornstarch and water, combine all ingredients. Cook on low for around 6 to 8 hours, covered.
- Increase to the maximum. Inside a small-sized bowl, combine cornstarch and cold water; stir till smooth & cornstarch is dissolved. Stir into the liquids in the Crock-Pot. Cook on HIGH for around 15 to 30 minutes, keeping the cover slightly ajar to let steam to escape.
- Serve with rice or Chinese noodles on the side.

14. Chicken Cordon Bleu

(Preparation time: 10 minutes | Cooking time: 7 hours | Servings: 6)
Per serving: Calories 427, Total fat 20g, Protein 40g, Carbs 21g

Ingredients:

- 1/4 cup of dry white wine
- 4 boneless chicken breast halves
- 4 slices of Swiss cheese

- 1 can (10 1/2 ounces) of condensed golden mushroom soup
- 4 thin slices of ham
- 1/2 cup of water

Instructions:

- Between the sheets of plastic wrap, pound chicken breasts till thin and even in the thickness.
- On every chicken breast half, place 1 slice of ham and 1 piece of cheese.
- Roll up & place inside the Crock-Pot's bottom.
- Combine 1/4 cup of dry white wine, 1/2 cup of golden mushroom soup, and 1/2 cup of water. Combine all ingredients and pour over the chicken in a Crock-Pot.
- Cook on low for around 6 to 7 hours, covered.
- Serve with the rice or noodles as a side dish.

15. Chicken Divan with Broccoli and Noodles

(Preparation time: 10 minutes | Cooking time: 7 hours | Servings: 6)
Per serving: Calories 186, Total fat 8g, Protein 15g, Carbs 12g

Ingredients:

- 1/3 cup of mayonnaise
- 3 cups of cooked, diced chicken
- 2 celery ribs, sliced
- 1 tablespoon of lemon juice
- 2 tablespoons of chopped onion
- 1 (10 oz.) pkg. frozen broccoli cuts, around 1 1/2 to 2 cups
- 1 (10 3/4 oz.) can cream of chicken soup
- 3 tablespoons of flour
- 1 pound of pasta or noodles
- 1/2 teaspoon of curry powder, or to taste

Instructions:

- Combine all ingredients (excluding noodles) inside a medium-sized mixing

bowl. To properly combine the components, stir them together.

- Pour the ingredients into a Crock-Pot that has been lightly greased. Cook on LOW for around 5 to 7 hours or HIGH for around 2 1/2 to 3 1/2 hours, covered.
- Cook the pasta according to package directions under boiling salted water when the chicken & broccoli combination is nearly done. Over hot buttered noodles or spaghetti, serve.

16. Chicken Lasagna

(Preparation time: 20 minutes | Cooking time: 6 hours | Servings: 6)
Per serving: Calories 555, Total fat 24g, Protein 37g, Carbs 46g

Ingredients:

- 6 to 9 lasagna noodles
- 1 can of cream of mushroom soup
- 2 large chicken breast halves, boneless
- 1/2 teaspoon of thyme
- 1 package (1 ounce) of dry chicken gravy mix
- 2 ribs of celery chopped
- 1 package of frozen spinach, thawed & squeezed dry
- 1 can of tomatoes with green chilies
- salt and black pepper to taste
- 3/4 cup of reserved broth
- 6 ounces of fresh mushrooms, thickly sliced
- 1 small onion, chopped
- 1 1/2 cups of shredded Cheddar

Instructions:

- Cook chicken breasts with salt, celery, onion, thyme, and pepper in a 2-quart pot till cooked, around 25 minutes. Remove the chicken and set it aside to cool before cutting it into bite-size pieces or shredding it. 3/4 cup broth should be set aside. Alternatively, you can discard the excess broth or freeze it to use in another dish. Break lasagna noodles into half and boil for around 5 to 8 minutes, or till they are just slightly flexible. To make handling easier, drain & rinse with cold water.
- Combine the soup, tomatoes, gravy mix, and saved broth inside a medium-sized mixing dish. Pour 3/4 cup of the soup mixture into a Crock-Pot. 4 to 6 lasagna noodle halves should be placed on top of the soup mixture. Combine 1/3 of the spinach, 1/3 of the chicken, 1/3 of the mushrooms, and 1/2 cup of shredded cheese. Pour the remaining 3/4 cup of soup mixture over everything. Continue layering two more times, finishing with the leftover soup mixture. Cook on low for around 4 to 5 hours, covered. The noodles may turn mushy if cooked for too long, so check after 4 1/2 hours.

17. Chicken with Bacon and Wine

(Preparation time: 20 minutes | Cooking time: 8 hours | Servings: 4)
Per serving: Calories 459, Total fat 21g, Protein 25g, Carbs 22g

Ingredients:

- 1 1/2 cups of sliced green onions
- 4 to 5 chicken breasts & thighs
- 8 ounces of small whole mushrooms
- 1/4 teaspoon of pepper
- 1 cup of chicken broth
- Chopped parsley for the garnish
- 8 bacon slices, diced
- 16 small new potatoes, scrubbed
- 1 to 2 tablespoons of each, water and flour
- 8 small white onions peeled

- 2 teaspoons of salt
- 2 medium potatoes, quartered
- 3 cloves of garlic, crushed & minced
- 1 teaspoon of dried thyme leaves
- 1 cup of dry red wine

Instructions:

- Cook diced bacon and green onions inside a large pan till bacon is crisp. Remove and drain them onto paper towels. Cook the chicken pieces in the skillet till they are golden brown on all sides. Remove the browned chicken from the pan and set it aside. Inside a crockpot, combine the mushrooms, onions, potatoes, and garlic. Add the browned chicken pieces, salt, bacon, thyme, green onions, pepper, and chicken broth together. Cook on LOW for around 6 to 8 hours or HIGH for around 3 to 4 hours, covered.
- One hour before the end of the cooking time, add the wine. Transfer the chicken to a serving plate. Thicken fluids with a mixture of 1 to 2 tablespoons flour and cold water if required. Arrange the vegetables around the chicken, then pour the liquids over everything. Serve with chopped parsley as a garnish.

18. Chicken with Biscuits

(Preparation time: 20 minutes | Cooking time: 7 hours | Servings: 6)
Per serving: Calories 654, Total fat 35g, Protein 39g, Carbs 42g

Ingredients:

- 1/4 teaspoon of poultry seasoning
- 1 1/2 to 2 pounds of boneless chicken breast halves, cut in large chunks
- 2 cups of frozen mixed vegetables, thawed
- 1 can (10 3/4 ounces) of condensed cream of chicken soup, undiluted
- 1/2 cup of chopped onion
- Dash black pepper
- 6 frozen biscuits
- 1 cup of chopped celery

- 1 jar (12 ounces) of chicken gravy
- 1/2 teaspoon of dried leaf thyme

Instructions:

- Layer the uncooked chicken breasts with the chopped onion & celery inside a Crock-Pot.
- Pour the soup & gravy over the chicken, along with thyme, poultry spice, and pepper.
- Cook on LOW for around 5 to 6 hours, covered.
- Turn the Crock-Pot to HIGH and add the thawed mixed veggies. Cook for another 20 to 30 minutes, or till the vegetables are soft.
- Meanwhile, bake the biscuits according to the package directions.
- Split a biscuit in half, then spoon some of the chicken and veggies on the bottom side to serve. Cover the chicken and gravy with the top half of the biscuit.

19. Chicken with Garlic and Pineapple

(Preparation time: 20 minutes | Cooking time: 6 hours | Servings: 6)
Per serving: Calories 419, Total fat 4g, Protein 29g, Carbs 49g

Ingredients:

- 1 clove of minced garlic
- 3 1/2 pounds of chicken
- 4 ounces of sliced water chestnuts, drained
- Salt and black pepper
- 1/4 cup of soy sauce
- 1/4 teaspoon of ground ginger
- 1 cup of chicken broth
- 1/4 cup of cornstarch
- 8 1/2 ounces of pineapple, sliced in syrup, reserve the syrup
- 1 tablespoon of vinegar
- 4 green onions, thinly sliced

Instructions:

- Season the chicken using salt and black pepper before placing it in the Crock-Pot.

- Add the ginger, chicken broth, garlic, and pineapple syrup. Pineapple slices should be quartered.
- Place pineapple slices and sliced water chestnuts on top of the chicken. Pour the garlic ginger sauce over everything.
- Simmer for around 1 hour on HIGH, then decrease to low and cook for another 3 to 5 hours, or till chicken is cooked. Toss in the green onions. Combine cornstarch, soy sauce, & vinegar inside a crockpot and stir to combine.
- Cook for around 10 to 15 minutes longer on HIGH, or till slightly thickened.
- Serve with the steaming rice.

20. Chicken with Noodles

(Preparation time: 20 minutes | Cooking time: 9 hours | Servings: 6)
Per serving: Calories 629, Total fat 42g, Protein 48g, Carbs 40g

Ingredients:

- 2 thinly sliced ribs celery
- 1 broiler-fryer chicken (around 3 pounds), cut up
- 2 teaspoons of chicken bouillon granules
- 1 tablespoon of all-purpose flour
- 3/4 teaspoon of poultry seasoning
- 2 tablespoons of sliced pimento
- 1 tablespoon of chopped fresh parsley
- 1/4 cup of water
- 1/3 cup of diced Canadian bacon or smoked ham
- 2 tablespoons of grated Parmesan cheese
- 1 (16 oz.) package of wide egg noodles, cooked & drained
- 2 to 3 thinly sliced carrots
- 1 thinly sliced small onion
- 1 (10 3/4 oz.) can of condensed cheddar cheese soup

Instructions:

- Combine chopped parsley, chicken bouillon, and poultry seasoning inside a small-sized bowl; leave aside.
- Layer Canadian bacon or ham, celery, carrots, and onion inside a Crock-Pot. Fill the container halfway with the water.
- Remove the skin & excess fat out from the chicken before rinsing and patting it dry. Half of the chicken should be placed inside the Crock-Pot. Half of the saved seasoning mixture should be sprinkled on top. Sprinkle the remaining seasoning mixture on top of the remaining chicken.
- Do not whisk the soup & flour together before spooning it over the chicken.
- Cover & cook on HIGH for around 3 to 3 1/2 hours or low for around 6 to 8 hours, or till chicken is cooked and juices from the bone flow clear and vegetables are soft.
- Fill a shallow 2 to 2 ½-quart broiler-safe serving dish halfway with hot cooked noodles. Place the chicken on top of the noodles. Inside a crockpot, combine the soup and vegetables and stir till well combined. Vegetables along with some of the liquid, should be spooned over the chicken. Pimiento slices and Parmesan cheese are sprinkled over the top.
- Broil for around 5 to 8 minutes, or till gently browned, at a distance of 4 to 6 inches from the heat source.
- If desired, garnish with a parsley sprig.

- 2 cups of great northern dried beans, (soaked for overnight)
- 2 small zucchinis, cubed
- 3 cups of boiling water
- 1 tomato, chopped, for the garnish, or halved cherry tomatoes
- 1 cup of chopped onion
- 2 to 3 jalapeno peppers canned, chopped
- 1 tablespoon of lime juice
- 1 tablespoon of ground cumin
- 1 to 1 1/2 pounds of chicken breasts boneless, chopped into 1-inch pieces
- sour cream for the garnish
- 1 can (12 to 15 ounces) of whole kernel corn, drained
- 1/4 cup of fresh cilantro chopped, and extra for the garnish
- 1/2 cup of sour cream

Instructions:

- Inside a Crock-Pot, combine the beans and the boiling water. Allow standing while you prepare the rest of the ingredients. Inside the crockpot, combine the chopped onion, cumin, minced garlic, jalapeño pepper, & chili powder. Place the chicken over the top of that. Toss in the diced squash. Cook for around 7 to 8 hours on low flame, or till beans are soft. Combine the corn, lime juice, salt, sour cream, and chopped cilantro. Fill bowls with the mixture. If desired, serve with a teaspoon of sour cream, diced tomato, & fresh chopped cilantro.

21. Crockpot Chicken Chili

(Preparation time: 20 minutes | Cooking time: 8 hours | Servings: 6)
Per serving: Calories 232, Total fat 7g, Protein 33g, Carbs 33g

Ingredients:

- 2 minced garlic cloves
- 1 teaspoon of chili powder
- 2 1/4 teaspoons of salt

22. Crockpot Chicken Drumsticks

(Preparation time: 20 minutes | Cooking time: 8 hours | Servings: 6)
Per serving: Calories 162, Total fat 8g, Protein 19g, Carbs 10g

Ingredients:

- 1 teaspoon of Dijon mustard
- 12 to 16 chicken drumsticks, skin removed
- 1/2 cup of soy sauce

- 1 tablespoon of cold water
- 1 cup of maple syrup
- Sliced green onions or fresh chopped cilantro
- 1 can (14 ounces) of whole berry cranberry sauce
- 1 tablespoon of cornstarch

Instructions:

- If you want to keep the skin on the drumsticks, place them inside a big pot with enough water to cover them and bring to the boil over high flame. Cook for around 5 minutes at a low temperature. Some of the extra fat out from the skin can be removed by parboiling.
- Remove the chicken, pat dry, and add the drumsticks inside the Crock-Pot.
- Combine the cranberry sauce, maple syrup, soy sauce, and mustard inside a mixing bowl. Pour the mixture over the drumsticks.
- Cook for around 6 to 7 hours on LOW or around 3 hours on HIGH, covered. The chicken should be extremely tender but not fall apart.
- Transfer the chicken drumsticks to a serving plate and keep them warm.
- Inside a cup or small-sized dish, combine the cornstarch & cold water. Stir till the mixture is completely smooth.
- Raise the temperature of the Crock-Pot at high & stir in the cornstarch mixture. Cook for around 10 minutes, or till the sauce has thickened.
- Alternatively, combine the ingredients inside a saucepan and bring to the boil. Cook, constantly stirring for a minute or two, till the sauce has thickened.
- If desired, garnish with the sliced green onions or chopped cilantro.

23. Chicken Stroganoff

(Preparation time: 20 minutes | Cooking time: 5 hours | Servings: 4)

Per serving: Calories 456, Total fat 31g, Protein 34g, Carbs 20g

Ingredients:

- 1 cup of sautéed sliced mushroom
- 1 cup of fat-free sour cream
- 1 1/2 cups of Bisquick baking mix
- 1 pound of boneless and skinless chicken breast, cut into 1-inch pieces
- 1 tablespoon of all-purpose flour
- 1/2 cup of 1% low-fat milk
- 1 envelope of chicken gravy mix (approximately 1 ounce)
- 10 ounces of potatoes, peeled and cut into 1-inch pieces
- 1 cup of water
- 4 green onions, chopped (1/3 cups)
- 16 ounces of frozen California blend vegetables, thawed
- 1 cup of frozen peas

Instructions:

- Inside a crockpot, whisk together the gravy mix, sour cream, flour, and water till smooth. Combine the chicken, veggies, and mushrooms. Cook for around 4 hours on low flame, or till chicken is tender and the sauce has thickened. Add the peas and mix well. Combine the baking mix and the onions. Stir in the milk till it is just moistened. Drop rounded tablespoonful of dough onto the chicken-vegetable combinations. Cook for around 45 to 50 minutes on the high heat setting, or till toothpick placed in the middle of dumplings comes out clean.

24. Chicken with Leeks

(Preparation time: 20 minutes | Cooking time: 5 hours | Servings: 4)

Per serving: Calories 286, Total fat 11g, Protein 25g, Carbs 12g

Ingredients:

- 1 package of leek soup mix
- 3 to 4 pounds of chicken parts, bone-in

- 1/2 to 1 cup of water
- 4 to 6 potatoes, sliced about 1/4-inch thick
- Seasonings
- 1 thinly sliced leek or 4 sliced green onions
- Paprika

Instructions:

- Inside the bottom of a Crock-Pot, layer potatoes, onion or leek, & chicken. (If you are making multiple layers of chicken, season the bottom layers as you place them in.) Season the top layer first.) Combine 1/2 cup of leek soup with 1/2 cup of water and pour over everything. Season the top layer of chicken using salt and black pepper. Also, add paprika at this time to give it some color.

- Season with minced garlic and fresh rosemary, if desired.

- Cook for around 6 to 7 hours on low, adding extra water if necessary.

25. Crock-Pot Pulled Chicken

(Preparation time: 20 minutes | Cooking time: 5 hours | Servings: 8)
Per serving: Calories 254, Total fat 14g, Protein 26g, Carbs 10g

Ingredients:

- 1 1/2 cups of tomato ketchup
- 2 teaspoons of liquid smoke
- 1 tablespoon of butter
- 1/4 teaspoon of ground black pepper
- 1 pound of boneless chicken breasts
- 1 cup of chopped onions
- 3 tablespoons of cider vinegar
- 1/2 teaspoon of minced garlic
- A dash of allspice
- 1/2 cup of apricot preserves or peach preserves
- 1 pound of boneless chicken thighs
- 2 tablespoons of Worcestershire sauce
- 2 tablespoons of molasses

- 1/8 to 1/4 teaspoon of ground cayenne pepper

Instructions:

- Melt the butter inside a medium-sized saucepan on medium flame. When the butter has foamed up, put the chopped onions & simmer, constantly stirring, till softened and gently browned. Cook, constantly stirring, for around 1 minute more after adding the minced garlic. Ketchup, Worcestershire sauce, apricot preserves, vinegar, black pepper, liquid smoke, molasses, allspice, and cayenne pepper are added to the pan. Cook for around 5 minutes on low flame.

- Inside the Crock-Pot's crockery insert, pour 1 1/2 cups of the sauce.

- Save the excess sauce in a container & keep it refrigerated till ready to serve. Fill the Crock-Pot with the chicken pieces. Cook on LOW for around 4 1/2 to 5 hours, or till chicken is extremely soft and readily shreds. Shred the chicken chunks using a fork.

- Serve with coleslaw and extra barbecue sauce on split and toasted buns.

26. Country Captain Chicken

(Preparation time: 20 minutes | Cooking time: 7 hours | Servings: 6)
Per serving: Calories 255, Total fat 4g, Protein 28g, Carbs 26g

Ingredients:

- 2 tablespoons of raisins or currants
- 1 teaspoon of ground ginger
- 2 medium-size Granny Smith apples (unpeeled) cored and diced
- 1/4 cup of finely chopped onion
- 1 pound of medium to large shrimp, uncooked, shelled and deveined, optional
- 6 boneless chicken breast halves, skin removed
- 1 small green bell pepper, seeded & finely chopped

- 3 cloves of minced garlic
- Kosher salt
- 2 to 3 teaspoons of curry powder
- 1/4 teaspoon of ground red pepper, or to taste
- 1 cup of long-grain converted white rice
- Chopped parsley
- 1 can (around 14 1/2 oz.) of diced tomatoes
- 1/2 cup of chicken broth
- 1/3 cup of slivered almonds

Instructions:

- Combine chopped apples, ginger, bell pepper, garlic, golden raisins or currants, onion, curry powder, and ground red pepper inside a Crock-Pot; mix in tomatoes.
- Arrange the chicken on top of the tomato mixture, slightly overlapping pieces. Chicken broth should be poured over the chicken breast halves. Cover and simmer on LOW for around 4 to 6 hours, or till chicken is extremely tender when probed using a fork. Transfer the chicken to a warm dish and keep it warm in a 200°F.
- Combine the rice and the cooking liquid. Increase the temperature at high; cover & cook, stirring once or twice, for around 35 minutes, or till rice is almost tender. Stir in the shrimp. If using; cover & cook for an additional 15 minutes, or till the shrimp are opaque in the middle; test using a knife.
- Meanwhile, roast almonds inside a small-sized nonstick frying pan on medium flame, tossing periodically till golden brown. Set them aside.
- Season the rice mixture using salt to taste before serving. Arrange chicken on top of the mound inside a heated serving dish. Parsley and almonds should be sprinkled on the top.

27. Crockpot Glazed Chicken

(Preparation time: 20 minutes | Cooking time: 8 hours | Servings: 6)

Per serving: Calories 496, Total fat 21g, Protein 38g, Carbs 37g

Ingredients:

- 1/8 teaspoon of ground nutmeg
- 6 ounces of orange juice, frozen concentrate, thawed
- 1/4 cup of cold water
- 6 chicken of breast halves
- 2 tablespoons of cornstarch
- 1/2 teaspoon of ground marjoram or thyme
- A dash of garlic powder

Instructions:

- Combine the garlic powder, thawed orange juice concentrate, marjoram, & crushed nutmeg inside a small-sized bowl. Wash the chicken & pat it dry before coating it completely inside the orange juice mixture. Place inside a Crock-Pot. Over the chicken, spread the remaining orange juice mixture. Cook for around 6 to 8 hours on low, or till chicken is cooked and juices flow clear.
- Remove the chicken to a serving tray when it is done.
- Pour the remaining sauce into a saucepan. Combine the cornstarch with water inside a mixing bowl, then stir it into the juice in the pan. Cook, stirring regularly, till thick and bubbling on medium flame. Pour the sauce on top of the chicken and serve.

28. Crockpot Smothered Chicken

(Preparation time: 20 minutes | Cooking time: 8 hours | Servings: 6)

Per serving: Calories 372, Total fat 23g, Protein 19g, Carbs 22g

Ingredients:

- 1 tablespoon of butter
- 1 can (10 3/4 ounces) of condensed cream of mushroom soup
- 2 cups of sliced/diced vegetables of your choice
- 4 to 6 boneless chicken breast halves, without the skin
- Freshly ground black pepper
- 1 tablespoon of extra virgin olive oil
- 1 large sliced onion
- 1 can (10 3/4 ounces) of condensed cream of chicken soup
- 12 ounces of small Portobello or crimini mushrooms, sliced
- 1 can (10 3/4 ounces) of condensed French onion soup

Instructions:

- Inside a skillet or sauté pan, heat the olive oil & butter on medium-high flame. Cut the chicken into bite-size pieces and brown them rapidly inside the heated fat.
- Cook the onion till softened and gently browned, then remove the chicken out from the pan and set it aside. Cook for another 5 minutes after adding the mushrooms.
- Inside the bottom of the Crock-Pot, layer the sliced or chopped vegetables. 1/2 of the mushroom & onion mixture should be on top.
- The browned chicken goes on top, followed by the remaining mushroom & onion combination.
- Fill the pan with all 3 cans of condensed soup. Cook, constantly stirring, till the mixture is heated, scraping off any browned bits out from the pan's bottom. Inside the Crock-Pot, pour the hot soup combination over the chicken mixture.
- Add freshly ground black pepper to taste.
- Cook for around 2 1/2 to 3 hours at HIGH, or till the chicken is done and the vegetables are soft. Alternatively, simmer the dish on LOW for around 5 to 6 hours.
- Serve with the veggies, noodles, cooked rice, or biscuits.

29. Cranberry Glazed Chicken

(Preparation time: 20 minutes | Cooking time: 8 hours | Servings: 6)
Per serving: Calories 242, Total fat 6g, Protein 23g, Carbs 24g

Ingredients:

- 4 chicken breast halves
- 1/2 teaspoon of dried thyme
- 1 medium peeled and diced yellow onion
- 1/2 teaspoon of salt
- 1/4 teaspoon of pepper
- 1 – 14 ounces can of whole cranberry sauce
- 1/2 teaspoon of ground ginger
- 1 cup of barbecue sauce

Instructions:

- Place the diced onions inside the bottom of a Crock-Pot that has been coated using nonstick cooking spray.
- Sprinkle the chicken breasts using salt & black pepper. If desired, brown them with a little butter or oil first.
- Pour the bbq sauce over the chicken, then top with the cranberry sauce. Add ginger, thyme, and pepper to taste.
- Cook for around 7 to 8 hours on low or around 4 to 5 hours on high. Remove the chicken breasts and serve with the mashed potatoes & cranberry sauce.

30. Chinese Cashew Chicken

(Preparation time: 20 minutes | Cooking time: 8 hours | Servings: 6)
Per serving: Calories 544, Total fat 42g, Protein 31g, Carbs 12g

Ingredients:

- 1-1/2 pounds of chicken tenders

- 1 – 10 3/4 ounces can of golden mushroom soup
- 3/4 cup of whole or halved cashews
- 2 – 1/2 teaspoons of low salt soy sauce
- 1/4 teaspoon of salt
- 2 teaspoons of fresh shredded ginger or 1 teaspoon dry ground ginger
- Cooked brown or white rice
- 1 – 4 ounces can of sliced mushrooms that have been drained
- 1/4 teaspoon of pepper
- 1 – 16 ounces' package of frozen Asian vegetables (also called stir fry vegetables)

Instructions:

- Using a nonstick spray, coat the Crock-Pot.
- Combine the soup, salt, soy sauce, ginger, and pepper.
- Arrange the chicken on top, then cover with the frozen vegetables & canned mushrooms.
- Cook on low for around 6 to 8 hours or high for around 3 to 4 hours with the cover on.
- Mix in the cashews just before serving. Serve over steaming rice.

31. Crockpot Sesame Chicken

(Preparation time: 30 minutes | Cooking time: 6 hours | Servings: 6)

Per serving: Calories 242, Total fat 6g, Protein 23g, Carbs 26g

Ingredients:

- 2 minced garlic cloves
- ¼ cup of water
- 4 tablespoons of tomato paste or puree
- Toasted sesame seeds & quinoa or rice to serve
- ½ cup of organic honey
- 2 cups of chopped and cut into bite-sized pieces' broccoli florets
- 1 small finely chopped onion
- 2 teaspoons of sesame oil
- ½ cup of low-sodium soy sauce
- 6 bone-in, skinless chicken thighs

- 3 teaspoons of cornstarch or corn flour

Instructions:

- In your crockpot, place the chicken thighs. Pour over the chicken the garlic, onion, soy sauce, oil, and tomato puree mixture.
- Cook for around a minimum of 4 hours & up to 6 hours on low, turning the thighs occasionally.
- Around 20 minutes before the serving time, prepare your rice or quinoa according to the package directions.
- Inside a small-sized bowl or cup, combine the water with cornstarch.
- Add this to the Crock-Pot's sauce. Increase the flame and let the sauce to thicken. While you wait for this, shred the chicken using a fork. Remove and discard the bones. Stir in the shredded chicken into the thickening sauce every now and then.
- Inside a frying pan or skillet, heat 1 teaspoon of sesame oil on medium flame.
- Stir in the broccoli pieces till they acquire a deep green color and appear moist on the exterior but remain firm to eat.
- Place the broccoli on top of the rice or quinoa and drizzle with the chicken sauce mixture.
- Sprinkle the sesame seeds on top before serving.

32. Chicken with Potatoes and Carrots

(Preparation time: 30 minutes | Cooking time: 4 hours | Servings: 6)

Per serving: Calories 307, Total fat 4g, Protein 34g, Carbs 32g

Ingredients:

- 1 teaspoon of paprika
- 2 cups of fresh baby carrots
- 6 ounces of boned and skinned chicken thighs
- 1 teaspoon of garlic, minced
- Cooking spray
- 6 small round red potatoes cut into quarter-inch sizes

- ¾ teaspoon of salt, divided
- 1 tablespoon of fresh thyme, chopped
- ½ teaspoon of black pepper freshly ground and divided
- Fresh chopped thyme, optional
- ½ cup of dry white wine
- 1 teaspoon of olive oil
- ½ cup of low-sodium fat-free chicken broth
- 1 ¾ cups of onions, vertically sliced

Instructions:

- Add onions to a Crock-Pot that has been coated using nonstick cooking oil. Add the potatoes and carrots to the top. Pour the broth over the vegetables, along with half a teaspoon of salt, a quarter teaspoon of pepper, half a cup of dry white wine, one tablespoon of fresh thyme, one teaspoon of minced garlic, half a teaspoon of salt, and a quarter teaspoon of pepper.
- Combine the pepper, paprika, and the remaining quarter teaspoon of salt. This should be rubbed all over the chicken. Heat a large-sized nonstick skillet on medium flame, then drizzle in the oil and stir to coat.
- Cook the chicken for around 3 minutes on each side, or till browned. Place the chicken on top of the vegetables. Cover and cook on low for around 3-4 hours, or till veggies are soft and chicken is cooked through. If desired, garnish with thyme.

33. Cheesy Saucy Chicken and Veggies

(Preparation time: 30 minutes | Cooking time: 6 hours | Servings: 4)
Per serving: Calories 500, Total fat 20g, Protein 45g, Carbs 37g

Ingredients:

- 1 sweet red bell peppers
- 2 cups of chicken stock
- 3 cloves of garlic, minced
- 1/4 teaspoon of freshly ground black pepper
- 4 medium-sized chicken breasts, boneless and skinless

- 1 teaspoon of Dijon mustard
- 1 pound of green beans
- 1 onion, cut into wedges
- 1/2 teaspoon of dried marjoram
- 3 medium-sized potatoes, peeled & diced
- 1/2 cup of cream cheese, cut into cubes
- 2 tablespoons of balsamic vinegar

Instructions:

- Inside a Crock-Pot, combine all ingredients except for the cheese, mustard, & balsamic vinegar.
- Cook on low for around 5 to 6 hours, covered. Remove the chicken and vegetables out from the Crock-Pot and set them aside to keep warm.
- Inside the Crock-Pot, combine the cheese, mustard, & vinegar to make the sauce. Stir till all the ingredients are completely combined, and the cheese has melted.
- In four soup bowls, divide the chicken & vegetables.
- Using a spoon, pour the sauce over the chicken & vegetables. Warm the dish before serving.

34. Chicken Paprikash with Noodles

(Preparation time: 30 minutes | Cooking time: 8 hours | Servings: 8)
Per serving: Calories 616, Total fat 21g, Protein 36g, Carbs 57g

Ingredients:

- 2 bay leaves
- 1 tablespoon of paprika
- 2 tablespoons of olive oil
- 1/4 cup of dry white wine
- 1 cup of cream cheese
- 1 large-sized onion, peeled & diced
- 2 cloves of garlic, minced
- 3 pounds of chicken thighs, boneless & skinless
- 1/2 cup of chicken broth
- 1 teaspoon of sea salt
- Egg noodles, cooked

- 1/2 teaspoon of ground black pepper, to taste

Instructions:

- Heat olive oil inside a big skillet on medium flame. Cook till the onions and garlic are just soft. 1/4 cup dry white wine
- Chicken thighs should be cut into small pieces.
- Stir-fried the chicken for around 5 to 6 minutes inside the skillet.
- Transfer to a Crock-Pot.
- Cover & cook on low for around 8 hours, adding bay leaves, chicken broth, sea salt, black pepper, paprika, and white wine.
- Serve over the cooked noodles with a dollop of cream cheese.

35. Crock-Pot Buffalo Chicken

(Preparation time: 20 minutes | Cooking time: 4 hours | Servings: 3)
Per serving: Calories 484, Total fat 32, Protein 40g, Carbs 8g

Ingredients:

- 1 whole stalk of celery
- 3/4 cups of chicken broth
- Salt & pepper to taste
- 1 clove of garlic
- 1 tablespoon of butter
- 1/2 small onion (quartered)
- 1 whole carrot or radish
- 5 1/3 tablespoon of buffalo sauce
- 1 pound of boneless chicken

Instructions:

- Combine the chicken breasts, entire garlic cloves, whole garlic, onions, whole carrots, celery ribs, and chicken broth inside a Crock-Pot.
- Season to taste using salt and black pepper.
- Then, on high, cook for around 4 hours inside your Crockpot.

- Remove everything from the pot except the 1/3 cup of the cooking liquid and the vegetables.
- Now shred the chicken with two forks into small pieces. If you want to add the buffalo sauce & butter, do so now and cook for an additional 15 minutes.

36. Chocolate Chicken Mole

(Preparation time: 20 minutes | Cooking time: 8 hours | Servings: 4)
Per serving: Calories 402, Total fat 21, Protein 37g, Carbs 20g

Ingredients:

- 1/4 teaspoon of ground cinnamon powder
- 2 tablespoons of creamy almond butter
- ½ chopped medium onion
- 1/4 teaspoon of chili powder
- ½ teaspoon of sea salt
- ½ teaspoon of cumin powder
- 1 lb. of chicken pieces of bone-in breasts & legs, without the skin
- 25 oz. (35.4 g) of dark chocolate 70% or above
- 2 cloves of garlic crushed or minced
- Black pepper to taste
- 2 ½ dried New Mexico chili peppers rehydrated & chopped
- Sea salt
- 3-4 whole tomatoes peeled, seeded & chopped
- Avocado, cilantro and jalapeno, chopped
- 1 tablespoon of ghee

Instructions:

- Set aside the chicken after seasoning it using salt and pepper. Place a skillet on medium flame and add the ghee.
- After the butter has melted, add the chicken & brown it on all sides. You can cook the chicken in batches if it is huge.
- Place the chicken inside a crockpot now. After that, add the onion to the pan with

the chicken and cook till golden. Sauté for around a minute after adding the garlic.

- Once the garlic and onion are done, add the spices, chili peppers, salt, dark chocolate, almond butter, and tomatoes to the crockpot.
- Cook for around 6 to 8 hours, or till the chicken is soft and easily pulled apart.
- Serve with cilantro, jalapeno, & avocado on top.

37. Crockpot Creamy Salsa Chicken

(Preparation time: 20 minutes | Cooking time: 5 hours | Servings: 4)
Per serving: Calories 255, Total fat 18, Protein 40g, Carbs 15g

Ingredients:

- 1/2 can of cream mushroom soup
- 1/2 jar salsa (16 ounces)
- 3 large boneless chicken breasts

Instructions:

- Place the chicken breasts inside the bottom of a Crock-Pot, followed by the salsa & soup cans.
- Set the Crock-Pot to low flame and place it over the chicken breasts.
- Cook for at least 4 hours, then shred the chicken using a fork by stirring it around.
- If it does not shred, simmer it for another 30 minutes.
- You can eat it plain or with a flour tortilla. If desired, add avocado, onion, or cheese to the top.

38. Crock-Pot Balsamic Chicken

(Preparation time: 20 minutes | Cooking time: 4 hours | Servings: 4)

Per serving: Calories 380, Total fat 20, Protein 31g, Carbs 18g

Ingredients:

- 3 tablespoons of tomato paste
- ¼ cup of flat-leaf parsley leaves
- 1 bay leaf
- ½ cup of pomegranate seeds
- Kosher salt
- 1 tablespoon of butter
- 5 minced garlic cloves
- Black pepper, freshly ground
- 1 to 2 tablespoons of extra virgin olive oil
- ¼ cup of coconut sugar
- 8 ounces of white button mushrooms, quartered
- 1 cup of chicken stock
- 2 stems of fresh rosemary
- ¾ cup of balsamic vinegar
- 8 to 10 boneless and skinless chicken thighs
- 1 16 ounces' package of white pearl onions, frozen

Instructions:

- Season both sides of the chicken thigh using salt & pepper.
- Heat olive oil inside a large-sized frying pan on medium flame.
- In batches, brown the thighs using oil for around 5 minutes on each side. Remove them from the pan once golden brown & put them aside.

- Inside a Crock-Pot, layer the onions, mushrooms, rosemary, garlic, and bay leaves.
- Inside the Crockpot, place the browned chicken breasts. Season using pepper & salt after mixing together balsamic vinegar, tomato paste, brown sugar, & chicken stock inside a bowl.
- Cook for around 3 hours at high with the mixture poured over the breast. Check for doneness, and if necessary, simmer for another 15-30 minutes or till the chicken is no pinker.
- Cover the chicken using foil or a lid after transferring it to a serving dish. After that, remove the liquid out from the vegetables and combine them with the chicken.
- Inside a pan, combine the liquid and cook on a medium-high flame. Boil for around 5 minutes, or till it has reduced by half. Whisk in the butter till the sauce has thickened & the butter has melted.
- Serve the chicken with parsley & pomegranate seeds as a garnish. Serve with a balsamic reduction sauce.

39. Chicken Tikka Masala

(Preparation time: 20 minutes | Cooking time: 6 hours | Servings: 3)
Per serving: Calories 493, Total fat 41, Protein 26g, Carbs 17g

Ingredients:

- 1/2 cup of heavy cream
- 1 1/2 tablespoons of tomato paste
- ½ chopped fresh cilantro
- 1 teaspoon of onion powder
- 1/2 cup of coconut milk
- 1 teaspoon of smoked paprika
- 5 ounces can of tomatoes, diced
- 3/4 lbs. (12 ounces) of chicken thighs, bone-in skin-on
- 2 teaspoons of kosher salt
- 1/2 inch grated ginger root

- 2 1/2 teaspoons of garam masala
- 1/2 lb. of chicken thighs, skinless & boneless
- 1/2 teaspoon of arrowroot powder
- 1 1/2 cloves of minced garlic
- 1 tablespoon of olive oil

Instructions:

- Remove the bones out from the chicken thighs before chopping them into bite-sized chunks. The chicken skin should not be removed.
- Inside a Crock-Pot, place the chicken thigh and grate 1-inch of ginger on the top.
- Then combine the tomato paste & canned diced tomatoes.
- Cook on high for around 3 hours or low for around 6 hours after adding 1/2 cup of coconut milk and stirring thoroughly.
- Once the chicken is done, stir in the arrowroot powder, heavy cream, & any remaining coconut cream.
- Serve with your choice of veggies or cauliflower rice.

40. Easy Crockpot Cassoulet

(Preparation time: 20 minutes | Cooking time: 7 hours | Servings: 6)
Per serving: Calories 548, Total fat 26g, Protein 36g, Carbs 40g

Ingredients:

- 1 teaspoon of dried thyme leaves
- 4 boneless and skinless chicken thighs, coarsely chopped
- 1 tablespoon of extra virgin olive oil
- 2 tablespoons of water
- 1 finely chopped large onion
- 1/4 pound of cooked smoked sausage, such as kielbasa or spicier andouille, diced
- 3 tablespoons of chopped fresh parsley
- 3 cloves of minced garlic
- 1/2 teaspoon of black pepper
- 3 cans (about 15 ounces each) of great northern beans, rinsed and drained

- 4 tablespoons of tomato paste

Instructions:

- Inside a large-sized skillet, heat the olive oil on medium flame.
- Cook, occasionally turning, till the onion is soft, around 4 minutes.
- Combine the chicken, thyme, sausage, garlic, and pepper. Cook for around 5 to 8 minutes, or till the chicken and sausage are golden browns.
- Add the tomato paste and water to the Crock-Pot and stir to combine. Cover and simmer on LOW for around 4 to 6 hours, stirring great northern beans into the chicken mix.
- Sprinkle chopped parsley over the cassoulet just before serving.

41. Greek Chicken & Vegetable Ragout

(Preparation time: 20 minutes | Cooking time: 4 hours | Servings: 4)

Per serving: Calories 326, Total fat 20, Protein 29g, Carbs 23g

Ingredients:

- 1/3 cup of lemon juice
- Pepper, freshly ground
- 1 large egg
- 1 14-ounce can of chicken broth, reduced-sodium
- 1/3 cup of chopped fresh dill
- ¾ teaspoon of salt
- 2 large egg yolks
- 1 pound of rutabagas, 1¼-inch-wide wedges
- 1 15-ounces can of artichoke hearts, rinsed
- 4 cloves of minced garlic
- 3 cups of baby carrots
- 1/3 cup of dry white wine
- 2 pounds of boneless and skinless chicken thighs, trimmed

Instructions:

- The rutabagas & carrots should be evenly distributed inside the Crock-Pot. After that, arrange the chicken on top of them.
- Inside a medium-sized saucepan on a medium-high flame, bring the salt, garlic, wine, & broth to a simmer.
- Cover the cooker and pour the broth combination over the vegetables & chicken. Cook on low for around 4 to 4 1/2 hours or high for 2 1/2 to 3 hours.
- Add artichokes, cover, and simmer for around 5 minutes on High heat once the vegetables are tender & the chicken is cooked through.
- Meanwhile, whisk together the egg yolks, lemon juice, and egg inside a medium-sized mixing bowl till thoroughly combined. Transfer the vegetables & chicken to a serving bowl using a slotted spoon. To keep warm, cover.
- 1/2 cup of the cooling liquid should now be spooned into the lemon mixture and whisked till smooth. Inside the Crockpot, whisk the combination into the remaining liquid.
- Cook, covered, for around 15 to 20 minutes, whisking occasionally. Remove the sauce out from the flame once it has thickened slightly and reached a temperature of 160°F.
- Spoon the sauce over the vegetables and chicken after adding the pepper and dill.

42. Herbed Chicken with Wild Rice

(Preparation time: 20 minutes | Cooking time: 7 hours | Servings: 6)

Per serving: Calories 572, Total fat 29g, Protein 34g, Carbs 38g

Ingredients:

- 1 tablespoon of vegetable oil
- 1 (6 oz.) box of Uncle Bens (chicken flavor) long grain and wild rice
- 1 to 1 1/2 pounds of chicken tenders

- 1 teaspoon of herb mixtures, such as fine herbes or a mixture of your favorites; thyme, parsley, tarragon, etc.
- 6 to 8 ounces of sliced mushrooms
- 2 to 3 slices of crumbled bacon
- 1 cup of water
- 1 teaspoon of butter
- 1 can of cream of chicken soup, with the herbs or plain

Instructions:

- Cook the chicken and mushrooms with oil and butter till the meat is gently browned. Bacon should be placed on the bottom of a Crock-Pot. Place the rice on top of the bacon. Seasonings should be kept in a separate package. Place chicken tenders over rice, or chop chicken breasts into strips or cubes if using chicken breasts. Pour the soup over the chicken, then cover with water. Season using salt & pepper, then sprinkle with the herb combination. Cook for around 5 1/2 to 6 1/2 hours on LOW, or till rice is tender (but not mushy).

43. Honey Barbecued Chicken with Sweet Potatoes

(Preparation time: 20 minutes | Cooking time: 9 hours | Servings: 6)
Per serving: Calories 305, Total fat 12g, Protein 28g, Carbs 50g

Ingredients:

- 1/4 cup of finely chopped onion
- 3 cups of peeled and sliced sweet potatoes
- 1/2 teaspoon of dry mustard
- 1 can (8 ounces) of pineapple chunks in juice, undrained
- 1/3 cup of barbecue sauce
- 4 to 6 chicken leg quarters (legs with thighs, skin removed)
- 1/2 cup of chicken broth
- 1/2 teaspoon of ground ginger
- 2 tablespoons of honey

Instructions:

- Mix sweet potatoes, chopped onion, pineapple juice, chicken broth, & ground ginger inside a Crock-Pot; stir well to combine. Combine honey, barbecue sauce, and dry mustard inside a small-sized mixing dish and toss well to combine. Coat the chicken with the barbecue sauce mixture on all sides. Arrange the coated chicken inside a single layer on top of the sweet potato & pineapple mixture, overlapping as needed. Any leftover barbecue sauce combination should be spooned over the chicken.
- Cover and cook on low for around 7 to 9 hours, or till the chicken is fork-tender & the juices flow clear, and the sweet potatoes are cooked.

44. Hearty Chicken Stew

(Preparation time: 30 minutes | Cooking time: 6 hours | Servings: 4)
Per serving: Calories 272, Total fat 16g, Protein 22g, Carbs 9g

Ingredients:

- 1 red bell pepper, chopped
- 1 can (10 ¾ ounces) of reduced-sodium condensed cream of chicken soup
- 1 cup of sliced onion
- 1 minced poblano pepper
- 1 ¼ cups of 2% reduced-fat milk
- 1 cup of water

- 1/2 teaspoon of dried rosemary
- 1 green bell pepper, chopped
- 1/4 teaspoon of ground black pepper
- 1 pound of chicken breasts, boneless, skinless and cubed
- 1/2 cup of carrot, thinly sliced
- 1/4 cup of cold water
- 1/2 cup of turnip, diced
- 1/2 teaspoon of celery salt
- 1/2 teaspoon of dried oregano
- 2 tablespoons of cornstarch
- 1/4 teaspoon of red pepper flakes, crushed

Instructions:

- Inside a Crock-Pot, combine milk, cream of chicken soup, and water. Cover and cook on low for around 5 to 6 hours, stirring in the other ingredients except for cornstarch and water. After that, whisk in the cornstarch & cold water mixture for around 2 to 3 minutes, stirring regularly. If preferred, serve with boiled potatoes.

45. Italian Style Chicken in the Crockpot

(Preparation time: 20 minutes | Cooking time: 9 hours | Servings: 4)
Per serving: Calories 540, Total fat 45g, Protein 25g, Carbs 8g

Ingredients:

- 1/2 cup of sliced pitted ripe olives
- 1 teaspoon of dried leaf oregano
- A pinch of dried leaf thyme
- 1 pound of boneless chicken thighs, skin removed, or 4 chicken leg quarters, skin removed
- 1/4 cup of cold water or chicken broth
- 1/2 cup of chopped onion
- 1/2 teaspoon of dried rosemary, crumbled
- 1 can (14.5-ounces) of diced tomatoes, undrained
- 1/2 teaspoon of salt
- 1 tablespoon of cornstarch
- 1/4 teaspoon of garlic powder

Instructions:

- Place the chicken inside a Crock-Pot.
- Add chopped onion with sliced olives to the top. Combine tomatoes, thyme, oregano, salt, rosemary, and garlic powder. Pour the tomato sauce over the chicken. Cook for around 7 to 9 hours on LOW, or till chicken is fork-tender & juices flow clear. Transfer the chicken and veggies to a warm serving plate using a slotted spoon. Keep warm by wrapping inside the foil. Increase the crockpot's setting to HIGH.
- Combine water or broth with the cornstarch inside a cup or small-sized bowl and whisk till smooth. Inside the crockpot, stir in the liquids. Cook, covered, till the sauce has thickened. Serve the chicken with the thickened sauce.

46. Lemon Chicken

(Preparation time: 20 minutes | Cooking time: 8 hours | Servings: 4)
Per serving: Calories 322, Total fat 12g, Protein 46g, Carbs 10g

Ingredients:

- 2 cloves of minced garlic
- 1 broiler-fryer, cut up, or around 3 1/2 pounds of chicken pieces
- 1/4 cup of dry wine, chicken broth, sherry, or water
- 1 teaspoon of crumbled dry leaf oregano
- Salt and black pepper
- 2 tablespoons of butter
- 3 tablespoons of lemon juice

Instructions:

- Using salt and black pepper, season the chicken pieces. Half of the garlic and oregano should be sprinkled over the chicken.
- Inside a sauté pan on medium flame, melt the butter and brown the chicken on all sides.
- Place the chicken inside the crockpot. Garnish with the rest of the oregano and garlic. Pour the wine or sherry into the

pan after stirring to loosen the brown pieces in the sauté pan.

- Cook on LOW for around 7 to 8 hours, covered. Last but not least, add the lemon juice.
- Remove the fat out from the juices and strain them into a serving bowl; thicken the juices if desired.
- Serve the chicken along with juices.

47. Roasted Whole Chicken

(Preparation time: 20 minutes | Cooking time: 7 hours | Servings: 6)
Per serving: Calories 341, Total fat 15g, Protein 46g, Carbs 6g

Ingredients:

- 1/2 teaspoon of garlic powder
- 1 large peeled onion cut into wedges
- 2 teaspoons of paprika
- 1 teaspoon of salt
- 1 – 4 pounds of whole chicken
- 1/4 teaspoon of pepper
- 1 teaspoon of onion powder
- 1 teaspoon of dried thyme
- 1/4 teaspoon of cayenne pepper

Instructions:

- Place the onion wedges in the bottom of the crock that has been sprayed using nonstick cooking spray.
- Inside a small-sized bowl, combine the salt, pepper, paprika, garlic powder, onion powder, cayenne, and thyme.
- Discard any giblets from the inside of the chicken's cavity. (You can chop and sauté them before putting them back in the cavity.)
- In the bowl, apply the spice rub on the outside and interior of the cavity. On the breasts & thighs, get some under the skin.
- Invert the chicken and set the breast side down on top of the onions inside the Crock-Pot.

- Cook for around 4 hours on high or around 7 hours on low. When the chicken is done, it will fall off the bone.

48. Sweet and Sour Chicken

(Preparation time: 20 minutes | Cooking time: 8 hours | Servings: 6)
Per serving: Calories 448, Total fat 4g, Protein 29g, Carbs 48g

Ingredients:

- 1 cup of broccoli florets
- 1 large can of chunk pineapple (drain and reserve the juice)
- 2 to 4 skinless chicken breasts
- Salt and black pepper to taste, optional
- 1 roughly chopped large onion
- Water/wine/orange juice/white grape juice etc. as needed for the extra liquid
- Cloves, optional
- 2 bell peppers roughly chopped (one green, one red)
- 1/2 cup of carrot chunks
- Hot sauce to taste, optional
- Allspice, optional
- 1/4-1/2 cup of brown sugar (can use reg. sugar)
- 1 tablespoon of cornstarch for every cup of liquid you end up with
- Curry powder, optional
- Cinnamon, optional

Instructions:

- Inside a Crock-Pot, place the chicken breasts. Combine the broccoli, onion, peppers, & carrots. Whisk together the cornstarch, sugar, liquids, and spices till smooth and lump-free. Pour the sauce over the chicken. If there is not enough of the juice, add whatever liquid you want to get it to the right consistency.
- Cook on LOW for around 6 to 8 hours, covered. You can occasionally change up the recipe by using a fruit cocktail with a little less sugar, pineapple, apricot

preserves, or orange marmalade. (When using preserves, no cornstarch or sugar is required.) Make up your own scenario. Keep in mind that sweet and sour is simply fruit juice & vinegar.

49. White Chicken Chili

(Preparation time: 20 minutes | Cooking time: 5 hours | Servings: 6)
Per serving: Calories 232, Total fat 7g, Protein 33g, Carbs 33g

Ingredients:

- 2 cloves of finely chopped garlic
- 1 lb. of chicken, cut up into small chunks
- 1 or 2 chopped red, green or yellow bell peppers, or a combination of both
- 1/2 teaspoon of dried oregano leaves
- 1 cup of chopped onion
- 1 can of chicken broth
- jalapeno chili peppers, fresh, canned or jarred, optional or 'to taste
- 2 teaspoons of Cumin seed (ground will not withstand long cooking as well)
- 3 -15 oz. cans of white beans (great northern or cannellini), drained & rinsed

Instructions:

- Combine the chicken, onions, cumin, chicken broth, garlic, and oregano inside a Crock-Pot.
- Allow simmering on low for a while (approximately 3 to 5 hours).
- Drain the beans and add them to the pot.
- Now comes the crucial step if you do not want your chili to be mushy. No sooner than an hour or hour and a half before serving, add the bell peppers and jalapeño peppers (if using).
- If preferred, garnish each serving with grated Monterey jack cheese and broken tortilla chips.

50. Wine & Tomato Braised Chicken

(Preparation time: 20 minutes | Cooking time: 7 hours | Servings: 4)
Per serving: Calories 240, Total fat 12, Protein 24g, Carbs 15g

Ingredients:

- 11.2 ounces of chopped whole tomatoes
- 1/2 teaspoon of pepper, freshly ground
- 1 ½ tablespoons of fresh parsley, finely chopped
- 1 1/2 cloves of minced garlic
- 4 bone-in chicken thighs, skin removed, trimmed
- 1½-2 slices of bacon
- Salt
- 6 tablespoons of dry white wine
- 1/2 teaspoon of dried thyme
- 1/2 bay leaf
- 1/2 teaspoon of fennel seeds
- 1/2 thinly sliced large onion

Instructions:

- Cook the bacon for around 4 minutes inside a large-sized skillet on medium flame. Transfer to a paper towel to drain and cool once crisp. Crumble.
- Remove 2 tablespoons of the grease from the pan & set aside. Then, on medium flame, add the onion & sauté for around 3-6 minutes.
- When softened, add in the bay leaf, garlic, fennel seeds, thyme, and pepper. Cook for a minute, stirring constantly.
- Then add the wine and cook for about 2 minutes, scraping away any browned bits as you go. Now, along with the juice, add the tomatoes. Toss in the salt and whisk to combine.
- Place the chicken thighs inside a Crockpot and top with the bacon. Cover the Crock-Pot with the wine & tomato mixture.
- Cook on low for around 6 hours or high for around 3 hours, or till chicken is tender. Discard the bay leaf from the cooker and garnish using parsley.

Chapter 4:
Crock-Pot Beef and
Lamb Recipes

1. Autumn Vegetable Beef Stew

(Preparation time: 20 minutes | Cooking time: 9 hours | Servings: 6)
Per serving: Calories 367, Total fat 11g, Protein 31g, Carbs 37g

Ingredients:

- 2 cups of beef broth
- 1 to 1 1/2 pounds of lean stewing beef, cut in 1-inch cubes
- 1/8 teaspoon of black pepper
- 2 tablespoons of cold water
- 1 slice of bacon, diced
- 2 thinly sliced ribs celery
- 1 cup of chopped onions
- 1 1/2 pounds of potatoes (around 5 or 6 medium potatoes), diced
- 1 bay leaf
- 1 cup of apple cider
- 1 tablespoon of fresh chopped parsley
- 2 medium carrots, peeled, thinly sliced
- 1 1/2 cups of diced rutabaga
- 1/2 teaspoon of dried rosemary, crumbled
- 2 tablespoons of flour

Instructions:

- Inside a large-sized skillet, sauté the bacon, meat, & onions on medium flame till the steak is browned and the bacon is cooked.
- Combine the meat, onions, bacon, beef broth, carrots, apple cider, potatoes, rosemary, celery, rutabaga, bay leaf, and pepper inside a Crock-Pot.
- Cook for around 7 to 9 hours, covered. To get a smooth mixture, combine flour with cold water.
- Stir into the beef combination, increase the temperature to HIGH, and simmer for another 15 minutes.

2. Beef & Red Wine Stew

(Preparation time: 20 minutes | Cooking time: 7 hours | Servings: 3)
Per serving: Calories 477, Total fat 27, Protein 39g, Carbs 14g

Ingredients:

- 2 tablespoons of tomato paste
- ½ chopped fresh flat-leaf parsley
- 1 chopped large celery rib
- 1/2 tablespoon of unsalted butter
- 1/2 teaspoon of Dijon mustard
- 1/2 tablespoon of canola oil
- 1/2 cup of dry red wine
- 1/2 (8-ounces) package of cremini mushrooms
- Black pepper, freshly ground
- 2 cloves of chopped garlic
- Kosher salt
- 1 cup of beef stock
- 1 1/2 lbs. of pot roast, trimmed & cut into 4 pieces
- 3 sprigs thyme
- 1/2 chopped large red onion
- 1/2 lb. of carrots or rutabaga cut into small pieces
- 1 ½ tablespoons of flour

Instructions:

- Whisk together flour, mustard, and beef stock inside a Crock-Pot. Then add in thyme, garlic, mushrooms, celery, onion, and carrots.

- Heat the oil inside a big skillet on medium flame before seasoning the meat using pepper and salt.
- Cook, rotating periodically, for around 10-12 minutes or till browned.
- Inside a Crock-Pot, combine the ingredients. Toss in the tomato paste and simmer for a minute, stirring constantly.
- Cook for around 30 seconds while scraping up the browned parts with the wine. Place inside a Crockpot.
- Remove the thyme and toss it out. Remove the steak & shred it using two forks. Return the Crock-Pot to the stovetop & add the butter.
- Cook for around 5-6 hours on high or around 7 to 8 hours on low, covered. Serve with parsley on top once cooked.

3. Beef Chuck Pot Roast

(Preparation time: 20 minutes | Cooking time: 5 hours | Servings: 3)
Per serving: Calories 380, Total fat 14, Protein 34g, Carbs 12g

Ingredients:

- 1/4 packet of onion soup dry mix
- 1/4 can of cream of celery soup or cream of mushroom soup
- 1 lb. of beef for the roasting

Instructions:

- Begin by piercing the beef using a fork or knife in a few places, then placing it inside the crock-pot with the fatty facing side up.
- Apply the dry onion soup to the top, then pour the mushroom or celery soup over it.
- Spread it out a little on top, then cover and turn on the Crock-Pot!
- Cook for around 3 hours on high or around 5 hours on low setting at this point.
- Serve & enjoy.

4. Beef & Broccoli

(Preparation time: 20 minutes | Cooking time: 10 hours | Servings: 4)
Per serving: Calories 430, Total fat 19, Protein 54g, Carbs 14g

Ingredients:

- 1 head of broccoli
- 3 tablespoons of sugar
- 1 red bell pepper
- 3 minced garlic cloves
- 1/2 teaspoon of salt
- 2/3 cup of soya sauce
- 1/4 - 1/2 teaspoon of red pepper flakes
- 1 teaspoon of sesame seeds
- 1 teaspoon of grated ginger
- 2 lbs. of flank steak
- 1 cup of beef broth

Instructions:

- Set your Crock-Pot to a low setting to begin. After that, cut a flank steak into the chunks.
- Once the crockpot is hot, add the meat, salt, beef broth, pepper, garlic, sweetener, and soya sauce.
- Cook for around 5 to 6 hours, depending on the ingredients. Prepare the bell pepper & broccoli in the meantime. Simply chop the broccoli into florets and slice the bell pepper into 1-inch pieces.
- Stir the steak once it is done cooking, then add the red pepper and chopped broccoli.
- Cook for about 1 hour, or till crisp, and then toss the ingredients together.
- Sprinkle with the sesame seeds & serve garnished with sesame seeds if desired. Serve over the cauliflower rice if desired.
- Thicken the sauce with corn flour if necessary. Simply combine 2 tablespoons of water and 1 tablespoon of corn flour inside a small-sized bowl and stir into the steak mixture once it is cooked through. Pour in as much as you need till you reach the appropriate consistency.

5. Beef Stroganoff

(Preparation time: 30 minutes | Cooking time: 8 hours | Servings: 6)
Per serving: Calories 679, Total fat 40g, Protein 29g, Carbs 48g

Ingredients:

- 1 medium peeled and sliced thin sweet onion
- 1 teaspoon of paprika
- 2 cups of sliced mushrooms
- 1 – 1 pound of round steak about 1-inch thick trimmed of fat
- 1/2 teaspoon of pepper
- 2 cups of cooked egg noodles
- 1 teaspoon of olive oil
- 2 tablespoons of minced garlic
- 1 cup of beef broth
- 1/2 teaspoon of salt
- 1 – 8 ounces' container of sour cream
- 1 teaspoon of dried parsley
- 1/3 cup of flour

Instructions:

- Inside a skillet, cook the steak in diagonal strips with olive oil & garlic. Place inside a Crock-Pot coated using nonstick cooking spray. Combine the pepper, onion, salt, and parsley. Top with the browned strips.
- Mix together the flour, paprika, and beef broth inside a small-sized dish and pour over the top. Cook on low for around 8 hours with the lid on. Add the mushrooms and crank the heat up to high during the last 1/2 hour of cooking.
- Add the sour cream right before serving and whisk well. Wait around 10 minutes before serving the beef mixture over the steaming hot egg noodles.

6. Beef Steak with Mushroom Gravy

(Preparation time: 15 minutes | Cooking time: 8 hours | Servings: 12)
Per serving: Calories 296, Total fat 18g, Protein 19g, Carbs 12g

Ingredients:

- 2 pounds of beef round steak, boneless
- 1 (12-ounces) jar of beef gravy
- 2 medium onions, peeled & sliced
- 3 cups of sliced mushrooms
- 1 (1-ounce) envelope of dry mushroom gravy mix
- 1 cup of sliced turnips

Instructions:

- On the bottom of your Crock-Pot, place the onions.
- Remove the fat out from the beef round steak before cutting it into eight pieces.
- The beef should be placed on top of the onions, followed by the mushrooms. Serve with sliced turnips on top.
- Combine the beef gravy & mushroom gravy mix.
- Cover and simmer on low for around 8 hours with this gravy mixture in the Crock-Pot. If preferred, serve over mashed potatoes.

7. Basque Beef Stew

(Preparation time: 20 minutes | Cooking time: 10 hours | Servings: 4)
Per serving: Calories 475, Total fat 19g, Protein 42g, Carbs 31g

Ingredients:

- 1 green bell pepper, cut in 1-inch squares
- 1 tablespoon of olive oil
- 2 tablespoons of balsamic vinegar
- 6 slices of bacon, diced
- 2 pounds of lean beef stew meat, cut into 1/2- to 1-inch chunks
- 1/2 teaspoon of dried ground marjoram
- 8 ounces of sliced mushrooms
- 1 (14.5 oz.) can of tomatoes
- 1 red bell pepper, cut into 1-inch squares
- 1/4 teaspoon of pepper
- 1 bunch of green onions sliced into 1/2-inch, about half of the green included
- 1 can (4 oz.) of sliced ripe olives

- 3 tablespoons of tomato paste
- 1/4 cup of chicken broth
- 1/2 teaspoon of salt

Instructions:

- Inside a large-sized skillet, heat the olive oil & cook the bacon. Sauté for 2 minutes with the peppers, mushrooms, and green onions. Cook for around 1 minute longer with the vinegar, scraping up the browned bits from the base of the pan. Set them aside.
- Place the beef inside a Crock-Pot with a capacity of 3 1/2-quarts or more. Toss in the sautéed bacon and veggie mixture, followed by the olives. Inside a mixing dish, combine the remaining ingredients.
- Inside the Crock-Pot, pour over the beef and vegetables. Cook on low for around 8 to 10 hours, covered.

8. Beer Beef Stew

(Preparation time: 20 minutes | Cooking time: 10 hours | Servings: 6)
Per serving: Calories 340, Total fat 18g, Protein 20g, Carbs 21g

Ingredients:

- 2 minced cloves of garlic
- 1 1/2 teaspoons of salt
- 2 1/2 pounds of lean beef stew meat, cut into 1-inch cubes
- 1 teaspoon of oregano
- 1 large chopped onion
- 2 ribs of celery, cut into 1/2-inch slices
- 3 tablespoons of melted butter
- 1 cup of beer
- 3 carrots, cut into 1-inch slices
- 2 medium potatoes, cut into 1-inch cubes
- 1 cup of beef broth, or use all beer
- 2 tablespoons of tomato paste
- 1/3 cup of all-purpose flour
- 1/2 teaspoon of pepper

Instructions:

- Combine the stew beef, onion, potatoes, garlic, carrots, celery, beer, oregano, beef broth, salt, pepper, and tomato paste inside the Crock-Pot.
- Cook on low for around 8 to 10 hours, covered.
- Combine melted butter and flour inside a mixing bowl; stir into the stew. Season using salt and black pepper to taste.
- Cook on high for around 15 to 20 minutes, or till the sauce has thickened.

9. Beef Curry Stew

(Preparation time: 20 minutes | Cooking time: 10 hours | Servings: 4)
Per serving: Calories 356, Total fat 19g, Protein 22g, Carbs 23g

Ingredients:

- 2 medium sliced onions
- 4 teaspoons of curry powder, or more to taste
- 2 tablespoons of olive oil or vegetable oil
- 1 teaspoon of salt
- 1 1/2 pounds of lean stew beef, cut into cubes
- 1 can (14.5 ounces) of diced tomatoes, drained
- 1/4 cup of flour
- 1 teaspoon of Creole or Cajun seasoning
- 1 jar (around 12 ounces) of small white onions, drained
- 1/2 teaspoon of garlic powder
- 3/4 cup of beef broth

Instructions:

- Inside a large-sized skillet, heat the vegetable oil.
- Combine the Creole seasoning, flour, salt, and garlic powder inside a food storage bag or shallow dish; toss the beef with the mixture, then brown in the hot oil with the cut onions.

- Cook for around 4 to 6 minutes, turning occasionally, or till beef is browned & onions are soft.
- Fill a 4 to 6-quart Crock-Pot halfway with the contents.
- Scrape up any browned bits out from the bottom of the skillet and pour over the beef & onions inside the Crock-Pot.
- Stir in the tomatoes, curry powder, and small white onions.
- Cook for around 8 to 10 hours on low, covered.

10. Beef Stew with Red Wine and Herb Dumplings

(Preparation time: 20 minutes | Cooking time: 10 hours | Servings: 8)
Per serving: Calories 730, Total fat 52g, Protein 42g, Carbs 48g

Ingredients:

- 2 medium celery ribs sliced, about 1 cup
- 1 teaspoon of dry mustard
- 2 pounds of lean stew beef, cut in 1-inch pieces
- 3/4 cup of dry red wine or beef broth
- 1/4 cup of water
- 4 medium carrots, cut into 1/4-inch slices, around 1 1/2 cups
- 2 medium sliced onions
- 1 1/2 teaspoons of salt, or to taste if the beef broth is used
- 1 can (14.5 ounces) of diced tomatoes with the juices
- 1/4 cup of all-purpose flour
- 8 sliced mushrooms
- 1 teaspoon of dried thyme leaves
- 1/4 teaspoon of pepper

For the Herb Dumplings:

- 1/4 teaspoon of dried sage leaves, crumbled
- 1 1/2 cups of baking mix (Bisquick)
- 1/2 cup of milk
- 1/2 teaspoon of dried thyme leaves

- 1/4 teaspoon of dried rosemary, crumbled

Instructions:

- Combine stew meat, carrots, tomatoes, celery, onions, mustard, mushrooms, wine or beef broth, salt, thyme, and pepper inside a 3 1/2 to 6-quart Crock-Pot.
- Cook for around 8 to 10 hours on LOW (or around 4 to 5 hours on HIGH) or till vegetables & beef are cooked.
- Stir together the water and flour, then gradually add it to the beef mixture.
- Combine sage, baking mix, thyme, & rosemary to make herb dumplings. Stir in the milk till it is just moistened.
- Drop spoonful of dough onto the boiling beef stew liquid.
- Cook for around 25 to 35 minutes on HIGH, or till a toothpick placed in the middle of the dumplings pulls out clean.

11. Beef Enchilada Casserole

(Preparation time: 30 minutes | Cooking time: 8 hours | Servings: 8)
Per serving: Calories 626, Total fat 24g, Protein 33g, Carbs 57g

Ingredients:

- 2 cups of grated cheddar cheese, divided
- 1.5 lbs. of beef flank steak
- 3.8 oz. can of black olives divided
- 28 oz. can of red enchilada sauce
- 10 corn tortillas (Package of soft corn tortillas)

Instructions:

- Inside a Crock-Pot, combine the beef & enchilada sauce.
- Cook for around 4 hours on HIGH or around 6-8 hours on LOW. Inside the Crock-Pot, shred the beef using two forks.
- Cut the tortillas into strips and mix them in with the chicken and sauce. Stir. Half of the cheese and half of the olives should be

added to the sauce & beef mixture. Stir once more.

- Make a flat surface for the mixture.
- On top, sprinkle the remaining cheese and olives.
- Cook for another around 40–60 minutes on low.
- Serve with a dollop of sour cream on the top (optional).

12. Beef Ragu

(Preparation time: 20 minutes | Cooking time: 5 hours | Servings: 8)

Per serving: Calories 375, Total fat 25g, Protein 22g, Carbs 11g

Ingredients:

- 1 large diced onion
- 2 tablespoons of olive oil
- 1 teaspoon of dried thyme
- 7 cups of canned crushed tomatoes
- Salt & pepper for seasoning the beef
- 2 cups of chopped fresh mushrooms
- 1 large diced carrot
- Shaved parmesan cheese & fresh herbs for the serving, if desired (optional)
- 2 pounds of stewing beef cubes
- 1 teaspoon of dried basil
- 4 cloves of minced garlic
- 1 1/2 cups of red wine (substitute beef broth and 1 tablespoon of balsamic vinegar, if desired)
- 1/2 teaspoon of dried parsley

Instructions:

- Preheat a big skillet over medium-high flame. Pour in the oil.
- Season the beef cubes on all sides using salt and black pepper before browning them inside the skillet. If the beef is overcrowded, it will steam rather than brown. Brown the meat cubes in batches on all sides. At this point, do not worry about fully cooking the meat; instead, aim

for a deep golden brown color on the outside.

- When the beef cubes have completed browning, remove them to a plate & add the carrots, onions, garlic, & mushrooms to the hot skillet.
- Cook for a few minutes, or till the onions & carrots have softened, and also the mushrooms have released their juices.
- Turn the flame off and transfer the browned beef & sautéed vegetables to the Crock-Pot. Stir in the wine, then add the herbs & tomatoes that have been smashed.
- Combine all of the ingredients and stir until well blended.
- Cook on high for around 5 to 6 hours or low for around 8-10 hours in your Crock-Pot.
- Shred the beef in the sauce before serving.
- Serve with freshly shaved parmesan & fresh herbs, if desired, over Linguine or Pappardelle noodles (flat, long noodles) cooked according to the package directions.

13. Beef Bourguignon

(Preparation time: 10 minutes | Cooking time: 8 hours | Servings: 8)

Per serving: Calories 453, Total fat 21g, Protein 29g, Carbs 12g

Ingredients:

- 4 strips of bacon, diced
- 2 tablespoons of olive oil
- 1 cup of beef stock
- 16 oz. of mushrooms (cremini or baby Bella), halved
- 3 lbs. of lean chuck roast, diced into 1–2” cubes, patted dry
- 2 minced garlic cloves
- Flat-leaf parsley for the garnish
- 1 roughly chopped yellow onion
- Salt & pepper to season
- 4 carrots, chopped into 1” cubes
- 1 bunch of thyme (tied using cooking string)

- 3 cups of red wine
- optional: 1 tablespoon of cornstarch with 1 tablespoon of water
- 3 tablespoons of tomato paste
- 10 oz. of pearl onions

Instructions:

- Dry the meat using a paper towel. Add salt & pepper to taste.
- Preheat a large-sized skillet to medium-high flame. Toss in some olive oil into the pan. Then add the meat and fry it for around 2 to 3 minutes on each side, till it is lightly browned. Inside the Crock-Pot, place the seared meat.
- Toss in the bacon into the skillet. Cook till golden brown. Approximately 3–4 minutes Inside the Crock-Pot, add the bacon.
- After that, add the garlic and onions to the skillet. Sauté for around 2-3 minutes, or till onions are transparent. Toss onions into the Crock-Pot.
- After that, pour red wine onto the heated skillet. Scrape all of the brown bits from the pan's bottom using a wooden spoon. Add the beef stock & tomato paste to the pan, whisk together, and scrape the bottom of the pan till all everything is clear.
- Add the mushrooms, carrots, and pearl onions to the Crock-Pot with the thyme bundle. Fill the Crock-Pot with the red wine mixture. Cover & stir gently.
- Cook for around 6-8 hours on LOW, or till the meat is cooked. Add more thyme or the flat-leaf parsley as a garnish.
- Serve!

14. Coffee- Braised Brisket

(Preparation time: 20 minutes | Cooking time: 10 hours | Servings: 4)
Per serving: Calories 329, Total fat 18, Protein 32g, Carbs 18g

Ingredients:

- 1/2 teaspoon of garlic powder
- 1/2 tablespoon of balsamic vinegar

- 1/2 (3-pounds) of boneless beef brisket
- 4 cups of strong brewed coffee
- 1/2 tablespoon of ground coffee
- 1 large sliced onion
- 1/2 teaspoon of salt
- 1 tablespoon of brown sugar
- 1/2 teaspoon of ground black pepper
- 1/2 tablespoon of paprika

Instructions:

- Brown sugar, salt, paprika, garlic powder, pepper, & ground coffee are combined inside a bowl.
- Then cut the fat from the brisket & rub the mixture all over the beef's surfaces. If necessary, chop the meat to fit into a Crock-Pot.
- Place the beef inside the Crock-Pot with the onions on top of the brisket. After that, combine the vinegar & coffee and spread over the onions. Cover and cook for around 10 hours on low or around 5 hours on high.
- After the meat has finished cooking, transfer it to a cutting board & slice it against the grain. Then, using a slotted spoon, remove the onions from the cooking fluid. Serve the meat with the onion mixture.

15. Crock-Pot Meatballs

(Preparation time: 30 minutes | Cooking time: 2 hours | Servings: 4)
Per serving: Calories 413, Total fat 18, Protein 47g, Carbs 12g

Ingredients:

For the meatballs:

- 1/2 tablespoon of cumin
- 1 cup of bone broth
- A small handful of fresh parsley, diced
- 1 heaping tablespoon of tomato paste
- Sea salt & pepper
- 1 lb. of ground beef
- 1/2 teaspoon of paprika

For the cauliflower:

- 2 tablespoons of butter or ghee
- Pepper
- Sea salt
- 1/2 large head of a cauliflower

Instructions:

- Combine the paprika, meat, pepper, salt, & cumin inside a mixing bowl.
- To combine, whisk everything together thoroughly.
- Make one-inch meatballs with the meat and place them inside the bottom of your crockpot.
- Then, in a dish, combine the paste and broth & spoon over the meatballs. Cook for roughly around 2 hours on high inside the crockpot.
- When the meatballs are done, cut the cauliflower into florets & steam them till they are tender.
- Remove the water and season using butter, salt, & pepper. Using an immersion blender, combine the ingredients till it is completely smooth.
- Place the cauliflower mash onto a serving tray and top with meatballs and sauce to taste.
- Enjoy with a parsley garnish.

16. Curried Lamb

(Preparation time: 20 minutes | Cooking time: 9 hours | Servings: 4)
Per serving: Calories 341, Total fat 15g, Protein 33g, Carbs 8g

Ingredients:

- 2 teaspoons of coriander
- 1-14 ounces can of coconut milk
- 1/8 teaspoon of saffron threads
- 1-1/2 teaspoons of cumin
- 1 teaspoon of pepper
- 1 teaspoon of turmeric
- 4 pounds of lamb stew meat
- 1 tablespoon of paprika

- 1/2 teaspoon of salt
- 3 peeled and minced cloves of garlic
- 1-1/2 tablespoons of grated fresh ginger
- Plain yogurt for the garnish
- 1-14 ounces can of diced tomatoes
- 2 tablespoons of olive oil

Instructions:

- Inside a saucepan, combine the milk, ginger, coriander, turmeric, cumin, paprika, and saffron threads, if using. On medium flame, occasionally stir till the mixture is smooth, creamy, and steaming, around 5 minutes.
- Spray the Crock-Pot using nonstick cooking spray before pouring in the milk. Inside the Crock-Pot, combine the diced tomatoes, salt, & black pepper.
- Inside a skillet, heat the oil & add the garlic. Add the stew meat to the pan and brown lightly from all sides. Add this into the Crock-Pot & cook on low for around 8 hours with the lid on.
- Remove the cover and give it a good swirl. Reduce the flame to high and leave the cover off for 30 minutes to an hour. Because this meal contains a lot of liquid, leaving the top off allows the liquid to solidify.
- Serve over rice with a dollop of plain yogurt on top.

17. Crock-Pot Braised Lamb Shanks

(Preparation time: 20 minutes | Cooking time: 6 hours | Servings: 6)
Per serving: Calories 572, Total fat 25g, Protein 32g, Carbs 34g

Ingredients:

- 1 medium peeled & diced yellow onion
- 2 peeled & diced carrots
- 4 lamb shanks trimmed of fat
- 2 stalks of celery diced
- 2 crushed cloves of garlic
- 1 – 14.5 ounces can of crushed tomatoes
- 1 bay leaf
- 2 tablespoons of tomato paste
- 2 tablespoons of olive oil
- 1 teaspoon of fresh thyme chopped
- 1 cup of red wine
- 2 cups of chicken stock
- Salt & pepper to taste

Instructions:

- Place the carrots, celery, onion, crushed tomatoes, and tomato paste inside the crock after spraying it using a nonstick spray. Pour the stock on top of the garlic and herbs. To thoroughly incorporate the ingredients, gently stir them together.
- Season the shanks using salt and black pepper. Heat the olive oil inside a sauté pan on medium flame till it is very hot. Brown the shanks on all sides. It should take roughly 5 minutes to complete this task. Inside the Crock-Pot, place the browned shanks.
- Pour the wine into the hot pan when it has been removed from the flame. Return the flame and simmer the wine, constantly swirling to incorporate all of the brown bits before pouring them into the Crock-Pot.
- Cook for around 6 hours on high, covered.
- Place the shanks onto a serving plate.
- Remove the bay leaf from the sauce and purée it inside the Crock-Pot using a stick blender till smooth. With the shanks, serve your sauce.

18. Crock-Pot Meatloaf

(Preparation time: 30 minutes | Cooking time: 10 hours | Servings: 8)
Per serving: Calories 362, Total fat 23g, Protein 21g, Carbs 16g

Ingredients:

- 1/2 peeled and chopped onion
- 1 teaspoon of pepper
- 2/3 cup of unseasoned bread crumbs
- 1 cup of Ketchup
- 1 tablespoon of garlic powder
- 1/2 cup of milk
- 1 teaspoon of salt
- 2 eggs
- 1 tablespoon of Worcestershire Sauce
- 1 teaspoon of dried Italian seasoning herbs
- 1-1/2 pound of ground beef

Instructions:

- Bread crumbs, salt. garlic powder, onion, eggs, pepper, Italian Seasoning, and milk are combined inside a large-sized mixing dish. Mix thoroughly before adding the ground meat. Knead everything together using your hands and form into two loaves. Place inside the bottom of an oblong Crock-Pot that has been sprayed using a nonstick spray.
- Whisk together the ketchup & Worcestershire sauce inside a 4 cup measuring cup & pour on top of the meatloaves.
- Cook for around 8 to 10 hours on low. Remove the loaves out from the Crock-Pot with care and serve. You will always have a hard time pulling these out of the Crock-Pot without breaking them up, so slice them in half and remove the slices using a cake server or spatula.

19. Corned Beef, Cabbage and Potatoes

(Preparation time: 20 minutes | Cooking time: 9 hours | Servings: 8)

Per serving: Calories 269g, Total fat 10g, Protein 13g, Carbs 32g

Ingredients:

- 2 medium peeled & sliced onions
- 1 can of beer
- 1 to 2 cups of baby carrots
- 1 bay leaf
- 6 medium red potatoes, skins on, cut into quarters
- 1 small cabbage wedges
- 1 – 3 to 4-pounds of corned beef brisket

Instructions:

- Spray the inside of the Crock-Pot using nonstick cooking spray. Inside the bottom of the pot, place the carrots, onions, potatoes, and bay leaf.
- Trim the brisket of excess fat and place it on top.
- Cook on low for around 8 to 9 hours after pouring the beer on top.
- Turn up at high for the last 45 minutes of cooking & add the cabbage wedges.
- Place the cabbage inside a dish after removing it from the pot. If the brisket is not falling apart, remove it and cut it against the grain. Remove the potatoes, carrots, & onions from the pot and combine them with cabbage to serve. Discard the bay leaf.

20. Crock-Pot Lamb Shoulder

(Preparation time: 20 minutes | Cooking time: 8 hours | Servings: 10)
Per serving: Calories 324, Total fat 27g, Protein 17g, Carbs 6g

Ingredients:

- 1 large chopped onion
- 4 pounds of lamb shoulder
- 6 tablespoons of tomato paste
- 3 bay leaves
- 6 large carrots, peeled, chopped into 1-cm pieces
- Salt to taste

- 6 cloves of grated garlic
- Pepper powder to taste
- Vegetable or lamb stock as required
- 2 teaspoons of Worcestershire sauce

Instructions:

- Preheat a nonstick skillet to medium flame. Cook till the lamb is brown on both sides. Season using salt & pepper. Carrots should be placed inside the Crock-Pot. On top of the vegetables, place the lamb.
- In the same skillet, sauté the onions till they are transparent. Place it on the top layer of a Crock-Pot. Then add enough stock to cover the lamb, place tomato paste, garlic, Worcestershire sauce, and bay leaves. Cook on Low for around 8 hours, or till the meat easily falls off the bone.
- Remove the bone out from the lamb and serve alongside mashed potatoes and the juice from the boiled carrots.

21. Crock-Pot Kielbasa

(Preparation time: 15 minutes | Cooking time: 8 hours | Servings: 6)
Per serving: Calories 135, Total fat 9g, Protein 10g, Carbs 4g

Ingredients:

- 1/2 cup of dry red wine
- 1 medium chopped green pepper
- 1/2 pound of lean ground beef
- 1/4 teaspoon of ground black pepper
- 1 teaspoon of crushed dried oregano
- 1 pound of kielbasa or smoked sausage, sliced around 1/2-inch thick
- 1-pound pasta of your preference
- 1 (28 ounces) can of tomatoes, undrained
- 3 cloves of minced garlic
- 1 1/2 to 2 cups of frozen French-style green beans
- 4 ounces of freshly grated Parmesan cheese
- 1 can of whole ripe olives, around 6 ounces, drained

- 1 onion, sliced & separated into rings
- 1 teaspoon of crushed dried leaf basil
- 1/2 teaspoon of crushed dried leaf thyme

Instructions:

- Brown the lean ground beef inside a medium-sized skillet. Transfer to a Crock-Pot after browned. Except for the pasta and Parmesan cheese, combine all other ingredients. Cook on LOW for around 6 to 8 hours, covered. Cook the pasta according to the package directions. Inside large serving bowls, spoon kielbasa over spaghetti to serve. To garnish, pass the Parmesan cheese.

22. Carne Guisado

(Preparation time: 20 minutes | Cooking time: 12 hours | Servings: 4)
Per serving: Calories 553, Total fat 37g, Protein 37g, Carbs 18g

Ingredients:

- 10 1/2 ounces of condensed beef broth, undiluted
- 1 teaspoon of chili powder
- 1 pound of stew beef
- 1/2 cup of water
- 2 tablespoons of vegetable oil
- 1 or 2 chopped small jalapeno or serrano chili peppers
- 2 tablespoons of tomato paste, optional
- 1/2 teaspoon of ground black pepper
- 2 teaspoons of cornstarch, dissolved in a small amount of cold water
- 2 cloves of crushed garlic
- 1/2 teaspoon of cumin

Instructions:

- All sides of the meat should be browned in oil. Excess grease should be poured away. Tomato paste, chili peppers, beef broth, salt & pepper, garlic, chili powder, cumin, and water are all added to the Crock-Pot.
- Cook for around 8 to 12 hours on low, or till meat is extremely soft.

- Turn the heat to high and whisk together 2 teaspoons of cornstarch with a small amount of cold water, then gently pour into the simmering stew till the liquids are thickened.
- Serve with warm tortillas and rice, as well as refried beans & garnishes.

23. Crockpot Leg of Lamb Off the Bone

(Preparation time: 30 minutes | Cooking time: 10 hours | Servings: 6)
Per serving: Calories 476, Total fat 30g, Protein 46g, Carbs 13g

Ingredients:

- 2 peeled and chopped cloves of garlic
- 1 cup of baby carrots
- 1/2 teaspoon of ground cinnamon
- 1 medium peeled & chopped yellow onion
- 2 tablespoons of flour
- 1-1/2 pounds of lamb shoulder
- 1 teaspoon of paprika
- 1/2 teaspoon of ground ginger
- 1/2 cup of halved dried apricots
- 1/2 teaspoon of pepper
- 1 teaspoon of ground cumin
- 1/2 cup of vegetable stock
- 1/4 teaspoon of salt

Instructions:

- After spraying the Crock-Pot using a nonstick spray, layer the carrots, onion, garlic, salt, apricots, spices, flour, and pepper in it.
- Remove the fat out from the lamb shoulder & cut it into 1-inch chunks. Fill the Crock-Pot with the pieces.
- Over the top, pour the vegetable stock.
- Set the Crock-Pot on low for around 5 hours & high for around 8 hours with the lid on. Serve with couscous on the side.

24. Crock-Pot Lamb Chops

(Preparation time: 30 minutes | Cooking time: 5 hours | Servings: 6)

Per serving: Calories 566, Total fat 52g, Protein 16g, Carbs 10g

Ingredients:

- 1 teaspoon of garlic powder
- 1 teaspoon of oregano
- 1/8 teaspoon of pepper
- 1/4 teaspoon of salt
- 1/2 teaspoon of thyme
- 1 medium peeled & chopped yellow or sweet onion
- 2 minced cloves of garlic
- 8 lamb chops
- 1 teaspoon of onion powder

Instructions:

- Combine the salt, herbs, and pepper inside a bowl and rub into the lamb chops.
- Place the chops on top of the onion inside the bottom of a Crock-Pot that has been coated using a nonstick spray. Garlic should be sprinkled on top.
- Cook on low for around 4 to 5 hours, covered. Because there is no moisture added to this dish, it should not be cooked on high.

25. Cheesy Everyday Meatloaf

(Preparation time: 30 minutes | Cooking time: 6 hours | Servings: 4)

Per serving: Calories 362, Total fat 23g, Protein 21g, Carbs 16g

Ingredients:

- 1 cup of quick-cooking oats
- 1/2 pound of lean ground pork
- 1/4 cup of tomato ketchup
- 1/2 teaspoon of ground black pepper
- 1/2 pound of lean ground beef
- 1/2 teaspoon of ground ginger
- 1/2 cup of reduced-fat cream cheese
- 1 clove of minced garlic
- 2 tablespoons of Worcestershire sauce
- 1/2 cup of chopped onion
- 1 medium-sized egg
- 1 chopped green bell pepper
- 1/2 cup of grated reduced-fat Cheddar cheese
- 1 teaspoon of sea salt

Instructions:

- Combine all of the ingredients, except for the Cheddar cheese, inside a large-sized mixing dish. Make a meatloaf out of it.
- Inside a Crock-Pot, place the meatloaf on a Crock-Pot liner.
- Cook for around 6 hours on low.

- Strew grated cheese around and place a slice of cheddar cheese on the top and set aside till it melts. Serve.

26. Curried Peanut Meat Loaf

(Preparation time: 20 minutes | Cooking time: 6 hours | Servings: 4)
Per serving: Calories 332, Total fat 21g, Protein 24g, Carbs 10g

Ingredients:

- 1 chopped sweet red bell pepper
- 1 cup of quick-cooking oats
- 1 teaspoon of dried basil
- 1 teaspoon of curry powder
- 1/4 cup of chutney, chopped
- 1/2 teaspoon of ground black pepper
- 1 teaspoon of grated ginger
- 1 ½ pounds of ground beef and pork, mixed
- 1/2 cup of milk
- 1 teaspoon of granulated garlic
- 1 egg
- 1/2 cup of chopped onion
- 1 teaspoon of sea salt
- 1/3 cup of chopped peanuts

Instructions:

- Using a large strip of aluminum foil, line your Crock-Pot.
- Combine oats, ginger, bell pepper, milk, egg, chutney, onion, garlic, sea salt, basil, peanuts, curry powder, and black pepper inside a large-sized mixing bowl.
- To blend, whisk everything together thoroughly.
- Mix in the ground meat one more. Form the dough into a circular loaf.
- Place inside the Crock-Pot, cover, and cook on low for around 6 hours.
- Warm or at the room temperature is fine.

27. Chipotle Beef Barbacoa

(Preparation time: 10 minutes | Cooking time: 4 hours | Servings: 9)
Per serving: Calories 244, Total fat 14g, Protein 21g, Carbs 7g

Ingredients:

- 2 tablespoons of apple cider vinegar
- 1 tablespoon of dried oregano
- 2 medium chipotle chilies in adobo with the sauce 4 teaspoons
- 1 teaspoon of black pepper
- 2 teaspoons of cumin
- 3 lbs. of beef brisket (trimmed & cut into 2-inch pieces)
- 2 whole bay leaves
- 1/2 cup of beef broth
- 2 tablespoons of lime juice
- 1/2 teaspoon of ground cloves
- 5 cloves of minced garlic
- 2 teaspoons of sea salt

Instructions:

- Inside a blender, combine the broth, adobo chipotle chilies, lime juice, garlic, apple cider vinegar, black pepper, dried oregano, cumin, sea salt, and ground cloves (everything except the beef & bay leaves). Puree till completely smooth.
- Inside a Crock-Pot, place the meat chunks. On top, pour the pureed contents from the blender. Add the bay leaves (whole).
- Cook on high for around 4 to 6 hours or low for around 8-10 hours, or till the beef is cooked.
- Remove the bay leaves from the dish. Using two forks, shred the meat and swirl it into the liquids. Cover and set aside for around 5-10 minutes to let the beef absorb extra flavor. To serve, use a slotted spoon.

28. Crock-Pot Ropa Vieja

(Preparation time: 20 minutes | Cooking time: 4 hours | Servings: 6)

Per serving: Calories 559, Total fat 41g, Protein 34g, Carbs 6g

Ingredients:

- 1 large sliced onion
- 2- 2 1/2 pounds of beef flank steak, skirt or roast
- 1 thyme spring
- 2 bell peppers (red, green), seeded & sliced into strips
- 1 teaspoon of ground cumin
- 2-3 tablespoons of parsley/cilantro
- Salt, cumin, pepper and Sazon (adjust to taste)
- 1-2 packets of Sazon (sub beef or chicken bouillon)
- ¼ cup of vegetable oil or more
- Salt & pepper to taste
- 2 tomatoes sliced into strips
- 1 large bay leaf
- 4-5 garlic cloves minced
- 1 can (8 ounces) of tomato sauce
- 1 teaspoon of smoked paprika
- 1-2 cups of beef broth

Instructions:

- Remove any excess fat out from the beef, then season using salt, cumin, pepper, and sazon. Taste and adjust as needed.
- Inside a medium-sized skillet, heat about 2 tablespoons of oil, then arrange the beef inside a single layer & sear on both sides till brown. Each side should take around 3-4 minutes. After browning one side, add bay leaves.
- On medium-high flame, add the remaining oil to the skillet. Then add the onions, tomato sauce, garlic, bell peppers, tomatoes, cumin, thyme, paprika, and salt and pepper to taste. Cook for around 3-5 minutes at a low temperature. Pour in the broth. Remove the pan from the flame and pour 3/4 of the sauce into the Crock-Pot.
- Cook for around 3 1/2--4 hours on High or around 7 -8 hours on Low, or till meat is soft and readily shredded with two forks.

Remove the steak from the pan and set it aside.

- Toss in 1-2 cups of the crockpot sauce with the remaining sauce. Cook for 2 minutes or longer if desired. If necessary, add more seasoning (sazon). Toss in some parsley. Season to taste.
- Finally, mix in the shredded beef for a minute. Serve with beans, rice, & tostones as a side dish.

29. Crock-Pot Steak Fajitas

(Preparation time: 20 minutes | Cooking time: 8 hours | Servings: 6)
Per serving: Calories 467, Total fat 20g, Protein 28g, Carbs 44g

Ingredients:

- 1 teaspoon of ground coriander
- 1 beef flank steak (around 1-1/2 pounds)
- 1/2 teaspoon of salt
- 1 jalapeno pepper, seeded & chopped
- 1 medium sweet red pepper, julienned
- 12 flour tortillas (around 6 inches), warmed
- 1 teaspoon of ground cumin
- 1 medium julienned green pepper
- 1 can (14-1/2 ounces) of diced tomatoes with garlic & onion, undrained
- 2 minced garlic cloves
- 1 teaspoon of chili powder
- 1 medium sliced onion
- Optional: Sour cream, fresh cilantro leaves, salsa and lime wedges
- 1 tablespoon of minced fresh cilantro

Instructions:

- Slice the steak thinly across the grain into strips and set them inside a 5-quart Crock-Pot.
- Combine the tomatoes, chili powder, jalapeno, garlic, coriander, cumin, and salt in a large mixing bowl. Cook on low for around 7 hours, covered.

- Combine the peppers, onion, and cilantro in a mixing bowl. Cook, covered, for around 1-2 hours, or till the meat is soft.
- Spoon roughly 1/2 cup of beef mixture down the middle of each tortilla using a slotted spoon.
- Fold the bottom of the tortilla over the filling, then roll it up. Serve with the cilantro, sour cream, salsa, and lime wedges, if desired.

30. Crock-Pot Schwartz's Rouladen

(Preparation time: 30 minutes | Cooking time: 6 hours | Servings: 6)
Per serving: Calories 472, Total fat 30g, Protein 40g, Carbs 7g

Ingredients:

- 1/4 cup of finely chopped onion
- 3 chopped bacon strips
- 1 chopped celery rib
- 2 tablespoons of Dijon mustard & Worcestershire sauce
- 1-1/2 pounds of beef top round steak
- 3 medium carrots, quartered lengthwise
- 1 small parsnip, peeled & chopped
- 1/3 cup of dry red wine
- 2 tablespoons of minced fresh parsley
- 1 can (10-3/4 ounces) of condensed golden cream of mushroom soup, undiluted
- 6 dill pickle spears
- 1 cup of sliced fresh mushrooms

Instructions:

- Cook bacon inside a large-sized skillet on medium flame till crisp.
- Using a slotted spoon, transfer to paper towels to drain, reserving the drippings.
- Meanwhile, cut the steak into six serving-size pieces & pound to 1/4-inch thickness using a meat mallet. Mustard should be spread on the tops. 2 carrots pieces & 1 pickle spear on top of each; onion on top. Each one should be rolled up from the short side and secured using toothpicks.

- Brown all roll-ups in bacon drippings inside a large-sized skillet on medium-high flame. Inside a 4-quart Crock-Pot, place the roll-ups. Add celery, mushrooms, parsnip, and fried bacon to the top.
- Whisk together the soup, wine, & Worcestershire sauce inside a small-sized bowl. Pour the liquid over the top. Cover & cook on low for around 6-8 hours, or till beef is cooked. Serve with a parsley garnish.

31. Eye of Round Roast and Vegetables

(Preparation time: 20 minutes | Cooking time: 8 hours | Servings: 4)
Per serving: Calories 415, Total fat 7g, Protein 50g, Carbs 31g

Ingredients:

- 1 teaspoon of garlic powder
- 3/4 cup of baby carrots
- 1 teaspoon of oregano
- 1 teaspoon of ground pepper
- 1 teaspoon of paprika
- 1 whole onion, diced
- 1 teaspoon of dried onion powder
- 1-1/2 cup of beef broth
- 1/2 teaspoon of salt
- 1 – 3 to the 4-pounds eye of round roast
- 1 tablespoon of flour
- 6 to 8 red potatoes quartered (do not peel the skin)
- 2 stalks of diced celery
- 1 – 1.2 ounces' package of dry beef gravy mix

Instructions:

- Combine the garlic, oregano, paprika, onion powder, salt, & pepper inside a small-sized bowl and stir well. Set aside the roast after rubbing it using the mixture. Wrap the roast under plastic wrap and place it in the refrigerator overnight.
- After coating the crock using a nonstick spray, stack the potatoes, celery, carrots,

and onions inside the bottom and top with the roast.

- Whisk together the beef broth with dry gravy mix inside a large glass measuring cup and pour it over the edges of the roast. Cook for around 8 hours on low or around 5 hours on high. After around 5 minutes of sitting, remove the roast and place it on a platter for carving. Using a slotted spoon, remove the vegetables & place them in a bowl.
- Whisk in the flour till the gravy thickens, then serve in a gravy boat on the side.

32. Easy Crock-Pot Beef

(Preparation time: 10 minutes | Cooking time: 7 hours | Servings: 8)
Per serving: Calories 292, Total fat 14g, Protein 36g, Carbs 6g

Ingredients:

- 1 10.75 oz. can of condensed cream of mushroom soup
- 1 small onion diced (around 1/3 cup)
- 1 tablespoon of cornstarch mixed with 1 tablespoon of water
- 2 lbs. of beef stew meat
- 1 .88 oz. of packet brown gravy mix
- Optional: Egg noodles or mashed potatoes prepared
- 1 cup of beef broth
- 1-2 cloves of garlic minced

Instructions:

- Combine gravy mix, cream of mushroom soup, onion, beef broth, and garlic inside a medium-sized mixing bowl. Combine all ingredients in a mixing bowl. It is fine if it is a little lumpy; the lumps will dissolve while it cooks in the Crock-Pot.
- Fill a 4-quart Crock-Pot halfway with the stew meat. Pour the gravy over the beef and toss gently to incorporate. Cook on LOW for around 7 hours, covered. Remove the meat using a slotted spoon once it is finished cooking & set it aside.

Incorporate the cornstarch/water combination. Return the steak to the Crock-Pot and simmer for another 5 minutes while the gravy thickens.

- Serve with egg noodles or the mashed potatoes as a side dish.

33. Italian Pot Roast

(Preparation time: 20 minutes | Cooking time: 10 hours | Servings: 6)
Per serving: Calories 504, Total fat 25g, Protein 57g, Carbs 8g

Ingredients:

- 2-1/2 pounds of boneless beef pot roast
- 1 teaspoon of toasted and crushed fennel seed
- 1 peeled and thinly cut onion
- 1 teaspoon of garlic powder
- 26-ounces jar of tomato pasta sauce
- 1/2 teaspoon of pepper
- 2 trimmed & cored fennel bulbs thinly cut
- 1/4 cup of fresh chopped Italian parsley
- 3 chopped carrots

Instructions:

- Place fennel seeds on a foil-covered pan sprayed using nonstick spray and roast them underneath the broiler for a few minutes. Using a mortar and pestle, crush the ingredients. To prepare a rub, combine the garlic powder & pepper inside a small-sized bowl.
- Trim the fat off the roast and massage all sides using the ingredients listed above. If you are starting the roast in the morning, keep it refrigerated overnight.
- Inside the bottom of a nonstick sprayed Crock-Pot, layer the sliced fennel, carrot, & onion, then top with the roast. If necessary, cut the meat to fit.
- Overtop, pour the tomato spaghetti sauce. Cover and cook on low for around 9 to 10 hours or high for around 5 hours.

- Remove the roast from the pot and chop it into pieces. Using a slotted spoon, remove the veggies to serve with roast.
- Cook some penne or rigatoni, drain and top with the sauce from the Crock-Pot.

34. Irish Lamb Stew

(Preparation time: 20 minutes | Cooking time: 10 hours | Servings: 6)

Per serving: Calories 672, Total fat 39g, Protein 46g, Carbs 26g

Ingredients:

- 2 tablespoons of vegetable oil
- 4 potatoes, quartered
- 2 1/2 pounds of boneless lamb, cut in 1 1/2-inch cube
- 1/2 teaspoon of pepper
- 4 carrots, sliced into 1/2-inch thick
- 2 tablespoons of chopped parsley
- 1 1/2 teaspoons of salt
- 2 medium sliced onions
- 4 turnips, cut into 1/2-inch cubes
- 2 tablespoons of flour

Instructions:

- Oil is used to brown the meat.
- Place all of the ingredients inside the Crock-Pot with the meat, except for the flour and parsley.
- Cook on low for around 8 to 10 hours, covered with 2 cups of water. Remove the top and set the temperature at high.
- Stir together 1/4 cup of flour and 1/4 cup of water to make a paste; gradually add to stew, frequently stirring till slightly thickened.
- Serve with the parsley on top.

35. Italian Meatball Stew

(Preparation time: 30 minutes | Cooking time: 10 hours | Servings: 4)

Per serving: Calories 641, Total fat 45g, Protein 40g, Carbs 65g

Ingredients:

- 2 tablespoons of grated Parmesan cheese
- 8 to 12 ounces of extra lean ground beef
- 1/4 teaspoon of pepper
- 2 eggs, beaten
- 1/4 cup of milk
- 1 teaspoon of salt
- 1/8 teaspoon of garlic powder
- 1/2 cup of fine dry bread crumbs, Italian seasoned
- 1/2 teaspoon of oregano
- 1 teaspoon of seasoned salt
- 4 to 6 carrots; peeled & sliced about 1/4-inch thick
- 1 cup of water
- 1 can (6 oz.) of tomato paste
- 1/2 teaspoon of basil
- 16 ounces of Italian vegetables (frozen)
- 1 cup of beef broth

Instructions:

- Set aside the first 8 ingredients, which should be mixed together & formed into firm meatballs. Place the bite-size carrot pieces in the base of the Crock-Pot, followed by the meatballs.
- Toss the meatballs inside a mixture of tomato paste, beef broth, water, oregano, basil, and seasoned salt.
- Cook on LOW for around 4 to 6 hours, covered. Turn the Crock-Pot on HIGH and add the thawed Italian veggies. Cover and simmer for another 1/2 hour on HIGH, or till the vegetables are tender.
- Serve over or with pasta or noodles.

36. Lamb Shanks with Cannellini Beans

(Preparation time: 20 minutes | Cooking time: 9 hours | Servings: 12)

Per serving: Calories 474, Total fat 12g, Protein 31g, Carbs 51g

Ingredients:

- 1 cup of chopped onions

- 1 (28-ounces) can of un-drained and diced tomatoes
- ¼ teaspoon of ground black pepper
- 2 cloves of garlic thinly sliced
- ½ teaspoon of salt
- 4 (around 1 ½ pounds) lamb shanks
- 2 teaspoons of dried tarragon
- ¾ cup of chopped celery
- 1 (19-ounces) can of rinsed and drained white beans of choice, preferably cannellini beans
- 1 ½ cup of carrots, peeled and diced

Instructions:

- Trim any excess fat from the lamb shanks.
- Inside a seven-quart Crock-Pot, combine the beans, one and a half cups peeled & diced carrots, three-quarter cup chopped celery, one cup chopped onion, and the two garlic cloves thinly sliced.
- Over the top of the bean mixture, place the lamb shanks. Season using salt, pepper, & tarragon if desired.
- Cover the lamb with tomato sauce.
- Simmer for around 1 hour on high, then reduce to low and cook for another 9 hours, or till the lamb is extremely soft.
- Remove the shanks out from the crockpot and strain the bean mixture into a dish using a strainer or a colander.
- Allow this liquid to sit for five minutes before skimming any fat that has risen to the surface.
- Return the bean mixture to the liquid, shredding the lamb to eliminate any bones.
- Toss the lamb with bean concoction & serve.

37. Lamb Chili

(Preparation time: 15 minutes | Cooking time: 8 hours | Servings: 6)
Per serving: Calories 430, Total fat 16g, Protein 29g, Carbs 35g

Ingredients:

- 2 cloves of minced garlic
- 1-quart of vegetable stock
- 1 teaspoon of Italian seasoning mix
- 2 cans (15-ounces) of pinto beans, rinsed and drained
- Salt, to taste
- 1 cup of partially cooked ham, diced
- Cayenne pepper, to taste
- 1 pound of cubed lamb
- 1 chopped rib celery
- 1 large-sized finely chopped red onion
- Sour cream for the garnish
- 1 large-sized carrot, chopped
- Black pepper, to taste
- 1 cup of tomato sauce

Instructions:

- Inside a Crock-Pot, combine all ingredients except for the sour cream.
- Cook your chili for around 7 to 8 hours on low inside a Crock-Pot.
- Serve with a dollop of sour cream on the top.

38. Lamb and Vegetable Stew

(Preparation time: 10 minutes | Cooking time: 9 hours | Servings: 8)
Per serving: Calories 174, Total fat 6g, Protein 11g, Carbs 21g

Ingredients:

- 2 to 3 medium potatoes
- 1 cup of chopped onions
- 2 pounds of lamb stew meat, or cubed lean boneless lamb
- 1 crushed garlic clove
- 2 cups of stock, chicken
- 1 small summer squash
- 2 medium tomatoes, peeled & seeded, chopped
- 1/2 cup of chopped bell peppers
- 2 tablespoons of flour
- 1 small zucchini
- 1 can of sliced mushrooms
- 2 teaspoons of salt

- 1/2 teaspoon of thyme leaves
- 2 tablespoons of butter
- 1 bay leaf

Instructions:

- Squash and zucchini should be sliced. Potatoes should be diced.
- Inside a Crock-Pot, combine the lamb with veggies. The stock should be seasoned with thyme, salt, garlic, and bay leaf before being poured over the meat and veggies.
- Cook for around 8 to 9 hours on low, till the lamb and veggies are soft.
- Set the volume to maximum. Combine the flour and butter inside a mixing bowl. Drop tiny pieces into the stew & heat till it thickens, stirring constantly.
- Serve with rice or hot cooked noodles on the side.

39. Mississippi Roast

(Preparation time: 20 minutes | Cooking time: 8 hours | Servings: 4)
Per serving: Calories 328, Total Fat 25, Protein 23g, Carbs 11g

Ingredients:

- 2 lbs. of boneless beef chuck roast
- 1/4 large onion, finely chopped
- 2 tablespoons of butter
- Black pepper, freshly ground
- 1/4 cup of beef broth
- 1/2 cup pf pepperoncini
- Kosher salt
- 1/2 packet of ranch seasoning

Instructions:

- Inside a Crock-Pot, combine the ranch seasoning, onion, and beef broth till well combined.
- Season the chuck roast using pepper and salt.
- Toss in the butter and pepperoncini.
- Cook for around 6 to 8 hours on low heat or 4 hours on high heat, covered.

- Then take the roast out of the Crockpot and place it inside a big mixing dish.
- Shred the meat using two forks, then toss with the Crockpot juices.
- Serve the roast warm over the toast.

40. Middle Eastern Beef

(Preparation time: 20 minutes | Cooking time: 8 hours | Servings: 4)
Per serving: Calories 424, Total Fat 22, Protein 51g, Carbs 16g

Ingredients:

- 1/4 teaspoon of ground cinnamon
- 2 tablespoons of coconut vinegar
- 1/4 teaspoon of whole peppercorns
- 1 1/2 cups of bone broth
- 1/2 teaspoon of whole fennel seeds
- 1/4 large sweet onion, chopped
- 1 1/2 lbs. of grass-fed beef brisket
- 1 1/2 tablespoons of tomato paste
- 1/2 teaspoon of cardamom powder
- 1/8 teaspoon of sea salt
- 1/2 teaspoon of cumin powder
- Sea salt & pepper
- 1/2 teaspoon of whole cloves

Instructions:

- Season the brisket on both sides using pepper & salt.
- Then, with a pestle and mortar, pound together cloves, peppercorns, and fennel seeds to a fine powder.
- Combine the combination onion and tomato paste inside a blender or food processor.
- After pureeing till smooth, add the vinegar and broth. To make a smooth sauce, puree it once more.
- Place the brisket inside the crockpot, then spoon the sauce over it at this point. Cook your brisket for around 7 to 8 hours on low inside the crockpot.
- When the meat is done, shred it using a fork & serve.

41. Mostaccioli

(Preparation time: 20 minutes | Cooking time: 6 hours | Servings: 6)

Per serving: Calories 433, Total fat 20g, Protein 21g, Carbs 34g

Ingredients:

- 2 teaspoons of granulated sugar
- 1 pound of Italian sausage, mild or sweet
- 1 (12 oz.) can of tomato sauce
- 1 bay leaf
- 1 teaspoon of dried sweet basil
- 1 pound of lean ground beef
- 1 teaspoon of salt
- 1 cup of chopped onion
- Parmesan cheese, for the serving
- 1 can (6 ounces) of tomato paste
- 1 teaspoon of oregano
- 1/4 teaspoon of freshly ground black pepper
- 16 ounces of Mostaccioli, penne, or any other pasta of your choice
- 1 can (14.5 ounces) of tomatoes with juice
- 1/2 teaspoon of garlic powder

Instructions:

- Drain fat after browning sausage & ground beef. Inside a Crock-Pot, combine all ingredients except for the pasta and Parmesan cheese.
- Cook on LOW for around 6 hours, stirring occasionally and adding a little water if the sauce becomes too thick at the end.
- Cook the mostaccioli, penne, or any other pasta according to package directions into boiling salted water just before the sauce is done. Drain the pasta and toss it with the sauce.

42. Old Fashion Tasting Salisbury Steak

(Preparation time: 20 minutes | Cooking time: 6 hours | Servings: 6)

Per serving: Calories 440, Total fat 32g, Protein 23g, Carbs 14g

Ingredients:

- 2 pounds of ground beef
- 1 package of onion soup mix
- 2 to 3 tablespoons of flour
- 1 tablespoon of butter
- 1/2 cup of bread crumbs
- 1/4 cup of beef broth
- 1 teaspoon of garlic powder
- 1 egg
- 1 large sweet onion, thinly sliced
- 1/4 cup of milk
- 2 cans of cream of mushroom soup mix

Instructions:

- Inside a large-sized mixing bowl, combine the soup mix, egg, bread crumbs, garlic powder, & milk and stir well to combine.

- Mix in the ground beef using your hands, making sure everything is completely blended. Make 8 patties and keep them aside.
- Heat the butter inside a skillet till it is melted, then sauté the onion till it is brown. Set the onion aside after removing it from the skillet.
- Dredge the patties gently into flour and brown them on each side just long enough to brown them but not completely. Place them inside a Crock-Pot sprayed using nonstick cooking spray.
- Inside the Crock-Pot, arrange the onions on top.
- Whisk together the cream of mushroom soup & the beef broth inside a 4-cup measuring cup. Pour this mixture over the patties.
- Cook for around 6 hours on low, then serve alongside mashed potatoes.

43. Orange-Spiced Brisket

(Preparation time: 20 minutes | Cooking time: 7 hours | Servings: 6)
Per serving: Calories 459, Total fat 11g, Protein 22g, Carbs 20g

Ingredients:

- 1/2 cup of chopped dates
- 1 fresh beef brisket (3 pounds)
- 1/2 teaspoon of ground coriander
- 1-1/2 cups of orange juice
- 1 minced garlic clove
- 1/8 teaspoon of ground cloves
- 1 chopped small onion
- 1 cinnamon stick (3 inches)

Instructions:

- Inside a 6-quart Crock-Pot, place the beef. Combine remaining ingredients inside a small-sized dish; pour over meat. Cook on low for around 7-9 hours, covered, or till vegetables are soft.
- Transfer the brisket to a serving plate and keep it warm. Remove the cinnamon stick

and discard it. Remove the fat from the cooking liquid. Cover and purée cooking fluids in a blender till smooth; pour into a small-sized saucepan. Bring to the boil. Cook, occasionally stirring, for around 13 to 15 minutes or till thickened, uncovered. Cut the steak into thin slices diagonally across the grain and serve with the sauce.

44. Pakistani Style Beef Stew

(Preparation time: 30 minutes | Cooking time: 10 hours | Servings: 6)
Per serving: Calories 289, Total fat 13g, Protein 16g, Carbs 27g

Ingredients:

- 2 whole bay leaves
- 1 ginger root, 1" cube, chopped fine
- 5 tablespoons of whisked yogurt
- 8 tablespoons of vegetable oil
- 1/3 cup of cumin seed
- 20 whole black peppercorns
- 1 teaspoon of cardamom (seeds only)
- 1/2 teaspoon of cayenne, optional
- 2 medium onions, finely chopped
- 6 whole cloves
- 6 cloves
- 1 teaspoon of cumin seed
- 6 whole cardamom pods
- 3 each cinnamon sticks, 3 inches' long
- 6 finely chopped cloves of garlic
- 2 pounds of beef, cubed, (1")
- 1 teaspoon of coriander seed, ground
- 1/4 cup of coriander seed
- 2 teaspoons of salt
- 2 pounds of chopped spinach, fresh or frozen
- 1/2 cup of whole black peppercorns

Instructions:

- Blend the ginger, onions, & garlic to a paste inside a blender container, pouring a Tablespoon of water as needed. Set it aside. Inside a separate bowl, combine the bay leaves, peppercorns, cloves, and cardamom pods.

- Inside another separate bowl, combine the ground cumin, cayenne, ground coriander, and 1 teaspoon of salt. Place the yogurt inside a separate bowl. Prepare the fresh spinach by washing, chopping, and draining it before adding it to the dish. (Alternatively, thaw frozen spinach.) Inside a separate bowl, add the remaining teaspoon of salt.

- Inside a large-sized dutch oven, heat the vegetable oil. Add the bay leaves, peppercorns, cloves, and cardamom pods once the pot is hot. Stir for a brief moment. Add the onions, garlic, & ginger now. Stir and cook till brown specks appear in the paste. Add 1 teaspoon of salt, ground cumin, cayenne, ground coriander, and ground cumin. Combine all of the ingredients, then add the meat. Stir and cook for another minute. Then, one spoonful at a time, stir in the yogurt till it is fully combined with the other components. Continue to cook till the meat is slightly browned. Bit by bit, add the spinach, folding in more as the spinach inside the pan wilts. Continue to toss and simmer till the spinach is thoroughly wilted. To cook the meat, it should release its fluids.

- Place the entire mixture inside the Crock-Pot and cook on high for around 6 to 8 hours or low for around 8-10 hours, until the meat is cooked.

- When the meat is done, add the garam masala (directions below) over it and stir it in, then continue to cook for another 5 minutes. If there is too much fluid, cook for 5-10 minutes, uncovered, until the sauce thickens.

- To make the Garam Masala, combine all of the ingredients inside a large-sized mixing bowl: Using a blender or a coffee grinder, combine all ingredients and grind extremely finely. Store with other spices inside a firmly sealed jar.

45. Pepper Steak

(Preparation time: 20 minutes | Cooking time: 4 hours | Servings: 6)

Per serving: Calories 533, Total fat 44g, Protein 28g, Carbs 6g

Ingredients:

- 1 onion, cut into ½-inch strips
- 2 pounds of sirloin, cut into 2-inch slices
- 1 teaspoon of Worcestershire sauce
- 2 teaspoons of garlic powder
- 1 can of stewed tomatoes with liquid, around 14.5 ounces
- 1/4 teaspoon of red pepper flakes add to taste
- 2 tablespoons of cornstarch
- 1 red or yellow bell pepper, cored & cut into ½-inch strips
- 1/2 tsp Salt
- ¼ cup of water
- 2 green bell peppers cored & cut into ½-inch strips
- 1/4 cup of soy sauce, low sodium
- 1 teaspoon of brown sugar (or 1 teaspoon of honey)
- 1/4 teaspoon of black pepper
- 1 tablespoon of canola oil
- 1 tablespoon of fresh minced ginger

Instructions:

- Inside a bowl, place the cut meat. Garlic powder, salt, & black pepper is sprinkled over the beef. Toss to coat evenly.

- Inside a large-sized skillet, heat the oil on a medium-high flame. Cook, occasionally turning, till the meat is lightly browned on all sides, around 3-5 minutes. Transfer the steak to the Crock-Pot, along with any cooking juices. (Note: If you are in a hurry, you can omit this step because it adds taste.) However, we do not recommend missing it because browning the beef first adds more flavor to the dish.)

- Inside a Crock-Pot, combine tomatoes, Ginger, onions, bell peppers, and red pepper flakes. Note: Based on how crispy you want your bell peppers, you can add them 1 hour before you are ready to eat. When served, they will be crisper as a result of this.

- Combine water, Worcestershire sauce, cornstarch, soy sauce, and brown sugar inside a small-sized bowl. Put everything in the Crock-Pot.
- Cook for around 6 to 7 hours on LOW, till the beef, is tender.
- Serve immediately with the rice.

46. Rustic Stew of Lamb

(Preparation time: 30 minutes | Cooking time: 10 hours | Servings: 4)
Per serving: Calories 349, Total fat 16g, Protein 22g, Carbs 21g

Ingredients:

- 1/4 cup of all-purpose flour
- 1 1/2 pounds of lean lamb stew meat boneless, cut into 1-inch cube
- 2 cups of water
- 1 teaspoon of salt
- 2 cups of diced rutabaga or turnips
- 1/2 teaspoon of pepper
- 1 cup of frozen peas, thawed
- 2 tablespoons of vegetable oil
- 1 cup of baby carrots
- 1 cup of thinly sliced onion

Instructions:

- Season the lamb using 1/2 teaspoon of salt & freshly cracked pepper. Flour the surface. Inside a 2-3 quart Dutch oven, heat the oil on a medium-high flame. Brown the

lamb inside the hot oil a few chunks at a time. Using a slotted spoon, transfer to the Crock-Pot. Reduce to a medium flame setting. Cook, occasionally stirring, for around 3-4 minutes, or till onion is lightly browned. Scrape off browned bits from the bottom of the pot as you stir in the water. Add the carrots and rutabaga, and onion mixture inside the Crock-Pot.

- Cook them on low for around 8 to 10 hours, adding peas 30-40 minutes before the end.

47. Shredded Beef Tacos

(Preparation time: 20 minutes | Cooking time: 8 hours | Servings: 10)
Per serving: Calories 399, Total fat 33g, Protein 21g, Carbs 8g

Ingredients:

- 1 teaspoon of ground cumin
- 1/4 cup of beef broth
- Salt & pepper to taste
- 1 jalapeno pepper, diced
- 1 teaspoon of smoked paprika
- 1 medium yellow onion, diced
- 2–3 lbs. of chuck roast
- 1 teaspoon of cayenne
- 1 teaspoon of minced garlic
- 2 tablespoons of tomato paste
- 1/4 cup of lime juice

Instructions:

- Season your chuck roast to taste using salt and black pepper.
- Sear the chuck roast from all sides in some oil in a pan on medium-high flame till browned, around 2 minutes on each side. Remove the item and place it away.
- Combine the beef broth with smoked paprika, cayenne, cumin, and garlic.
- Stir in the jalapeño, tomato paste, and lime juice.
- Place the roast inside a 6-quart Crock-Pot with the diced onions on top.

- Cook on low for around 6-8 hours or high for around 3-4 hours after pouring the beef broth combination over the roast.
- Using two forks, shred the steak & toss to coat in the juices.
- Serve immediately with tortillas & your preferred toppings.
- Enjoy!

48. Turkish Lamb with Vegetables

(Preparation time: 30 minutes | Cooking time: 8 hours | Servings: 8)
Per serving: Calories 174, Total fat 6g, Protein 11g, Carbs 21g

Ingredients:

- 4 thinly sliced large onions
- 3 pounds of lean boneless, leg of lamb, trimmed, make 1 ½-inch piece
- 2 cans (14 ounces each) of diced tomatoes
- 1 pound of trimmed green beans
- ½ teaspoon of salt, divided
- 2 medium zucchinis make ¼-inch thick slices
- 1/3 cup of chopped fresh parsley
- 8 cloves of minced garlic
- 3 tablespoons of extra virgin olive oil
- 2 large Yukon gold potatoes, peeled, make ¼-inch thick slices
- Ground black pepper powder to taste
- 1 teaspoon of dried oregano
- 5 bay leaves
- 2 small eggplants make ¼-inch thick slices

Instructions:

- Using salt and pepper, season the lamb. Preheat a large-sized skillet to medium-high. Approximately a spoonful of oil should be added. Cook the lamb in batches, browning it on both sides. If required, add more oil. Inside a Crock-Pot, place the lamb.
- One tablespoon of oil should be added to the skillet. Once the oil is hot, add the onions and cook till they are transparent.

- Add the garlic and oregano and cook for a few minutes, till fragrant.
- Stir in the tomatoes thoroughly. Allow it to cook for a while. Mash it using a potato masher while it is simmering. Half of the mixture should be applied to the lamb.
- Arrange the potatoes on top of the lamb. After that, cover the potatoes with eggplant, beans, and zucchini. Season each layer with salt and pepper.
- Over the zucchini layer, spread the leftover tomato mixture. On top of that, place the bay leaves.
- Cook on high for around 4 hours or low for around 8 hours, covered. Remove the bay leaves once they have been cooked. Serve garnished with parsley.

49. Vegetable Pot Roast

(Preparation time: 15 minutes | Cooking time: 8 hours | Servings: 6)
Per serving: Calories 567, Total fat 33g, Protein 36g, Carbs 30g

Ingredients:

- 2 stalks of celery, diced
- 1 pound of carrots
- 1 teaspoon of broth concentrate
- 3 medium-sized potatoes, quartered
- 1 cup of tomato juice
- 2 cloves of garlic, peeled & minced
- 1 large-sized chopped onion
- 1 sweet red bell pepper, seeded & diced
- 1 cup of water
- 3 pounds of chuck roast, boneless
- 1 tablespoon of soy sauce
- 1/2 teaspoon of black pepper

Instructions:

- Inside your Crock-Pot, arrange the vegetables.
- Split the chuck roast into individual servings. Arrange the roast pieces on top of the veggies.

- Combine broth concentrate, tomato juice, black pepper, water, and soy sauce inside a mixing dish.
- To combine the ingredients, whisk them together. Fill the Crock-Pot halfway with this liquid mixture.
- Cook on low for around 8 hours, covered.

Chapter 5:
Crock-Pot Pork Recipes

1. Baby Lima Beans with Ham B-B-Q Pork

(Preparation time: 10 minutes | Cooking time: 3 hours | Servings: 8)

Per serving: Calories 266, Total fat 13g, Protein 17g, Carbs 27g

Ingredients:

- 2 mediums coarsely chopped onions
- 1/4 teaspoon of ground black pepper
- 1 pound of dried baby lima beans
- 3 to 4 cups of water to cover
- 2 quarts of water for soaking
- Salt, to taste
- 1 meaty ham bone plus the leftover diced ham, as desired
- A dash of cayenne pepper
- 1 teaspoon of Cajun or Creole seasoning blend

Instructions:

- Soak the lima beans overnight in around 2 quarts of water.
- Drain the lima beans and place them inside the Crock-Pot. Add 3 to 4 cups of water to

just cover the beans, then add the chopped onions, ham bone, & ham.
- Cook on HIGH for around 3 hours, covered.
- Add the black and cayenne peppers, as well as the Creole spice. Cook on LOW for around 4 hours, or till vegetables are extremely soft.

2. BBQ Boston Butt

(Preparation time: 10 minutes | Cooking time: 10 hours | Servings: 8)

Per serving: Calories 700, Total fat 53g, Protein 30g, Carbs 20g

Ingredients:

- 1/4 cup of water
- Barbecue sauce
- 4 to 7 pounds of bone-in or boneless pork shoulder or Boston butt
- Salt and pepper lightly

Instructions:

- Inside a Crock-Pot, combine the salt, meat, water, and pepper.
- Cook for around 1 hour on HIGH, covered. Reduce to LOW and cook for another 7 to 9 hours, or till very tender. Remove the roast out from the pan and discard the fat and juices. Return the meat to the Crock-Pot after chopping or shredding it. To add flavor to the meat, mix in a little barbeque sauce. Cover and continue to simmer on LOW for another hour or till heated.
- Serve with coleslaw & extra bbq sauce on the side on warm split sandwich buns.

3. Braised Pork Loin

(Preparation time: 10 minutes | Cooking time: 10 hours | Servings: 8)

Per serving: Calories 344, Total fat 16g, Protein 34g, Carbs 11g

Ingredients:

- 1/2 teaspoon of each sage and thyme

- 3 to 4-pounds of boneless pork loin roast, trimmed
- 1/4 cup of dry white wine or chicken broth
- 4 cloves of sliced garlic
- 1/4 cup of flour
- Salt and black pepper
- 1 cup of chicken broth

Instructions:

- To remove the extra fat, brown the pork roast from all sides inside a wide skillet.
- Using a tiny knife, make slits in the roast & insert garlic slices; arrange inside Crock-Pot and season using pepper, salt, sage and thyme, or poultry seasoning. If using, add the broth and wine.
- Cook on LOW for around 8 to 10 hours, covered. Remove the roast and remove any excess fat from the juices; whisk together the flour and 3 tablespoons cold water till smooth.
- Increase the Crock-Pot's temperature to high and add the flour mixture. Cook, constantly stirring, till the sauce has thickened (this can also be done more rapidly on the stovetop).
- Serve with the rice or the potatoes and a side of sauce.

4. Brown Sugar Pork Loin

(Preparation time: 20 minutes | Cooking time: 10 hours | Servings: 8)
Per serving: Calories 381, Total fat 14g, Protein 27g, Carbs 34g

Ingredients:

- 1 1/3 cups of brown sugar, divided
- 1 boneless pork loin roast, around 4 to 6 pounds
- 1 tablespoon of balsamic vinegar
- 1 clove of garlic, halved
- 1/4 teaspoon of cinnamon
- Salt and freshly ground black pepper
- 1 tablespoon of Dijon mustard or a grainy mustard

Instructions:

- Trim the pork if it has an excessive layer of fat.
- A very little fat will assist the roast to stay juicy during the long cooking process.
- Rub the garlic halves all over the roast, season using salt and black pepper, and puncture the roast all over using a fork or skewer.
- Combine mustard, 1 cup of brown sugar, and vinegar inside a cup or bowl.
- Rub the roast all over. Transfer to the Crock-Pot.
- Cook on LOW for around 7 to 9 hours, or till vegetables are soft but not falling apart.
- Remove any extra fluids using a strainer.
- Spread the leftover 1/3 cup brown sugar over the top of the roast, along with the cinnamon. Cover and cook for an additional hour on LOW.

5. B-B-Q Pork

(Preparation time: 20 minutes | Cooking time: 9 hours | Servings: 8)
Per serving: Calories 409, Total fat 18g, Protein 28g, Carbs 34g

Ingredients:

- 1 tablespoon of granulated sugar
- 1/2 cup of cider vinegar
- 1 teaspoon of Worcestershire sauce
- 1/4 teaspoon of black pepper
- 3-4 pounds of boneless pork shoulder roast, trimmed and tied
- 1 teaspoon of ground paprika
- 2 tablespoons of ketchup
- 1/4 cup of chopped onion
- 1 teaspoon of Tabasco or hot pepper sauce
- Few dashes of liquid smoke, if liked
- 8 heated hamburger buns
- 1 teaspoon of salt

Instructions:

- Combine Worcestershire sauce, chopped onion, cider vinegar, & hot pepper sauce inside a large-sized non-metallic mixing bowl. Place the pork, cover, & marinate for around 6 to 10 hours inside the refrigerator. Turn the roast every now and then to keep the marinade on it.

- Scrape the onion back inside the marinade after removing the meat from it. Using paper towels, lightly wipe dry the roast. Pour the Liquid Smoke into the marinade inside a Crock-Pot.
- Inside the Crock-Pot, place either a Crock-Pot meat's rack or a foil ring.
- Inside a cup, combine the paprika, sugar, salt, and black pepper. Place the pork roast onto the rack inside the crockpot and rub with the seasoning mixture.
- Cook the dish on LOW for around 8 to 9 hours, or till the meat is very soft. Move the pork to the cutting board & keep it warm by covering it using foil.
- Skim all the fat out from the cooking liquid's surface. Pour the ketchup into a bowl after stirring it in.
- Pull your pork apart using two forks into the shreds or slice the pork into smaller bits.
- Serve pork alongside beans, coleslaw, or your favorite side dishes on warm split buns. The sauce should be served separately.

6. Brown Sugar and Maple Glazed Ham

(Preparation time: 20 minutes | Cooking time: 4 hours | Servings: 8)
Per serving: Calories 367, Total fat 11g, Protein 31g, Carbs 37g

Ingredients:

- 1/2 cup of prepared honey Dijon mustard
- 1/2 cup of packed brown sugar
- 1 – 5 to 6 pounds of fully cooked boneless ham
- 1/2 cup of maple syrup

Instructions:

- Coat a Crock-Pot using nonstick cooking spray.
- Place the ham inside the Crock-Pot with diamond cuts on the top.
- Combine the syrup, mustard, and brown sugar inside a large-sized measuring cup. Blend everything together with a whisk till it is completely smooth. It will be a thick one. Spoon over the ham & spread evenly so that it is completely covered.
- Cook on low for around 3 to 4 hours with the lid on the Crock-Pot. A meat thermometer must read 140 degrees F. Turn the Crock-Pot off once it achieves this internal temperature.
- Cover the ham loosely using foil after removing it from the Crock-Pot. Allow for a 15-minute rest period.
- Meanwhile, pour the cooking fluids into a gravy boat or measuring cup & set them aside.
- Slice the ham & serve it with the juices.

7. Cherry Glazed Pork Roast

(Preparation time: 20 minutes | Cooking time: 10 hours | Servings: 8)
Per serving: Calories 262, Total fat 9g, Protein 27g, Carbs 43g

Ingredients:

- 3 tablespoons of wine vinegar
- 1 pork loin roast, boneless, around 3 pounds
- 1 cup of cherry jam, or use pineapple or apricot preserves
- 1 can (10 1/2 ounces) of condensed chicken broth
- 1/4 teaspoon of seasoned pepper (or use regular ground black pepper)
- 1 bunch of green onions, with the green, sliced into 1-inch lengths
- Drop or 2 of red food coloring, optional
- 1 teaspoon of dried rosemary

Instructions:

- Place the pork roast inside the Crock-Pot after trimming it. Inside a small-sized mixing bowl, combine all ingredients except for the jam or preserves & food coloring. Pour the sauce over the roast. Cook on low for around 8 to 10 hours, covered. Turn the Crock-Pot to HIGH just before serving.
- Remove the roast and place it on a warm serving plate. Inside a Crock-Pot, combine cherry jam, juices, as well as a pinch of red food coloring, if preferred; heat to the serving temperature. Serve with sliced pork.

8. Chinese Pork Roast

(Preparation time: 20 minutes | Cooking time: 10 hours | Servings: 10)
Per serving: Calories 351, Total fat 22g, Protein 22g, Carbs 15g

Ingredients:

- 2 teaspoons of curry powder
- 1 pork shoulder roast, around 4 pounds
- 1/4 cup of cold water
- 16 ounces of frozen Chinese mixed vegetables, cooked till crisp-tender
- 1 teaspoon of salt
- 2 tablespoons of vegetable oil
- 2 cups of hot cooked rice
- 1 can (10 3/4 ounces) of condensed cream of mushroom soup or cream of celery soup
- 2 tablespoons of all-purpose flour

Instructions:

- Remove any excess fat out from the roast and, if necessary, chop it to fit into the Crock-Pot. Rub the roast with a mixture of salt & 1/2 teaspoon of curry powder. Inside a heated pan, brown the roast on all sides. Inside the crockpot, place the roast on a rack or a crumpled piece of foil. Pour the mushroom soup over the pork roast, along with the remaining 1 1/2 teaspoons of curry powder. Cover and cook for around 8 to 10 hours on the LOW setting.

Transfer the roast to a serving tray and set it aside to keep warm.

- Fill a pot halfway with the juices and skim off any extra fat. On the burner, bring the juices to the boil and then reduce to a low flame for around 15 minutes. Slowly pour cold water into flour and mix till smooth; toss in juices. Cook, constantly stirring, till the sauce has thickened; serve alongside hot cooked veggies, hot cooked rice, & pork roast.

9. Cider Pork Pot Roast

(Preparation time: 20 minutes | Cooking time: 8 hours | Servings: 8)
Per serving: Calories 235, Total fat 8g, Protein 21g, Carbs 19g

Ingredients:

- 4 to 6 carrots, cut into 1-inch pieces
- 1/8 teaspoon of pepper
- 1 teaspoon of chili powder
- 2 medium onions, halved and sliced
- 2 cups of natural apple juice or cider
- 1 boneless pork shoulder, around 3 1/2 to 4 1/2 pounds
- 2 tablespoons of cider vinegar
- 1/2 teaspoon of allspice
- 2 cloves of garlic, minced
- 1 teaspoon of dried leaf marjoram or thyme
- 1/2 teaspoon of salt

Instructions:

- Arrange the onions inside the Crock-Pot's bottom.
- Place the pork roast inside the Crock-Pot leave the netting.
- Carrots should be arranged around the roast, which should also be seasoned with garlic, chili powder, salt, pepper, allspice, and marjoram or thyme.
- Pour the juice & vinegar over the roast and toss to coat.
- Cook for around 1 hour on HIGH, covered. Reduce flame to LOW and simmer for

another 6 to 8 hours, or cook on HIGH for another 3 to 4 hours.

- Fill a pot halfway with juices and bring to the boil over high flame.
- Reduce the flame to medium and cook for another 5 minutes.
- Combine the flour & cold water inside a mixing bowl and whisk till smooth; add to the boiling liquids.
- Cook, constantly stirring, till the sauce has thickened. Serve alongside the pork.

10. Cranberry-Apple Pork Ribs

(Preparation time: 20 minutes | Cooking time: 10 hours | Servings: 8)
Per serving: Calories 220, Total fat 13g, Protein 12g, Carbs 15g

Ingredients:

- 1/3 cup of packed brown sugar
- 1/4 teaspoon of cinnamon
- 2 cups of cranberries (8 ounces)
- 1 tablespoon of cornstarch mixed with 1 to 2 tablespoons of cold water, optional
- 1 Granny Smith apple, diced, around 1 cup
- 3 to 4 pounds of boneless country-style ribs
- 1/2 cup of water
- 1/3 cup of maple syrup
- 1 bag (16 ounces) of frozen small white onions
- 1 teaspoon of Dijon mustard
- 1/4 teaspoon of mace or nutmeg

Instructions:

- Bring the cranberries, water, syrup, brown sugar, and apple to the boil inside a saucepan. Reduce the flame to medium-low & continue to cook for another 5 minutes. Combine the cinnamon, mustard, and mace or nutmeg.
- Arrange onions inside the bottom of a 5 to 7-quart Crock-Pot. Place the pork ribs on top of the onions, then equally distribute the cranberry sauce. Cook, covered, on LOW for around 7–9 hours, or till meat is tender.

11. Creamy Pork

(Preparation time: 20 minutes | Cooking time: 10 hours | Servings: 8)
Per serving: Calories 760, Total fat 61g, Protein 32g, Carbs 19g

Ingredients:

- 2 teaspoons of sugar
- 1/2 cup of chopped onion
- 1/4 teaspoon of ground nutmeg
- 1/2 cup of dry white wine
- 3 cloves of minced garlic
- 1/3 cup of whipping cream
- 2 Granny Smith apples, peeled, cored & sliced
- 1/2 teaspoon of crumbled dried leaf sage
- 2 to 3 pounds of boneless pork loin, trimmed and cut into 1-inch cubes
- Salt to taste
- 1/8 teaspoon of pepper
- 1/4 cup of all-purpose flour
- 1 tablespoon plus 2 teaspoons of cornstarch

Instructions:

- Combine garlic, chopped onion, sage, apples, sugar, and pepper inside a Crock-Pot. Coat the pork chunks using flour and place them inside the Crock-Pot. Pour the wine in. Cook on LOW for around 7 to 9 hours, covered. Whisk together the cornstarch & whipping cream inside a small-sized bowl. Turn the Crock-Pot to HIGH & pour the liquid into the meat mixture; simmer for another 15 to 20 minutes. Season using salt to taste. Serve with cornbread or cornmeal biscuits.

12. Crock-Pot Carnitas

(Preparation time: 20 minutes | Cooking time: 10 hours | Servings: 8)
Per serving: Calories 336, Total fat 15g, Protein 20g, Carbs 6g

Ingredients:

- 1 fresh jalapeno pepper
- 2 to 4 lbs. of pork shoulder roast
- 1 can of beer (12 ounces)
- 4 garlic cloves, peeled, each clove cut into 4 pieces
- Corn tortillas
- 1 bunch of fresh cilantro

Instructions:

- Cut numerous small slices into the roast using a knife.
- Insert slices of garlic cloves into the roast; set inside crockpot with whole pepper & half-chopped cilantro.
- Season using salt and black pepper to taste. Pour the beer in. Cook for around 4 to 6 hours on HIGH, or till fork tender (LOW for around 9 to 11 hours).
- Remove the meat and shred it. Serve with the warm tortillas with your favorite toppings.
- Diced tomatoes, salsa, guacamole, shredded lettuce, onions, sliced ripe olives, sour cream, cheese, and cilantro are suggested toppings.

13. Crock-Pot Herb Pork Roast

(Preparation time: 20 minutes | Cooking time: 10 hours | Servings: 8)
Per serving: Calories 472, Total fat 24g, Protein 46g, Carbs 14g

Ingredients:

- 1/4 teaspoon of crumbled dried leaf rosemary
- 1 scant teaspoon of dried leaf thyme
- 1/3 cup of water
- 4 large garlic cloves, quartered
- A dash of ground cloves or allspice
- 3 tablespoons of water, optional
- 1 pork loin roast, boneless, around 4 to 5 pounds
- 1/2 teaspoon of crumbled dried leaf sage
- 1 teaspoon of salt
- 1 teaspoon of grated lemon peel, optional

- 1/4 teaspoon of dried tarragon, crumbled, optional
- 3 tablespoons of cornstarch, optional

Instructions:

- Insert garlic slices into 16 tiny pockets cut into the meat. Combine the herbs, salt, and lemon peel inside a small-sized dish. Rub the roast using the spice mixture.
- Fill the Crock-Pot halfway with water, then add the roast. Cook on LOW for around 8 to 10 hours, covered. An instant-read thermometer should read at least 145°F for pork roast.
- Thicken juices if desired. Remove the roast from the pan juices. Pour up the cornstarch and 3 tablespoons of water till smooth, then stir it into the crockpot juices.
- Cook on HIGH till the sauce has thickened. With the pork roast, serve.

14. Crockpot Paprika Pork

(Preparation time: 20 minutes | Cooking time: 8 hours | Servings: 8)
Per serving: Calories 343, Total fat 21g, Protein 18g, Carbs 23g

Ingredients:

- 1/2 cup of chicken broth
- 3 to 4 pounds of country-style pork ribs, boneless
- 1/2 teaspoon of salt
- 1/3 cup of all-purpose flour
- 1 to 2 tablespoons of vegetable oil
- 4 teaspoons of Hungarian paprika
- 1/2 cup of sour cream
- A dash pepper
- 1 large onion, halved & sliced

Instructions:

- Inside a large skillet, heat the vegetable oil on medium-high flame. Brown the pork and onions for around 5 to 6 minutes, rotating once to brown all sides of the pork ribs. Inside a Crock-Pot, arrange the browned pork with onions. Scrape up the browned bits from the bottom of the heated pan and pour over the pork.

- Cook on LOW for around 6 to 8 hours, covered. Remove the pork out from the pan and keep it heated.
- Place the liquids inside a saucepan on medium flame. Simmer for around 5 to 8 minutes, or till the liquid has been reduced by 1/4 to 1/3. Remove from the flame & mix in the sour cream before serving the pork with the sauce.

15. Crockpot Pork Chops

(Preparation time: 20 minutes | Cooking time: 6 hours | Servings: 8)
Per serving: Calories 193, Total fat 8g, Protein 26g, Carbs 4g

Ingredients:

- 2 to 3 tablespoons of all-purpose flour
- 1 can (8 ounces) of tomato sauce
- 1/4 cup of light or dark brown sugar, packed
- 2 tablespoons of extra virgin olive oil
- 4 to 6 pork chops, bone-in or boneless
- 1/8 teaspoon of ground cloves
- Kosher salt & ground black pepper, to taste
- 1/4 teaspoon of ground cinnamon
- 1 large can (29 ounces) of peach halves or slices in the light syrup
- 1/4 cider of vinegar

Instructions:

- Place the pork chops on a parchment or wax paper-lined baking sheet. Both sides should be lightly seasoned using kosher salt and ground black pepper. Lightly dust the surface using flour.
- Add the olive oil to a big, heavy skillet or sauté pan on medium-high flame.
- Arrange the pork chops inside the pan once the olive oil is heated. Cook for around 3 minutes per side or till golden brown. Place the pork chops inside the Crock-Pot.

- Drain and set aside the peach syrup inside a bowl. Place the peaches on top of the pork chops.
- Combine 1/4 cup of peach syrup, tomato sauce, cinnamon, vinegar, brown sugar, and cloves inside a medium-sized mixing dish. Blend everything up thoroughly with a whisk.
- Inside the Crock-Pot, pour the sauce mixture on top of the peaches & pork chops.
- Cover & cook on LOW for around 4 to 6 hours, or till the pork is soft and done to your liking.

16. Crockpot Pork Chop and Potatoes

(Preparation time: 20 minutes | Cooking time: 8 hours | Servings: 6)
Per serving: Calories 705, Total fat 47g, Protein 33g, Carbs 38g

Ingredients:

- 2 to 3 tablespoons of vegetable oil
- 1 1/2 cups of fresh or frozen cut green beans
- 4 to 6 thick (3/4- to 1-inch), boneless pork chops, country ribs or steaks
- 1 jar of Alfredo sauce (16 oz.)
- 1/4 cup of flour seasoned with salt and pepper
- 3 tablespoons of dry sherry wine or white wine, optional
- Salt & pepper, to taste
- 3 large thinly sliced baking potatoes

Instructions:

- Using the flour mixture, coat the chops. Inside a large-sized skillet, heat the vegetable oil on a medium-high flame. Cook till the onions are soft. Brown the pork chops on the both sides. Place the chops with onions on a dish and put them aside. Remove the hot skillet from the flame and add the sherry, scraping off any browned pieces with a spatula. The majority of the wine will evaporate rapidly.

- Inside a 3 1/2-quart Crock-Pot, butter the sides and bottom.
- Place the potatoes and season lightly using salt and black pepper. Green beans should be placed on top of the potatoes. Pour the skillet drippings over the browned chops and onions inside the Crock-Pot. Over everything, pour Alfredo sauce. Cook on low for around 7 to 8 hours, covered. Season using salt and black pepper to taste.

17. Crockpot BBQ Pulled Pork

(Preparation time: 20 minutes | Cooking time: 6 hours | Servings: 10)

Per serving: Calories 486, Total fat 13g, Protein 15g, Carbs 54g

Ingredients:

- 2 thinly sliced medium onions
- 1 bottle (16 ounces) of barbecue sauce
- 4 pounds of pork shoulder roast
- 1 cup of chopped onion
- 1 1/2 cups of water

Instructions:

- Inside the bottom of the Crock-Pot, place 1/2 of the thinly sliced onions; add the pork and water, along with the remaining onion pieces. Cover and cook on LOW for around 8 to 10 hours, or HIGH for around 4 to 5 hours. Drain the liquid from the Crock-Pot; finely chop the meat and discard any excess fat. Return the pork to the Crock-Pot. Combine the barbecue sauce & chopped onion. Cover and continue to simmer on LOW for another 4 to 6 hours. Stir once in a while.
- Serve with coleslaw & toasty split buns.

18. Chinese-Style Pork with Vegetables

(Preparation time: 20 minutes | Cooking time: 10 hours | Servings: 6)

Per serving: Calories 450, Total fat 29g, Protein 30g, Carbs 25g

Ingredients:

- 1 can of water chestnuts, drained
- 1 to 1 1/2 pounds of cubed lean pork
- Salt & black pepper to taste
- 3 tablespoons of cornstarch
- 1/2 cup of chopped onion
- 1 cup of chicken broth
- 2 cans (4 ounces each) of mushrooms, drained
- 1 green bell pepper, cut into strips
- 1 tablespoon of soy sauce
- 16 ounces of frozen Chinese vegetables, thawed
- 3 tablespoons of water
- 1 teaspoon of ground ginger

Instructions:

- Brown the pork and add with the remaining ingredients inside the Crock-Pot.
- Cook on low for around 8 to 10 hours or on high for around 4 to 5 hours, covered.
- Turn to high & add the vegetables 45 minutes before the end of cooking time.
- Combine cornstarch & water inside a Crock-Pot and stir well to combine.
- Cook till the sauce has thickened, and the vegetables are tender.
- Serve alongside rice or noodles.

19. Country Pork Ribs with Ginger Sauce

(Preparation time: 20 minutes | Cooking time: 8 hours | Servings: 6)

Per serving: Calories 366, Total fat 20g, Protein 36g, Carbs 10g

Ingredients:

- 2 tablespoons of rice vinegar
- 4 pounds of country pork ribs
- 1 large onion, peeled & diced
- 1 ¼ cup of tomato ketchup
- 2 teaspoons of grated ginger
- 1/4 teaspoon of allspice
- 2 tablespoons of tamari sauce
- 1/4 teaspoon of red pepper flakes, crushed
- 1 clove of garlic, peeled & minced

Instructions:

- Pork ribs should be cut into individual serving-size chunks.
- Broil the ribs for around 5 minutes on each side, or till browned and aromatic.
- To make the sauce, mix rice vinegar, tomato ketchup, ginger, tamari sauce, allspice, onion, garlic, and red pepper together inside a Crock-Pot.
- Coat the pork ribs in the sauce and place them inside the Crock-Pot.
- Cook for around 8 hours on low, or till the ribs are tender.

20. Dutch Hot Pot

(Preparation time: 20 minutes | Cooking time: 8 hours | Servings: 8)

Per serving: Calories 365, Total fat 16g, Protein 17g, Carbs 38g

Ingredients:

- 1 teaspoon of crumbled dried leaf thyme
- 2 pounds of boneless pork shoulder, cubed
- 1/4 teaspoon of black pepper
- 6 carrots cut into 4" pieces
- 1/4 cup of all-purpose flour
- Boiling water or chicken broth
- 1 tablespoon of salt

- 2 tablespoons of butter
- 4 medium sliced onions
- 1 teaspoon of crushed coriander seeds
- 4 medium potatoes sliced into 1/4" slices (round, red, white, new potatoes, or other variety)
- 1 can (15 ounces) of kidney beans, white or red, liquid reserved

Instructions:

- Remove any visible fat out from the meat. Toss the pork chunks in flour to thoroughly coat them.
- Reserve the crushed coriander seed, salt, thyme, and pepper.
- Drain the liquid from the beans into the 2-cup measuring cup, then add 1-1/2 cups of boiling water.
- Inside the Crock-Pot, put half of each of the potatoes, beans, onions, pork, and carrots in the following sequence, dusting each layer with the spice mixture.
- For a second layer, repeat with the remaining vegetables, meat, & seasoning combination.
- Pour the liquid over the top and dot with butter. Cook, covered, for around 8 hours on low or around 4 hours on high, or till meat & veggies are cooked.

21. Fruited Pork Chops

(Preparation time: 20 minutes | Cooking time: 7 hours | Servings: 8)

Per serving: Calories 340, Total fat 13g, Protein 15g, Carbs 42g

Ingredients:

- 1 tablespoon of prepared mustard
- 4 boneless or bone-in pork chops, around 3/4 to 1-inch thick
- 1 can (17 oz.) of fruit cocktail, drained, syrup reserved
- 2 tablespoons of cold water
- 1/2 teaspoon of salt
- hot cooked rice for 4

- 1 dash pepper
- 2 tablespoons of wine vinegar
- 2 tablespoons of cornstarch
- 1/8 teaspoon of dried thyme or tarragon

Instructions:

- Season pork chops using salt and black pepper.
- Place inside a Crock-Pot. Combine the mustard, vinegar, & thyme or tarragon. Drain the fruit cocktail and add 1/2 cup of the syrup to the mustard mixture.
- Pour the sauce over the pork chops inside the crockpot. Cook for around 5 to 7 hours on LOW, or till meat is tender.
- Turn the crockpot to HIGH and remove the pork chops to keep them warm. Cornstarch should be dissolved in water and then stirred into the stew. Cover and simmer on high for around 20 minutes after adding the drained fruit cocktail.
- Serve the fruit sauce over the chops and rice.

22. "Green" Pork Loin

(Preparation time: 20 minutes | Cooking time: 7 hours | Servings: 8)

Per serving: Calories 238, Total fat 16g, Protein 18g, Carbs 11g

Ingredients:

- 2 tablespoons of olive oil
- 1 cup of julienne-cut carrots
- 1 tablespoon of ground cumin
- 2 pounds of boneless pork ribs or loin, trimmed & cut into bite-size cubes
- Hot sauce, to taste
- 2 cloves of minced garlic
- Salt & pepper
- 1 pound of tomatillos, husks removed, washed & diced
- 1/4 cup of flour
- 1 1/2 cups of diced celery
- Fresh chopped cilantro, optional

- 1 cup of chopped onion
- 3 to 6 tablespoons of drained jalapeno rings or chopped mild chili peppers
- A pinch of dried oregano
- 2 teaspoons of chili powder
- 2 cups of chicken broth
- Salt and black pepper, to taste
- 2 medium potatoes, cut into small cubes
- 2 cans (14.5 ounces each) of diced tomatoes

Instructions:

- Season the pork pieces using salt and black pepper before tossing them inside the flour. Inside a large-sized skillet, heat 2 tablespoons of olive oil; add pork and sauté, occasionally stirring, till beautifully browned; transfer to a 5 to 6-quart Crock-Pot. Sauté the celery and onion till soft in the very same skillet, adding a bit extra oil if necessary. Stir in the garlic, chicken broth, & jalapeño or mild peppers, scraping browned pieces from the bottom of skillet as needed.
- Set them aside.
- Meanwhile, add the potatoes, carrots, and tomatillos to the Crock-Pot. Add the onion & celery combination from the skillet on top of the tomatoes. To combine the components, stir them together. Cook on HIGH for around 3 hours or LOW for around 6 hours, covered. Season using salt and black pepper. Cook for an additional 1 to 2 hours on HIGH or 2 to 3 hours on LOW. Season using salt and pepper to taste. Serve with hot baked cornbread & a dusting of cilantro, if preferred.

23. Goulash

(Preparation time: 20 minutes | Cooking time: 10 hours | Servings: 6)

Per serving: Calories 632, Total fat 42g, Protein 48g, Carbs 14g

Ingredients:

- 1/2 cup of dry white wine

- 2 slices of bacon, diced
- 1/2 cup of chicken broth
- 8 ounces of light sour cream
- 1 cup of chopped onion
- 2 tablespoons of sweet Hungarian paprika
- 1 1/2 cups of sauerkraut, rinsed & squeezed dry
- 4 medium red potatoes, cut into 1-inch cubes
- 1 1/2 to 2 pounds of lean pork, cut into 1-inch cubes
- 1 large diced tomato
- 1/2 teaspoon of caraway seeds
- Salt and black pepper to taste
- 1 large green bell pepper, cut into 1-inch pieces

Instructions:

- Cook bacon & onion inside a large-sized skillet on medium flame, occasionally stirring, till bacon is crisp.
- Inside a Crock-Pot, combine the pork, paprika, broth, caraway seeds, wine, potatoes, peppers, & sauerkraut. Mix in the bacon & onions thoroughly.
- Cook on low for around 8 to 10 hours, covered.
- Add diced tomato & sour cream 15 to 20 minutes prior to serving. Serve immediately.

24. Hawaiian Pork Roast

(Preparation time: 20 minutes | Cooking time: 10 hours | Servings: 8)
Per serving: Calories 224, Total fat 13g, Protein 18g, Carbs 31g

Ingredients:

- 4 teaspoons of liquid smoke
- 2 ripe bananas, unpeeled
- 1 boneless pork shoulder roast (3-4 lbs.)
- 1/2 cup of water
- 4 teaspoons of soy sauce

Instructions:

- Put the pork roast on a heavy-duty aluminum foil sheet that is 22" x 18" in size. Sprinkle the liquid smoke and soy sauce over the roast. Place one unpeeled banana on each side of the pork roast after washing it. Pull the sides of the foil up around the pork roast; add water & tightly seal the foil; wrap with another big piece of foil. Refrigerate overnight, rotating many times inside a shallow baking pan or dish.
- Cook the foil-wrapped beef on low for around 8 to 10 hours inside the crockpot. Bananas and juices should be drained & discarded. To serve, shred the meat using a fork.

25. Honey-Chipotle Ribs

(Preparation time: 20 minutes | Cooking time: 10 hours | Servings: 4)
Per serving: Calories 627, Total fat 38g, Protein 45g, Carbs 28g

Ingredients:

- 1/4 cup of chopped onion
- 2 racks of baby back ribs, cut into 2 to 3 rib portions
- 1 tablespoon of Worcestershire sauce
- 2 tablespoons of cider vinegar
- 1/2 teaspoon of salt
- Salt & black pepper
- 1 tablespoon of prepared mustard
- 1 1/2 cups of ketchup
- 1 1/2 tablespoons of Tabasco Chipotle Sauce
- 1/3 cup of honey
- 2 teaspoons of chili powder
- 1/4 teaspoon of ground black pepper
- 1/2 teaspoon of garlic powder

Instructions:

- Preheat your oven at 375°F.
- The heavy-duty foil should be used to line a big baking sheet (with sides). Place the rib parts on the baking sheet with the rib sides down. Bake for around 1 hour in the oven.

- Inside a food processor or blender, combine the other ingredients and blend till smooth.
- Place the ribs inside the Crock-Pot, along with the onions, and the chipotle barbecue sauce. Cook for around 8 to 10 hours on LOW or around 4 to 5 hours on HIGH.

26. Honey Dijon Pork Tenderloin

(Preparation time: 20 minutes | Cooking time: 9 hours | Servings: 6)
Per serving: Calories 425, Total fat 12g, Protein 54g, Carbs 21g

Ingredients:

- 2 tablespoons of honey
- Salt and black pepper
- 1/2 teaspoon of dried leaf thyme, crumbled
- 1 tablespoon of cold water
- 2 pork tenderloins, around 1 pound each
- 1 small clove of minced garlic
- 1 tablespoon of cider vinegar or balsamic vinegar
- 4 tablespoons of grainy Dijon mustard or country-style
- 2 tablespoons of brown sugar
- 1 tablespoon of cornstarch

Instructions:

- Pork should be washed, trimmed, & patted dry before seasoning gently using salt & pepper. Inside a Crock-Pot, place the meat. Pour over the pork the garlic, mustard, vinegar, honey, brown sugar, & thyme mixture. Turn the pork to cover it completely. Cook on LOW for around 7 to 9 hours or HIGH for around 3 1/2 to 4 1/2 hours, covered.
- Place the pork on a platter and wrap it in foil to keep it warm. Fill a saucepan halfway with juices & bring to the boil on medium flame.
- Simmer for around 8 to 10 minutes, or till the liquid has been reduced by one-third. Combine the cornstarch & cold water inside a small-sized mixing bowl; whisk into

the reduced juices & cook for an additional minute. Sliced pork with thickened juices is served.

27. Hot and Spicy Pork Chops

(Preparation time: 20 minutes | Cooking time: 6 hours | Servings: 8)
Per serving: Calories 180, Total fat 6g, Protein 26g, Carbs 8g

Ingredients:

- 1 green bell pepper, cut into strips
- 2 sliced ribs celery
- 1/4 teaspoon of cayenne pepper, optional
- 1 cup of chopped onion
- 2 tablespoons of cornstarch, blended with 2 tablespoons of cold water
- 6 to 8 boneless pork chops, around 3/4 to 1-inch thick
- 1 red bell pepper, cut into strips
- 2 cups of spicy V-8 vegetable juice
- 1/4 teaspoon of cayenne pepper
- 1/2 teaspoon of coarsely ground black pepper

Instructions:

- Inside a crockpot, combine celery and diced onion. Remove the excess fat out from the pork chops and place them inside the Crock-Pot.
- Pepper slices should be strewn around and between the pork chops.
- Pour the V-8 juice over everything.
- Cook on LOW for around 6 hours, covered.
- Transfer the pork chops and veggies to a serving plate using a slotted spoon; keep heated.
- Into a measuring cup, strain the leftover juices and skim off the fat. In a saucepan, measure out cups of liquid.
- Combine the cornstarch & water inside a mixing bowl.
- Cook, constantly stirring, till the sauce has thickened and is bubbling.

- Cook for an additional 2 minutes, stirring often.
- Pork chops should be served with veggies and a hot spicy sauce.

28. Indonesian Pork

(Preparation time: 20 minutes | Cooking time: 9 hours | Servings: 8)

Per serving: Calories 682, Total fat 49g, Protein 42g, Carbs 22g

Ingredients:

- 1 cup of hot water
- 1/4 cup of orange marmalade
- 1 boneless pork loin roast, about 3 to 4 pounds
- 1/4 cup of prepared mustard
- Salt & black pepper to taste
- 1/4 teaspoon of ground ginger
- 1/4 cup of molasses
- 1 teaspoon of grated orange or lemon peel
- 1/4 cup of vinegar

Instructions:

- Inside the bottom of the Crock-Pot, place a metal rack or trivet. Alternatively, crumpled foil strips can be used to create a "rack."
- Season the pork roast using salt & ground black pepper all over before placing it on the rack. Pour boiling water all around the pork roast.
- Cover and cook on LOW for around 5 to 7 hours, or till an instant-read food thermometer placed inside the thickest part of the roast registers at least 145° F.
- Place the roast inside a roasting pan with a rack or a broiler pan with a rack. Preheat your oven at 400°F.
- Inside a saucepan, combine the remaining ingredients & stir to blend. Heat the mixture till it begins to boil.
- Place the roast inside the oven after brushing some of the glaze mix over it. Roast the pork for around 30 to 45

minutes, basting it periodically with the sauce.

29. Juicy Pork with Apple Sauce

(Preparation time: 20 minutes | Cooking time: 6 hours | Servings: 8)

Per serving: Calories 194, Total fat 5g, Protein 17g, Carbs 46

Ingredients:

- 4 cups of applesauce, unsweetened
- 1/4 cup of light brown sugar
- 1/2 teaspoon of ground black pepper
- 1/2 cup of dry red wine
- 1/4 cup of Dijon mustard
- 1/2 cup of chopped scallions
- 4 pounds of pork loin, fat removed

Instructions:

- Combine mustard, sugar, and black pepper inside a small-sized mixing dish or measuring cup. To blend, whisk everything together thoroughly.
- The pork loin should be rubbed with the mustard mixture.
- Inside a Crock-Pot, place the pork loin, applesauce, red wine, & scallions; cover using a lid.
- Cook for around 6 hours on low. Serve with additional mustard on the side.

30. Orange Pork Roast

(Preparation time: 20 minutes | Cooking time: 9 hours | Servings: 8)
Per serving: Calories 228, Total fat 6g, Protein 18g, Carbs 27g

Ingredients:

- 1/4 cup of brown sugar
- 1 pork shoulder roast, around 3 to 4 lbs., trimmed
- 1/8 teaspoon of ground allspice
- 1/2 teaspoon of salt
- 1/8 teaspoon of ground nutmeg
- 1/4 teaspoon of pepper
- 3 tablespoons of flour mixed with 3 tablespoons of cold water
- 1 can of frozen orange juice concentrate, thawed (6 oz.)

Instructions:

- Season the pork shoulder roast using salt and black pepper and place it inside the Crock-Pot. Combine the nutmeg, orange juice concentrate, brown sugar, and allspice inside a bowl & pour over the roast. Cook for around 1 hour on HIGH, covered. Reduce the heat to LOW & cook for a further 8 hours. Skim fat from juices before serving & transfer cooking liquid into a small-sized saucepan. Incorporate the flour-water combination. Bring to the boil, stirring constantly, and simmer till the sauce has thickened.
- Serve the pork roast with the thickened juices. For a complete dinner, serve with rice & a salad.

31. Pork Chops Stew with Cabbage

(Preparation time: 10 minutes | Cooking time: 8 hours | Servings: 8)
Per serving: Calories 370, Total fat 8g, Protein 21g, Carbs 34g

Ingredients:

- 2 tablespoons of olive oil or canola
- 1/4 teaspoon of salt
- 6 loin chops of pork
- 2 teaspoons of beef bouillon granules or beef base
- 1 chopped medium onion
- 1/2 cup of sour cream
- 4 tablespoons of flour, divided
- 1 small-sized cabbage, cut into the wedges
- 1 can (14 1/2 oz.) of stewed tomatoes, cut up
- 4 medium potatoes, red or Yukon gold, cut into cubes
- 1/4 cup of water
- 4 diced carrots
- 2 tablespoons of cornstarch
- 1/2 teaspoon of ground black pepper

Instructions:

- Trim the fat out from the chops and coat them in 2 tablespoons of flour.
- Inside a skillet on medium flame, brown the pork chops using heated oil.
- Inside a Crock-Pot, combine the onion, potatoes, and carrots. Toss the vegetables inside the remaining flour to coat them. Layer the cabbage wedges, salt, pepper, bouillon granules dissolved in 1/4 cup of water, browned pork chops, and stewed tomatoes on top of the potato mixture. The mixture should not be stirred.
- Cook on the HIGH for around 3-4 hours, or LOW for around 7-8 hours, covered.
- Mix together the sour cream with cornstarch inside a small-sized saucepan till smooth. Fill a two-cup measure halfway with cooking fluid, then pour enough milk or water to make 1 1/2 cups. Inside the saucepan, stir in the sour cream combination. Cook, constantly stirring, till the mixture thickens and comes to the boil on medium-low flame. Serve the pork chops with the sour cream mixture.

32. Peachy Pork Steak

(Preparation time: 20 minutes | Cooking time: 8 hours | Servings: 4)
Per serving: Calories 388, Total fat 9g, Protein 26g, Carbs 48g

Ingredients:

- 3/4 teaspoon of dried leaf basil
- 1 can (around 15 ounces) of peach slices in natural juice
- 1/4 cup of water
- 4 thick pork chops, around 1 1/2 inches thick, or pork cutlets or steaks
- 2 tablespoons of vinegar
- 1/4 teaspoon of salt
- 2 tablespoons of oil
- 4 cups of hot cooked rice
- 1/8 teaspoon of pepper
- 2 tablespoons of cornstarch
- 1 tablespoon of beef bouillon granules

Instructions:

- Trim any excess fat out from the meat. Brown pork on all sides in oil inside a pan on medium flame. Add basil, salt, & pepper to taste.
- Drain the peaches & keep the syrup. Inside a crockpot, arrange sliced peaches. Place the meat on top of the peaches. Pour over pork the saved peach juice, vinegar, & beef bouillon. Cook for around 8 hours on low, covered. Place steaks and peaches onto a serving plate with hot cooked rice and keep warm.
- Strain the cooking juices into a saucepan. Remove any extra fat out from the cooking liquid. Slowly combine cold water & cornstarch inside a small-sized dish or cup; whisk into the boiling liquid. Cook, constantly stirring, till the sauce has thickened and is bubbling. Serve the pork with the thickened liquids.

33. Pineapple Pork Loin

(Preparation time: 20 minutes | Cooking time: 10 hours | Servings: 8)
Per serving: Calories 201, Total fat 8g, Protein 24g, Carbs 6g

Ingredients:

- 1 tablespoon of soy sauce
- 1 boneless pork loin roast, around 2 to 3 lbs.
- 3 tablespoons of margarine
- 1 cup of chopped green and/or red bell peppers
- 1/2 teaspoon of ground ginger
- 1 can of crushed pineapple (20 oz.), undrained
- 1/2 teaspoon of allspice
- 1/2 cup of flour seasoned with 1/2 teaspoon of salt and 1/4 teaspoon of pepper
- 2 medium onions, halved & sliced
- 1 teaspoon of garlic powder
- 1 to 2 teaspoons of sugar
- 1 tablespoon of vinegar
- 1/2 teaspoon of cinnamon

Instructions:

- Pork loin should be cut into 3/4-inch thick slices. Using the seasoned flour as a dredging agent. Inside a large-sized nonstick skillet, melt margarine on medium flame. Brown both sides of the pork pieces with excess flour. Transfer the browned pork to a Crock-Pot (3 1/2 quart or bigger). Stir in the peppers and onions till they are slightly caramelized & tender. Bring the remaining ingredients to the boil, then pour over the pork.
- Cook on low for around 8 to 10 hours, covered. Serve over steaming rice.

34. Plantation Pork Chops

(Preparation time: 20 minutes | Cooking time: 8 hours | Servings: 4)

Per serving: Calories 172, Total fat 6g, Protein 14g, Carbs 4g

Ingredients:

- 2 tablespoons of melted butter
- 1/3 cup of orange juice
- 4 pork chops, loin (1 to 1 1/2-inch thick)
- Salt & black pepper
- 1 tablespoon of finely chopped pecans
- 1/2 teaspoon of orange peel, grated
- 1 1/2 to 2 cups of cornbread stuffing, prepared
- 1/4 cup of light corn syrup

Instructions:

- Cut a pocket in the side of each chop using a sharp knife to produce a filling pocket. Combine the stuffing, orange juice, butter, 1/4 teaspoon of salt, & pecans. Stuff pockets to the brim.
- Season pork chops using salt & black pepper before placing them inside the Crock-Pot. Brush with a corn syrup & orange peel combination. Keep the remaining corn syrup mix refrigerated. Cook on low for around 6 to 8 hours, covered.
- Cook for another 30 to 45 minutes on high, brushing chops using corn syrup & orange peel mixture again.

35. Pork and Rice

(Preparation time: 20 minutes | Cooking time: 8 hours | Servings: 8)
Per serving: Calories 557, Total fat 13g, Protein 26g, Carbs 60g

Ingredients:

- 1 medium chopped onion
- 2 teaspoons of dried parsley
- 1 to 1 1/2 pounds of pork cutlets, around 1/2-inch thick
- Salt & black pepper
- 1 1/2 cups of frozen peas (or a 10 oz. package), optional
- 1 large minced clove of garlic

- 1 3/4 cups of chicken broth
- 1/2 cup of flour
- 1 1/4 cup of rice
- 1 tablespoon of olive oil

Instructions:

- Toss the pork chops into flour.
- Brown the chops in the oil inside a large-sized skillet on medium flame, seasoning liberally using salt and black pepper.
- Cook till the onion is wilted, after adding the chopped onions & minced garlic. Place the rice inside a Crock-Pot, sprinkle with parsley, and afterward add the pork & onion mixture. To release browned bits, pour chicken broth into a heated skillet and stir. Inside the Crock-Pot, pour over the meat and rice.
- Cook on low for around 6 to 8 hours, covered. If desired, add the frozen green peas in the last half hour.

36. Pork & Cashews

(Preparation time: 20 minutes | Cooking time: 8 hours | Servings: 6)
Per serving: Calories 461, Total fat 24g, Protein 31g, Carbs 33g

Ingredients:

- 1 tablespoon of soy sauce
- 1/4 cup of brown sugar
- 1 1/2 pounds of lean pork - cut into narrow strips
- Peanut oil or other vegetable oil
- Hot cooked rice
- 5 chopped cloves of garlic
- 1 to 1 1/2 cups of roasted cashews

Instructions:

- Coat meat strips in soy sauce & set aside for around 10 minutes. Turn the crockpot to HIGH. Inside a heavy skillet on high flame, add a little oil & stir-fry the pork just to color it. Place the pork inside the crockpot. Garlic should be added. Cook on HIGH for around 2-3 hours or LOW for around 4 to 7 hours after adding the brown sugar. 30 minutes before serving, add cashews. Serve alongside steaming rice.

37. Pork Chili

(Preparation time: 10 minutes | Cooking time: 10 hours | Servings: 8)
Per serving: Calories 221, Total fat 16g, Protein 13g, Carbs 6g

Ingredients:

- 1/2 cup chopped onion
- 1 tablespoon chili powder
- 2 to 2 1/2 pounds of pork loin or lean pork shoulder, cut into 1-inch cubes
- Salt & black pepper to taste
- 2 tablespoons of vegetable oil
- 1 can (8 oz.) of tomato sauce
- 1 minced clove of garlic
- 1 large can (28 oz.) of diced tomatoes in juice
- 1/2 cup of salsa
- 1 small chopped bell pepper
- 1 can (16 oz.) of chili beans, undrained
- 1/4 teaspoon of cayenne pepper, or to taste
- Minced jalapeno or any other hot chili, to taste (optional)

Instructions:

- Brown pork cubes using heated oil inside a large-sized skillet on medium flame. Drain. Place the pork inside the Crock-Pot and add the rest of the ingredients. Cook on low for around 8 to 10 hours, covered.

38. Pork Loin with Stuffing

(Preparation time: 20 minutes | Cooking time: 9 hours | Servings: 6)
Per serving: Calories 360, Total fat 17g, Protein 40g, Carbs 9g

Ingredients:

- 1/2 cup of chopped onion

- 1 box, around 6 ounces, seasoned stuffing mix
- 1/2 cup of diced carrots, optional
- 1 cup of dried cranberries, optional
- 4 tablespoons of butter
- 1 cup of chicken broth
- 1/2 cup of chopped celery
- 1 tablespoon of chopped fresh parsley
- 1 boneless pork loin roast, around 2 to 3 pounds
- 1/2 teaspoon of salt
- For the pork rub:
- 1 teaspoon of Creole seasoning blend
- Dash of black pepper
- 1/2 teaspoon of sweet ground paprika
- 1 tablespoon of brown sugar
- 1/2 teaspoon of salt
- 1/2 teaspoon of garlic powder

Instructions:

- Oil a 5 to 6-quart Crock-Pot lightly.
- Inside a large-sized mixing bowl, combine the stuffing ingredients.
- Cook the celery, onion, and carrots in the butter inside a skillet or sauté pan on medium-low flame till softened. Combine the onion mixture and the stuffing ingredients in a mixing bowl. Combine the chicken broth, parsley, 1/2 teaspoon of salt, & dried cranberries and stir well.
- Fill the Crock-Pot halfway with the stuffing mixture.
- Mix the rub ingredients together and apply to the pork roast. Place the meat on top of the stuffing mix.
- Cook on LOW for around 7 to 9 hours, or till meat is well cooked.

39. Pork Marengo

(Preparation time: 20 minutes | Cooking time: 10 hours | Servings: 8)
Per serving: Calories 173, Total fat 5g, Protein 19g, Carbs 11g

Ingredients:

- 2 tablespoons of vegetable oil
- 3/4 teaspoon of ground marjoram
- 1/4 teaspoon of ground black pepper
- 1/2 cup of cold water
- 2 pounds of boneless pork loin, cut into 1-inch cubes
- 1/2 teaspoon of dried leaf thyme
- 1 medium chopped onion
- 1 can of diced tomatoes (14.5 ounces)
- 1 can (4 ounces) of sliced mushrooms, drained
- 1 chicken bouillon cube or granules
- 3 tablespoons of flour
- 1 teaspoon of salt

Instructions:

- Pork and onion should be combined & browned inside a skillet with heated oil. Remove out any excess fat. Place the pork and onions inside the crockpot. In the same skillet, combine the tomatoes, thyme, bouillon, marjoram, salt, and pepper, stirring and scraping out any browned bits. Inside the crockpot, pour over the meat & onion. Cook on LOW for around 8 to 10 hours, covered. Turn to HIGH and add the mushrooms at the end of the cooking time. Combine cold water & flour till smooth; stir into the meat mixture inside the crockpot.
- Cook till the gravy thickens, uncovered. To avoid sticking, stir occasionally. To thicken more rapidly, combine the liquids inside a saucepan and pour in the water & flour mixture. Cook on the stovetop, constantly stirring, till thickened. Over hot cooked rice, serve.

40. Pork Chop Casserole

(Preparation time: 20 minutes | Cooking time: 8 hours | Servings: 6)
Per serving: Calories 259, Total fat 18g, Protein 13g, Carbs 12g

Ingredients:

- 1/2 teaspoon of garlic salt

- 2 tablespoons of oil
- 1/3 cup of flour
- 1 can of condensed cream of chicken soup
- 4 to 6 lean pork chops
- 1 teaspoon of salt
- 1 teaspoon of dry mustard

Instructions:

- Dredge the chops inside a combination of mustard, flour, salt, & garlic salt. Inside a skillet, heat the oil & brown the chops from all sides. Add the soup to the chops inside the Crock-Pot. Cook for around 6-8 hours on low or around 3-4 hours on high. If you want extra gravy, you can pour more soup. Serve with rice or noodles.

41. Pork Chops with Apples

(Preparation time: 20 minutes | Cooking time: 9 hours | Servings: 6)
Per serving: Calories 285, Total fat 7g, Protein 25g, Carbs 30g

Ingredients:

- 6 tart apples, like Granny Smith, cored & thickly sliced
- 1 tablespoon of lemon juice
- 6 pork loin chops, around 1-inch thick, trimmed of the visible fat
- 1/4 cup of brown sugar
- 2 tablespoons of vegetable oil
- 1/4 cup of currants or raisins, optional
- Salt

Instructions:

- Chops are browned in oil on medium flame. Season using salt. Place the pork chops inside the Crock-Pot and pour the remaining ingredients over them. Cook on low for around 7 to 9 hours, or high for around 3 to 4 hours, covered.

42. Pork with Orange-Mustard Sauce

(Preparation time: 20 minutes | Cooking time: 9 hours | Servings: 6)

Per serving: Calories 259, Total fat 14g, Protein 25g, Carbs 6g

Ingredients:

- 1/2 to 1 cup of sliced green onions, with the green
- 1 tablespoon of Dijon mustard
- 6 boneless pork chops, about 2 pounds
- 1/2 cup of orange juice
- Ground black pepper
- 1 1/2 tablespoons of soy sauce
- 1/2 teaspoon of garlic powder
- 1 tablespoon of oil
- 1 1/2 teaspoons of honey

Instructions:

- Brown chops using oil on both sides inside a big skillet. Place the chops inside the Crock-Pot with the cut green onions on the top. Combine the other ingredients inside a mixing bowl & spoon over the pork chops. Cook on low for around 7 to 9 hours, covered.
- Serve & enjoy.

43. Pork Roast with Tasty Gravy

(Preparation time: 20 minutes | Cooking time: 10 hours | Servings: 8)

Per serving: Calories 354, Total fat 17g, Protein 40g, Carbs 8

Ingredients:

- 1 clove peeled & sliced garlic
- 1/2 teaspoon of salt
- 1 whole clove
- 2 tablespoons of cold water
- 1/4 teaspoon of pepper
- 1 tablespoon of olive oil
- 1 – 4 to 5-pounds of loin end roast
- 2 tablespoons of Worcestershire sauce
- 1 bay leaf

- 2 mediums thinly sliced sweet or yellow onions
- 2 tablespoons of cornstarch
- 1 cup of hot water

Instructions:

- Season the roast using salt and black pepper before cooking.
- Make incisions in the top of the roast & stuff garlic slices all over it.
- Brown the pork roast on all sides inside a heated skillet using olive oil.
- Inside the bottom of a Crock-Pot that has been coated using nonstick spray, place one of the sliced onions.
- Place the browned roast on top, followed by the second onion, the bay leaf, & the clove.
- Inside a large-sized measuring cup, combine the hot water with Worcestershire sauce to pour around the top of the roast.
- Cook for around 1 hour on high, then reduce to low for another 9 to 10 hours.
- Remove the meat and onions out from the Crock-Pot and place them on a plate to cool. Take out the clove & bay leaf and toss them out.
- Combine the cold water with cornstarch inside a mixing dish & stir till smooth paste forms. Set the Crock-Pot to high and mix the paste into the liquid inside. Cover and allow it to come to the boil, thickening into a delicious gravy. This will take an additional 10 to 15 minutes.
- After 10 minutes of sitting, slice the roast & serve with gravy.

44. Spicy Pork Roast with Vegetables

(Preparation time: 20 minutes | Cooking time: 6 hours | Servings: 4)

Per serving: Calories 582, Total fat 33g, Protein 44g, Carbs 30g

Ingredients:

- 1 chopped celery stalk

- 1 teaspoon of garlic powder
- 1 tablespoon of canola oil
- 1 (around 3-pounds) pork shoulder or butt roast
- 1 large-sized onion, sliced
- 1 jalapeño pepper, seeded & minced
- 1/4 teaspoon of ground black pepper
- 1 large-sized carrot, peeled & finely diced
- 1/2 teaspoon of dried basil
- Salt, to taste
- 1/2 teaspoon of five-spice powder
- 1 cup of vegetable broth
- 1/2 teaspoon of dried oregano

Instructions:

- Inside a cast-iron skillet, pour in the canola oil. On a medium-high flame, heat the canola oil, then add the vegetables. Sauté the vegetables for around 15 minutes, or till they are just soft.
- Incorporate garlic powder, salt, oregano, five-spice powder, black pepper, and basil inside a mixing bowl and whisk to combine.
- This spice mixture should be rubbed into the meat. Fill the Crock-Pot halfway with vegetable stock and add the pork roast. Cook on low for around 6 hours, covered.
- Using two forks, shred the meat. Serve the sauce over the pork while it is still heated.

- 1 pound of pork shoulder, boneless and fat removed
- 2 thinly sliced stalks celery
- 1 cup of chopped leeks
- 1 cup of chicken broth
- Salt to taste
- 2 cups of canned tomatoes, diced
- 1/2 teaspoon of dried thyme

Instructions:

- Bacon should be cut into small bits. Then, inside a nonstick skillet on a medium-high flame, cook the bacon for around 2 minutes, or till it begins to render fat. Fill your Crock-Pot halfway with water.
- Combine the remaining ingredients.
- Cook for around 6 hours on low, or till the pork shoulder is cooked.

45. Spicy Pork with Canadian Bacon

(Preparation time: 20 minutes | Cooking time: 6 hours | Servings: 4)

Per serving: Calories 344, Total fat 18g, Protein 26g, Carbs 20g

Ingredients:

- 2 minced cloves of garlic
- 1 ½ cups of canned beans, rinsed and drained
- 3/4 teaspoon of Italian seasoning blend
- 2 slices of Canadian bacon
- Freshly ground black pepper to taste

Chapter 6:
Crock-Pot Fish and
Seafood Recipes

1. Crockpot Citrus Fish

(Preparation time: 20 minutes | Cooking time: 2 hours | Servings: 6)

Per serving: Calories 157, Total fat 7g, Protein 18g, Carbs 5g

Ingredients:

- 1/2 cup of chopped onion
- 2 teaspoons of grated lemon rind
- Orange and lemon slices, for garnish
- 1 1/2 pounds of fish fillets
- 1 tablespoon of vegetable oil
- Salt & black pepper to taste
- 5 tablespoons of chopped fresh parsley
- Parsley sprigs for the garnish
- 2 teaspoons of grated orange rind

Instructions:

- Salt and pepper the fish fillets & butter the Crock-Pot. Put the salmon inside the crockpot. Over the fish, place the grated orange, onion, parsley and lemon peel, and oil. Cook on LOW for around 1 1/2 hours, covered.
- Serve with fresh parsley sprigs & slices of orange and lemon.

2. Crockpot Clam Chowder

(Preparation time: 20 minutes | Cooking time: 4 hours | Servings: 4)

Per serving: Calories 323, Total fat 8g, Protein 28g, Carbs 33g

Ingredients:

- 1 cup of chopped onion
- 4 cups of half and half cream or milk
- 3 1/2 teaspoons of salt
- 4 (6 1/2 oz.) cans of minced clams with juice
- Chopped fresh parsley, for the garnish
- 1/2 lb. of salt pork or bacon, diced
- 6 to 8 medium potatoes, peeled & cubed
- 3 to 4 tablespoons of cornstarch
- 3 cups of water
- 1/4 teaspoon of pepper

Instructions:

- If necessary, cut the clams into bite-sized pieces.
- Cook salt pork or bacon & onion in a pan till golden brown; drain. Combine all ingredients inside a Crock-Pot with the clams.
- Except for the milk, cornstarch, & parsley, combine all remaining ingredients.
- Cook for around 3 to 4 hours on high, or till soft.
- Mix 1 cup of milk or cream with cornstarch during the last hour of simmering. Stir in the cornstarch mixture & the remaining milk or cream till well combined; heat through.
- Serve alongside crackers or crusty French bread and a sprinkle of minced parsley on top of each serving.

3. Crockpot Jambalaya

(Preparation time: 20 minutes | Cooking time: 8 hours | Servings: 8)

Per serving: Calories 465, Total fat 20g, Protein 28g, Carbs 42g

Ingredients:

- 1/2 cup of dry white wine
- 1 pound of chicken breasts or tenders, boneless, cut into 1-inch cubes

- 2 teaspoons of Cajun seasoning
- 8 to 12 ounces of smoked sausage, sliced
- 1 pound of cooked shrimp
- 1/2 cup of chopped onion
- 1 large can (28 ounces) of crushed tomatoes
- 2 teaspoons of dried parsley
- 1 chopped green bell pepper
- 2 cups of cooked long-grain rice
- 1 cup of chicken broth
- 2 teaspoons of dried leaf oregano
- 1 teaspoon of cayenne pepper

Instructions:

- Inside a Crock-Pot, combine the chicken, sausage, diced bell pepper, & chopped onion. Gently whisk in the chicken broth, tomatoes, Cajun seasoning, wine, oregano, parsley, and pepper.
- Cook on LOW for around 6 to 8 hours or HIGH for around 3 to 4 hours, covered. Add cooked shrimp & hot cooked rice for around 30 minutes before serving; heat thoroughly.

4. Crock-Pot Shrimp Marinara

(Preparation time: 20 minutes | Cooking time: 8 hours | Servings: 4)
Per serving: Calories 198, Total fat 8g, Protein 20g, Carbs 10g

Ingredients:

- 1 minced clove of garlic
- 1 teaspoon of dried oregano
- 1 lb. of cooked shelled shrimp
- 1 (14.5 oz.) can of diced tomatoes
- 1 teaspoon of salt
- Hot cooked spaghetti or linguini
- 2 tablespoons of minced fresh parsley
- 1/2 teaspoon of dried leaf basil
- 1 (6 oz.) can of tomato paste
- 1/4 teaspoon of pepper
- Grated Parmesan cheese
- 1/2 teaspoon of seasoned salt

Instructions:

- Combine tomatoes, basil, parsley, garlic, salt, tomato paste, pepper, oregano, and seasoned salt inside a Crock-Pot. Cook on low for around 6 to 7 hours, covered. Increase the flame to high, mix in the cooked shrimp, cover, and simmer for another 15 minutes on high.
- Serve over spaghetti that has been cooked. Serve with a sprinkle of Parmesan cheese on top or on the side.

5. Cheesy Monkfish Chowder with Cauliflower

(Preparation time: 20 minutes | Cooking time: 8 hours | Servings: 4)
Per serving: Calories 290, Total fat 9g, Protein 27g, Carbs 25g

Ingredients:

- 1/2 cup of chopped green onions
- 1 can (14 ounces) of reduced-sodium chicken broth
- 1/2 head of cauliflower, broken into florets
- 1 pound of Yukon potatoes, peeled & cubed
- 1 large-sized chopped carrot
- Salt, to taste
- 1/2 cup of shredded reduced-fat Cheddar cheese
- 1 pound of cubed monkfish
- Crushed red pepper flakes to taste
- 3/4 teaspoon of hot pepper sauce

Instructions:

- In your Crock-Pot, combine the first five ingredients.
- Cook for around 8 hours on low inside the Crock-Pot.
- Then, inside a food processor, puree the cooked mixture till it reaches the desired consistency; return to the Crock-Pot.
- Add the remaining ingredients, except for the spicy sauce and cheese, and simmer for another 15 minutes on low.

- Allow to remain till the cheese has melted, then add the spicy pepper sauce. Serve hot at room temperature.

6. Cod and Shrimp Stew

(Preparation time: 20 minutes | Cooking time: 4 hours | Servings: 8)
Per serving: Calories 496, Total fat 29g, Protein 44g, Carbs 14g

Ingredients:

- 1/2 cup of finely chopped onion
- 1 cup of clam juice
- 2 bay leaves
- 1 can (28-ounces) of stewed tomatoes
- 1 teaspoon of dried basil
- 1/2 cup of dry white wine
- 1 pound of cod fillets, sliced
- 3 minced cloves of garlic
- Black pepper, to taste
- 1/2 teaspoon of dried thyme
- Salt, to taste
- 1 teaspoon of dried oregano leaves
- 1 ½ cups of shrimp, peeled & deveined

Instructions:

- Inside a Crock-Pot, combine all of the ingredients, except for the cod fillets & shrimp, and cover with a lid.
- Set the Crock-Pot at high and simmer for around 3 to 4 hours, adding the cod fillets & shrimp in the last 15 minutes. Remove bay leaves before serving with cornmeal.

7. Herbed Salmon Loaf with Sauce

(Preparation time: 20 minutes | Cooking time: 5-hours | Servings: 4)
Per serving: Calories 293, Total fat 16g, Protein 27g, Carbs 8g

Ingredients:

For the Salmon Meatloaf:

- 1 teaspoon of dried rosemary
- 1/4 cup of scallions, chopped
- 1 cup of fresh bread crumbs
- 1 teaspoon of mustard seed
- 1 can (7 ½ ounce) of salmon, drained
- 1 egg
- 1/3 cup of whole milk
- 1/4 teaspoon of white pepper
- 1 tablespoon of fresh lemon juice
- 1 teaspoon of ground coriander
- 1/2 teaspoon of salt
- 1/2 teaspoon of fenugreek

For the Sauce:

- 1/2 teaspoon of dill weed
- 1/2 cup of cucumber, chopped
- Salt, to taste
- 1/2 cup of reduced-fat plain yogurt

Instructions:

- Use foil to line your Crock-Pot.
- Combine all of the ingredients for the salmon meatloaf till well combined; shape into a loaf & place inside the Crock-Pot. Cover with the lid and cook for around 5 hours on low.
- To make the sauce, mix together all of the ingredients.
- Serve your meatloaf with the prepared sauce.

8. Poached Salmon with Onion

(Preparation time: 20 minutes | Cooking time: 1-hour | Servings: 4)
Per serving: Calories 405, Total fat 19g, Protein 49g, Carbs 4g

Ingredients:

- 1/2 cup of chicken broth
- 2 tablespoons of melted butter
- 1 sprig of fresh dill
- 1 thinly sliced small-sized onion
- Ground black pepper to taste
- 1 cup of water
- Sea salt, to taste
- 4 (6-ounces) salmon fillets
- 1 lemon, quartered, as the garnish

- 1 tablespoon of fresh lemon juice

Instructions:

- Using the butter, grease the interior of the Crock-Pot.
- Fill the Crock-Pot halfway with water and chicken stock, then add the onion slices. Cook for around 30 minutes on high in the Crock-Pot. Add the salmon fillets on top of the onions that have been cooked. Combine the lemon juice & fresh dill. Cook for another 30 minutes on high, or till the salmon is opaque. Add salt & black pepper to taste.
- Garnish the dish with lemons and enjoy!

9. Rich Tomato Shrimp Chowder

(Preparation time: 20 minutes | Cooking time: 5 hours | Servings: 6)
Per serving: Calories 400, Total fat 27g, Protein 22g, Carbs 16g

Ingredients:

- 2 cups of chicken broth
- 3 cups of whole kernel corn
- 1 cup of chopped red onion
- 1 cup of tomato juice
- 2 minced cloves of garlic
- 1 cup of clam juice
- 1/2 teaspoon of dried oregano
- 2 large-sized red potatoes, peeled & diced
- Salt to taste
- 1 chopped green bell pepper
- 1 ½ cups of cooked halved shrimp, peeled and deveined
- 1⁄4 cup of dry sherry, optional
- 1 teaspoon of dried basil
- 1⁄2 cup of whole milk
- 1⁄4 teaspoon of chili powder
- 1/2 teaspoon of ground black pepper

Instructions:

- Except for the shrimp and the milk, combine all of the ingredients inside your Crock-Pot.

- Cover and cook on high for around 4 to 5 hours, adding the shrimp and milk during the last 15 minutes of cooking.
- Serve after adjusting the seasonings to your liking.

10. Rich Seafood Soup with Bacon

(Preparation time: 20 minutes | Cooking time: 5 hours | Servings: 4)
Per serving: Calories 190, Total fat 12g, Protein 8g, Carbs 13g

Ingredients:

- 1 large-sized chopped sweet onion
- 1 pound of cubed halibut, cubed
- 1 ½ cups of clam juice
- 3/4 teaspoon of rubbed sage
- 1/4 cup of dry sherry wine
- Paprika to taste
- 4 large-sized Yukon gold potatoes, peeled & cubed
- 1 chopped rutabaga
- 1 chopped rib celery
- Salt, to taste
- 1 cup of 2% reduced-fat milk
- 2 slices of cooked bacon, crumbled
- A few drops of Tabasco sauce
- 1 teaspoon of dried parsley flakes

Instructions:

- To begin, combine the first 6 ingredients inside your Crock-Pot.
- Cook for around 4 to 5 hours on high. Transfer the prepared soup to a blender or food processor, along with the milk, and blend till smooth; return to the Crock-Pot.
- Except for the crumbled bacon, combine the remaining ingredients. Continue to cook for another 15 minutes.
- Distribute the soup into four serving bowls, sprinkle with bacon, & serve!

11. Summer Spiced Fish Stew

(Preparation time: 20 minutes | Cooking time: 5 hours | Servings: 8)

Per serving: Calories 339, Total fat 7g, Protein 27g, Carbs 41g

Ingredients:

- 1/2 cup of thinly sliced fennel
- 1 cup of clam juice
- 1/2 of chopped celery
- 1 cup of dry white wine
- 2 cans (14 ½ ounces) of tomatoes, undrained and diced
- 3/4 teaspoon of dill weed
- 1 cup of chopped leeks
- 1/4 cup of chopped parsley
- 1 clove of garlic, minced
- 1 pound of fish fillets, cubed
- 1/2 head of broccoli, chopped
- Black pepper, to taste
- 1 bay leaf
- 12 mussels, scrubbed
- 1/2 teaspoon of dried thyme
- Salt, to taste
- 1 teaspoon of grated lemon zest
- 2 tablespoons of cilantro
- 8 ounces of shrimp, peeled & deveined
- Cayenne pepper, to taste

Instructions:

- Inside a Crock-Pot, combine all of the ingredients except for the seafood; cover & cook on high for around 5 hours.
- Cook for another 15 minutes after adding the fish fillets, shrimp, & mussels to the Crock-Pot.
- Remove the bay leaf & serve immediately with cooked rice.

12. Salmon with Caper Sauce

(Preparation time: 20 minutes | Cooking time: 1-hour | Servings: 4)

Per serving: Calories 269, Total fat 26g, Protein 4g, Carbs 25g

Ingredients:

- 4 salmon steaks
- 1/2 cup of dry white wine
- 1/2 teaspoon of salt
- 3 tablespoons of flour
- 1/2 cup of water
- 2 teaspoons of lemon juice
- 1 thinly sliced yellow onion
- 1/4 teaspoon of black pepper
- 2 tablespoons of butter
- 3 tablespoons of capers
- 1 cup of chicken broth

Instructions:

- Inside a Crock-Pot, combine the wine, salt, water, onion, and black pepper; cover & cook on high for around 20 minutes.
- Place salmon & cook on high for around 20 minutes, or till salmon steaks are cooked.
- Melt butter inside a small-sized skillet on medium flame to prepare the sauce. Cook for around 1 minute after adding the flour.
- Whisk together the chicken stock and lemon juice for around 1 to 2 minutes. Add the capers, and the sauce is served with fish.

13. Shrimp and Rice

(Preparation time: 20 minutes | Cooking time: 8 hours | Servings: 4)
Per serving: Calories 286, Total fat 5g, Protein 25g, Carbs 32g

Ingredients:

- 1 chopped green bell pepper
- 1 can cream of celery soup
- 1 peeled and chopped yellow onion
- 2 to 3 cloves of garlic that have been finely chopped
- 1 chopped red bell pepper
- 2 cups of uncooked instant rice (do not use anything but the instant type)
- 1 cup of chicken broth
- 1 – 1/2 pounds of shrimp
- 1 can of cream of chicken soup
- 1 can of Ro-tel
- 1 teaspoon of dried parsley

Instructions:

- Inside a nonstick Crock-Pot, combine the garlic, onion, & peppers.
- Stir together the chicken broth, cream of chicken, & cream of celery soup inside a big measuring cup or bowl till smooth and lump-free. Pour the sauce over the vegetables.
- Inside a Crock-Pot, combine the Ro-tel, rice, & dried parsley.
- Place the frozen shrimp in the pot.
- Cook on low for around 6–8 hours then serve.

14. Salmon and Potato Casserole

(Preparation time: 20 minutes | Cooking time: 9 hours | Servings: 4)
Per serving: Calories 451, Total fat 28g, Protein 24g, Carbs 24g

Ingredients:

- 3 tablespoons of flour
- 1 can (10 3/4 ounces) of cream of mushroom soup
- 1 can (16 ounces) of salmon, drained & flaked
- A dash of nutmeg
- 4 to 5 medium potatoes, peeled & sliced
- Salt & black pepper
- 1/2 cup of chopped onion
- 1/4 cup of water

Instructions:

- Inside a greased Crock-Pot, place half of the potatoes. Sprinkle half of the flour on top, then season using salt and black pepper. Half of the flakes salmon should be on top, and half of the onion should be sprinkled on top. Layers should be repeated. Mix the soup and water together and pour over the potato & salmon mixture. Add a pinch of nutmeg to finish. Cook for around 7 to 9 hours on low, or till potatoes are soft.

15. Sweet and Sour Shrimp

(Preparation time: 20 minutes | Cooking time: 6 hours | Servings: 4)
Per serving: Calories 435, Total fat 20g, Protein 33g, Carbs 31g

Ingredients:

- 3 tablespoons of granulated sugar
- 1 package (6 ounces) of frozen Chinese pea pods
- 1 tablespoon of soy sauce
- 1 can (12 to 14 ounces) of pineapple tidbits in juice
- 2 tablespoons of cornstarch
- 1 bag (12 to 16 ounces) of frozen small to medium shrimp, cleaned & cooked
- 1 cup of chicken broth
- Hot cooked rice
- 1/2 cup of reserved pineapple juice
- 1/2 teaspoon of ground ginger
- 2 tablespoons of cider vinegar

Instructions:

- Place pea pods inside a colander and pour cold water over them till they are somewhat thawed. Drain pineapple and keeping a half cup of the juice, and set aside.

- Inside a Crock-Pot, combine pea pods & drained pineapple. Combine cornstarch & sugar inside a small-sized saucepan; pour chicken broth, saved pineapple juice, soy sauce, & ginger.
- Bring the mixture to the boil, stirring constantly, & simmer for around 1 minute.
- The sauce should be clear and thickened. Blend the sauce gently into the pea pods & pineapple. Cook on LOW for around 3 to 5 hours, covered.
- Add the shrimp and cook for another 30 minutes, or till the thawed cooked shrimp are heated thoroughly. Gently whisk in the vinegar.
- Serve alongside steaming rice.

16. Summer Seafood Treat

(Preparation time: 20 minutes | Cooking time: 4 hours | Servings: 8)
Per serving: Calories 442, Total fat 21g, Protein 46g, Carbs 18g

Ingredients:

- 1 ½ cup of tomatoes, undrained & diced
- 1 teaspoon of garlic powder
- 1/2 teaspoon of dried thyme
- 1 cup of fish stock
- 1/2 cup of water
- 1 cup of lobster tail, cooked & cut into small pieces
- 2 large-sized Yukon gold potatoes, diced
- Black pepper to taste
- 1 cup of spring onions, chopped
- Fresh cilantro, as the garnish
- 1/2 teaspoon of onion powder
- 1 cup of whole milk
- 1 teaspoon of dried tarragon leaves
- 1/2 teaspoon of cayenne pepper
- Paprika to taste
- 1/2 cup of small shrimp, peeled & deveined
- Salt to taste

Instructions:

- Fill your Crock-Pot halfway with water & fish stock. Tomatoes, onion powder, potatoes, tarragon, garlic powder, thyme, and cayenne pepper are then added.
- Cover and cook for around 4 hours on low.
- During the last 10 minutes of cooking, add the additional ingredients, except for the cilantro.
- Enjoy your summer chowder with the chopped fresh cilantro on top!

17. Scallop and Potato Chowder

(Preparation time: 20 minutes | Cooking time: 4 hours | Servings: 4)
Per serving: Calories 591, Total fat 31g, Protein 32g, Carbs 42g

Ingredients:

- 1/2 cup of dry white wine
- 1 cup of clam juice
- 1 minced clove of garlic
- 1/2 cup of water
- 2 large-sized red potatoes, peeled & cubed
- 1/2 cup of milk (2% low-fat)
- Salt to taste
- 1 pound of bay scallops
- Red pepper flakes, as the garnish
- 1/2 teaspoon of cumin

Instructions:

- Inside a Crock-Pot, combine the first five ingredients; cover & cook on high for around 3 to 4 hours.
- Blend till smooth and creamy in a blender, then return to the Crock-Pot. Except for the red pepper flakes, stir in the remaining ingredients.
- Cover and simmer on high for 10 minutes, or till scallops are cooked through.
- Serve heated, divided among soup bowls and sprinkled with red pepper flakes.

18. Salmon Chowder with Root Vegetables

(Preparation time: 20 minutes | Cooking time: 4 hours | Servings: 6)
Per serving: Calories 490, Total fat 26g, Protein 39g, Carbs 26g

Ingredients:

- 1/2 teaspoon of dry mustard
- 3 cups potatoes, peeled & cubed
- 1/2 cup of rutabaga
- 2 medium-sized thinly sliced carrots
- 1 teaspoon of celery seeds
- 1/2 cup of chopped scallions
- 2 tablespoons of cornstarch
- 1 cup of chopped turnips
- Black pepper, to taste
- 1 cup of water
- 1 cup of milk
- 2 cups of clam juice
- Salt, to taste
- 1/2 teaspoon of dried marjoram leaves
- 1 pound of salmon steaks, cut into bite-sized chunks

Instructions:

- Toss potatoes, carrots, onions, turnips, marjoram, clam juice, rutabaga, water, dry mustard, and celery seeds together inside a Crock-Pot.
- Cook for around 6 hours on high, covered.
- Return the chowder to the Crock-Pot after puréeing it in a food processor or blender till smooth & consistent. Cook for another 15 minutes after adding the salmon.
- Stir in the combined milk with cornstarch for around 3 minutes, stirring regularly. Add salt & black pepper to taste. Enjoy!

19. Tuna Noodle Casserole

(Preparation time: 20 minutes | Cooking time: 7 hours | Servings: 4)
Per serving: Calories 776, Total fat 42g, Protein 34g, Carbs 47g

Ingredients:

- 2 tablespoons of parsley flakes
- 1/4 cup of dry sherry
- 1/4 teaspoon of curry powder, or to taste
- 2/3 cup of milk
- 2 tablespoons of butter
- 10 ounces of frozen peas & carrots, around 1 1/2 to 2 cups
- 10 ounces of egg noodles, cooked till just tender
- 2 cans of tuna, drained

Instructions:

- Cream of celery soup, sherry, veggies, milk, parsley flakes, curry powder, and tuna together inside a large-sized mixing dish. Fold in the noodles and toss well to incorporate. Fill a greased Crock-Pot halfway with the mixture. Make a butter smear. Cover & cook on Low for around 5 to 7 hours, or till veggies are soft and noodles are cooked through.

20. Will's Fisherman's Stew

(Preparation time: 20 minutes | Cooking time: 8 hours | Servings: 6)
Per serving: Calories 413, Total fat 19g, Protein 37g, Carbs 16g

Ingredients:

- 3 minced cloves of garlic
- 1 large can (28 ounces) of crushed tomatoes with juice
- 1 chopped green pepper
- 1 can (8 ounces) of tomato sauce
- 1 teaspoon of thyme
- 1/2 teaspoon of paprika
- 1/2 cup of chopped onion
- Salt & pepper, to taste
- 1 cup of dry white wine
- 1/2 cup of parsley, chopped
- 1/3 cup of olive oil
- Water, if desired
- 2 teaspoons of basil
- 1 chopped hot pepper
- 1/2 teaspoon of cayenne pepper

- 1 teaspoon of oregano

For the Seafood:

- 1 dozen prawns
- 1 dozen mussels
- 1 deboned and cubed fillet of seabass, cod or any other whitefish
- 1 dozen clams
- 1 dozen scallops

Instructions:

- Except for the seafood, combine all ingredients inside a Crock-Pot. Cook on low for around 6 to 8 hours, covered.
- Add your seafood 30 minutes before the end of cooking time. Increase to HIGH & often stir (but gently).
- Serve with real sourdough bread if available.

Chapter 7: Crock-Pot Vegetarian Recipes

1. Bavarian-Style Red Cabbage

(Preparation time: 20 minutes | Cooking time: 10 hours | Servings: 6)
Per serving: Calories 136, Total fat 4g, Protein 2g, Carbs 25g

Ingredients:

- 6 tart apples, cored & quartered
- 2 cups of hot water
- 2/3 cup of cider vinegar
- 1 large head of red cabbage, washed & coarsely sliced
- 6 tablespoons of bacon grease or butter
- 2 medium onions, coarsely chopped, around 1 cup
- 2 teaspoons of salt
- 3 tablespoons of granulated sugar

Instructions:

- Inside a crockpot, combine the onions, cabbage, and apples. Season using salt. Pour over cabbage mixture a mixture of boiling water, vinegar, sugar, & bacon grease or butter. Cook on LOW for around 8 to 10 hours, covered. Before serving, give it a good stir.

2. Colcannon

(Preparation time: 20 minutes | Cooking time: 9 hours | Servings: 6)
Per serving: Calories 310, Total fat 16g, Protein 6g, Carbs 39g

Ingredients:

- 1 pound of chopped cabbage
- 1 dash of salt
- 1 pound of potatoes, sliced
- 2 medium leeks
- 1 dash of pepper
- 2 medium parsnips, peeled & sliced
- Parsley
- 1 cup of milk
- 1/4 teaspoon of nutmeg
- 2 tablespoons of butter
- 2 small cloves of garlic, minced

Instructions:

- Inside a kettle of water, cook the potatoes & parsnips till they are soft. While the veggies are cooking, chop the leeks (both light green & white) and stew them inside the milk till they are soft.
- Cook the cabbage & keep it warm in the oven.
- Season the potatoes & parsnips with salt, nutmeg, garlic, and pepper after draining. Using a fork, mash or beat the potato combination till it is smooth. Mix in the cooked leeks & milk till well combined.
- Combine the cooked chopped cabbage & butter.
- Garnish using fresh parsley,
- Cook the cabbage first in the Crock-Pot, then arrange all of the veggies in the crock, beginning with the potatoes. Cook for around 7 to 9 hours, or till veggies are soft, covered. Drain the vegetables and mash them using milk and butter before adding parsley on top.

3. Curry-Spiced Lentils & Spinach

(Preparation time: 20 minutes | Cooking time: 6 hours | Servings: 3)
Per serving: Calories 328, Total fat 8g, Protein 18g, Carbs 52g

Ingredients:

- 1 chopped medium onion
- 1 1/2 teaspoons of curry powder
- 1/4 cup of rice
- 1 can (1 1/2 cups) of vegetable broth
- 1/2 teaspoon of ground cumin
- 1/4 teaspoon of turmeric
- Chopped tomato & mint for the garnish, if desired
- 1 teaspoon of ginger
- 1 cup of lentils, rinsed
- 1/4 teaspoon of cayenne
- 2 cloves of garlic, crushed & minced
- 1 10-ounces package of chopped spinach or other greens
- Salt to taste

Instructions:

- Inside a Crock-Pot, combine all ingredients except for the sliced tomato and mint.
- Cook for around 6 hours on low, or till the rice & lentils are soft but not mushy.
- Season using salt and black pepper to taste, then serve with sliced tomato and mint, if desired.

4. Creamy Scalloped Potatoes

(Preparation time: 20 minutes | Cooking time: 7 hours | Servings: 4)
Per serving: Calories 310, Total fat 10g, Protein 13g, Carbs 45g

Ingredients:

- 3 tablespoons of butter
- 7 to 9 medium potatoes, peeled, thinly sliced, around 2 1/2 pounds
- 1 can (10 3/4 ounces) of condensed cream of mushroom soup
- 1 teaspoon of salt

- 1 thinly sliced medium onion
- 1 cup of cold water
- 6 ounces of American cheese, slices, cubed, or shredded
- 1/2 teaspoon of cream of tartar
- 1/4 cup of all-purpose flour
- 1/4 teaspoon of ground black pepper

Instructions:

- Drain potato slices after soaking them inside 1 cup of water & 1/2 teaspoon cream of tartar. Inside a buttered or greased 3 1/2 to 5-quart Crock-Pot, place half of the sliced potatoes. Half of the onion pieces, half of the flour, half of the salt, & half of the pepper. Half of the butter should be dotted on top. Rep layers, drizzling the remaining butter on top. Pour the soup on top.
- Cook on low for around 6 to 7 hours, or high for around 3 to 3 1/2 hours.
- Approximately 30 minutes before serving, add the cheese.

5. Corn Pudding

(Preparation time: 10 minutes | Cooking time: 3 hours | Servings: 4)
Per serving: Calories 239, Total fat 10g, Protein 7g, Carbs 34g

Ingredients:

- 1/4 cup of chopped fresh tomato
- 1/2 cup of evaporated milk
- 1/4 cup of chopped onion
- 1/2 teaspoon of salt
- 1/4 cup of chopped green pepper
- 1 16 oz. can of cream-style corn
- 1/4 teaspoon of pepper
- 4 large eggs

Instructions:

- Cook till the onion & green pepper are cooked, then add the tomato and cook for another minute.

- Whisk together the creamed corn, eggs, milk, and seasonings inside a medium-sized mixing bowl; stir in the cooked vegetables.
- Pour the ingredients into a 3 1/2-quart crockpot (or a soufflé dish that fits in a bigger crockpot) that has been lightly greased. Heat on HIGH for around 2 1/2 to 3 hours, then top with shredded cheese and cook till melted.

6. Creamy Fennel Soup with Walnuts

(Preparation time: 20 minutes | Cooking time: 4 hours | Servings: 6)
Per serving: Calories 222, Total fat 13g, Protein 5g, Carbs 26g

Ingredients:

- 1 medium-sized chopped carrot
- 3 ½ chicken broth
- 1/2 cup of chopped scallions
- 1 ½ cups of fennel bulbs
- 2 cloves of garlic, minced
- 1/2 cup of chopped celery
- 2 large-sized Idaho potato, peeled, cubed
- 1 tablespoon of soy sauce
- Salt to taste
- 1 tablespoon of apple cider vinegar
- Chopped toasted walnuts as the garnish
- 1/2 cup of 2% low-fat milk
- Ground black pepper to taste

Instructions:

- Combine the first seven ingredients inside a Crock-Pot. Cook for around 4 hours on high.
- Blend the prepared soup inside a food processor till it reaches a smooth consistency.
- Cook for another 5 minutes with the remaining ingredients, except for the chopped walnuts. Serve by dividing among serving bowls and scattering walnuts on top.

7. Creamed Root Vegetables

(Preparation time: 20 minutes | Cooking time: 5 hours | Servings: 6)
Per serving: Calories 235, Total fat 9g, Protein 3g, Carbs 37g

Ingredients:

- 2 medium sliced parsnips
- 4 small sliced potatoes
- 1/2 teaspoon of dried basil leaves
- 1/4 teaspoon of paprika
- 1 medium-sized sliced fennel bulb
- 1 sliced turnip
- 1/2 cup of half-and-half
- 1 large-sized sliced carrot
- 3 small leeks sliced (white parts only)
- 1/4 teaspoon of ground black pepper
- 2 minced cloves of garlic
- Salt, to taste
- 2 tablespoons of corn flour
- 1 cup of chicken broth
- 1 cup of sour cream

Instructions:

- In your Crock-Pot, combine all ingredients except for the sour cream and corn flour.
- Cook for around 5 hours on high, or till the vegetables are soft.
- Cook, constantly stirring, for around 2 to 3 minutes after adding the sour cream & corn flour mixture. Serve.

8. Delicious Cream of Asparagus Soup

(Preparation time: 20 minutes | Cooking time: 4 hours | Servings: 6)
Per serving: Calories 187, Total fat 15g, Protein 5g, Carbs 11g

Ingredients:

- 1 teaspoon of lemon zest
- 2 cups of vegetable stock
- 1 heaping tablespoon of fresh parsley
- 1 cup of water
- 1/4 teaspoon of white pepper

- 2 pounds of asparagus, reserving the tips for garnishing
- 1 teaspoon of dried marjoram
- 1 finely chopped onion
- Salt to taste
- 2 cloves of garlic, minced
- 1/2 cup of whole milk

Instructions:

- Inside a Crock-Pot, combine the water, stock, asparagus, marjoram, onion, lemon zest, garlic, and parsley.
- Cook for around 3 to 4 hours on a high.
- In the meantime, cook the asparagus tips till they are crisp-tender.
- Fill a food processor halfway with soup, then add the milk, salt, & white pepper and pulse till smooth. Serve at room temperature using steamed asparagus tips as a garnish.
- You can also cool your soup and serve it with chilled garnishes.

9. Eggplant Parmigiana

(Preparation time: 20 minutes | Cooking time: 5 hours | Servings: 4)
Per serving: Calories 481, Total fat 35g, Protein 14g, Carbs 30g

Ingredients:

- 1/3 cup of seasoned bread crumbs
- 4 mediums to large eggplant, peeled
- 32 ounces of marinara sauce
- Olive oil, extra virgin
- 2 eggs
- 16 ounces of Mozzarella cheese, sliced
- 1/3 cup of water
- 1/2 cup of Parmesan cheese
- 3 tablespoons of flour

Instructions:

- Cut eggplant into 1/2-inch slices & put in a bowl, adding salt on each layer. Allow draining excess moisture for 30 minutes before drying on paper towels. Combine the egg, 1/3 cup of water, & flour. Allow

extra batter to drip off eggplant slices as they are dipped in batter. Inside a skillet, briskly sauté a few slices of eggplant at a time in heated olive oil. Combine the seasoned bread crumbs and Parmesan cheese. Layer a quarter of the eggplant inside the crockpot, then top with 1/4 of the crumbs, 1/4 of the marinara sauce, & 1/4 of the Mozzarella cheese.
- Make 4 layers of eggplant, sauce, crumbs, and mozzarella cheese by repeating the process. Cook on LOW for around 4 to 5 hours, covered.

10. Everyday Tomato Casserole

(Preparation time: 20 minutes | Cooking time: 3 hours | Servings: 6)
Per serving: Calories 172, Total fat 12g, Protein 9g, Carbs 8g

Ingredients:

- 1 tablespoon of corn flour
- 8 ounces of cooked macaroni
- 1/2 cup of grated sharp cheese
- 1 can (16-ounces) of petite diced tomatoes, drained
- Salt, to taste
- 1/2 cup of chopped leeks
- 1/2 teaspoon of ground cinnamon
- 1 cup of whole milk
- Paprika, as the garnish
- 1 cup of water
- 3 lightly beaten eggs

Instructions:

- Inside a Crock-Pot, combine tomatoes, macaroni, & leeks.
- Combine the remaining ingredients inside a dish, excluding the paprika, and pour over the macaroni inside the Crock-Pot.
- Cook for around 3 hours on low or till set; divide among the serving dishes & top with paprika.

11. Hearty Bean and Vegetable Stew

(Preparation time: 20 minutes | Cooking time: 8 hours | Servings: 12)
Per serving: Calories 352, Total fat 6g, Protein 12g, Carbs 53g

Ingredients:

- 1/3 cup of apple or pineapple juice
- 1 lb. of beans, assorted, dry
- 1/2 cup of mushrooms, diced
- 1 teaspoon of parsley, dried
- 1 teaspoon of ground black pepper
- 2 cups of V-8 or tomato juice
- 1/2 cup of celery, diced
- 1/2 cup of dry white wine
- 3 cloves of minced garlic
- 1/3 cup of soy sauce
- Vegetable stock or water
- 1/2 cup of parsnips or turnips, diced
- 1 teaspoon of basil, dried
- 1/2 cup of carrots, diced
- 1 cup of rice or pasta, cooked
- 1 onion, diced
- 1 bay leaf

Instructions:

- After sorting and rinsing the beans, soak them under water for overnight. Drain the beans and place them inside a Dutch oven or kettle using fresh water. Simmer for around 1 hour, or till the vegetables are soft. Drain the beans and place them inside the Crock-Pot. Combine the soy sauce, vegetable juice, wine, and apple or pineapple juice. Cover in vegetable stock or water, depending on whether you want to make a soup or a thick stew. Cook for around 2 hours on high. Cook for around 5

to 6 hours on low till carrots & parsnips are soft, adding veggies, herbs, & spices as needed.
- When the vegetables are soft, add the rice or pasta & simmer for another hour.

12. Mediterranean Treat

(Preparation time: 20 minutes | Cooking time: 2 hours | Servings: 8)
Per serving: Calories 172, Total fat 14g, Protein 3g, Carbs 16g

Ingredients:

- 1 teaspoon of ginger root, ground
- 2 cups of green beans
- 1 tablespoon of rice wine vinegar
- 1/4 cup of finely chopped onion
- 1/2 teaspoon of sea salt
- 2 minced cloves of garlic
- 1 large-sized chopped red bell pepper
- 1 cup of canned black beans, drained
- 1 large-sized chopped carrot
- 1/4 teaspoon of ground black pepper
- 1/2 cup of water
- 2 teaspoons of tamari sauce

Instructions:

- Combine onion, green beans, garlic, ginger root, bell pepper, carrot, & water inside a Crock-Pot; cover with a lid & cook on high.
- Cook for around 1 1/2 hours and drain. Cook for another 30 minutes after adding the other ingredients. Serve after tasting and adjusting the seasonings.

13. Orange Wild Rice

(Preparation time: 20 minutes | Cooking time: 3 hours | Servings: 4)
Per serving: Calories 248, Total fat 14g, Protein 9g, Carbs 21g

Ingredients:

- 1 envelope of dry onion soup mix
- 1 1/2 cups of uncooked converted rice

- 1 bunch of green onions, chopped
- 1/4 cup of butter, melted
- 1/2 cup of uncooked wild rice
- 1 tablespoon of snipped parsley
- 8 oz. of fresh or canned mushrooms, sliced & drained
- 4 cups of water

Instructions:

- Inside a Crock-Pot that has been lightly oiled, combine all of the ingredients.
- Cook for around 2 1/2 hours on high, stirring periodically.
- Overcooked rice will turn mushy, so keep an eye on it.

14. Pasta with Lentils and Chard

(Preparation time: 20 minutes | Cooking time: 7 hours | Servings: 6)
Per serving: Calories 453, Total fat 18g, Protein 17g, Carbs 62g

Ingredients:

- 1 cup of lentils, rinsed & drained
- 2 cloves of garlic, minced
- 1 pound of fresh Swiss chard or spinach
- 6 ounces of light cream cheese at the room temperature
- 1/8 teaspoon of ground black pepper
- 12 ounces of dry spaghetti or linguine
- 1/2 cup of chopped onion
- 1/4 teaspoon of ground cumin
- 2 cups of water
- 1/2 teaspoon of crushed red pepper flakes
- Grated Parmesan cheese
- Salt

Instructions:

- Chard or spinach should be thoroughly rinsed & drained.
- Trim coarse stem ends, then cut thick stems crosswise into 1/4-inch pieces (if using chard).
- Refrigerate the chard or spinach leaves covered using plastic wrap.

- Combine garlic, sliced chard stems, lentils, diced onion, red pepper flakes, cumin seeds, and black pepper in a 3 1/2-quart or larger Crock-Pot.
- Fill the container halfway using water.
- Cover & cook on LOW for around 6 to 7 hours, or till lentils are soft when mashed using a fork.
- Crosswise chop chard or spinach leaves into 1/2-inch-wide strips & stir into Crock-Pot.
- Increase to HIGH; cover and simmer for another 15 minutes, or till chard or spinach is wilted & bright green.
- Meanwhile, cook linguine according to package directions into salted boiling water.
- Drain the linguine and place it inside a big serving bowl. Season the lentil sauce with salt to taste.
- Toss the spaghetti or similar pasta with the lentil sauce and cream cheese to mix well. If desired, serve with a side of Parmesan cheese.

15. Polenta

(Preparation time: 20 minutes | Cooking time: 9 hours | Servings: 8)
Per serving: Calories 110, Total fat 2g, Protein 3g, Carbs 24g

Ingredients:

- 1/4 teaspoon of paprika
- 2 cups of cornmeal or polenta
- 3 tablespoons of melted butter, divided
- 2 teaspoons of salt
- 6 cups of boiling water

Instructions:

- One tablespoon of butter should be used to grease the Crock-Pot's walls.
- Measure the other ingredients and combine them with the leftover butter inside the Crock-Pot. Cook, stirring periodically, on low for around 6 to 9 hours

(or around 3 to 4 hours on high), stirring occasionally.
- Fill a greased loaf pan halfway with polenta mixture. Chill completely before cutting into 1/4-inch slices & browning in butter.

16. Risotto with Zucchini and Yellow Squash

(Preparation time: 20 minutes | Cooking time: 2 hours | Servings: 4)
Per serving: Calories 63, Total fat 2g, Protein 5g, Carbs 12g

Ingredients:

- 1 cup of sliced cremini mushrooms
- 3 cups of vegetable broth
- 3/4 cup of cubed summer yellow squash
- 1 medium-sized chopped onion
- 1/4 cup of grated Pecorino cheese
- 2 cloves of garlic, minced
- 1/2 teaspoon of ground black pepper
- 1 cup of each zucchini, cubed
- 1 teaspoon of rosemary dried
- 1/2 teaspoon of cayenne pepper
- 1 ½ cups of short-grain rice
- 1 sweet potato, peeled and cubed
- 1/2 teaspoon of sea salt

Instructions:

- Inside your Crock-Pot, combine all ingredients except for the cheese.
- Cook for roughly 1 1/4 hours on high, or till rice is al dente.
- Stir in the cheese, then divide among 4 serving dishes.

17. Spaghetti with Beans and Asparagus

(Preparation time: 20 minutes | Cooking time: 3 hours | Servings: 4)
Per serving: Calories 200, Total fat 14g, Protein 5g, Carbs 19g

Ingredients:

- 2 medium-sized chopped carrots
- 1 cup of vegetable stock
- 1 teaspoon of onion powder
- 1/2 cup of green beans
- 8 ounces of cooked spaghetti
- 1 can (15-ounces) of Great Northern beans, rinsed & drained
- 1 pound of asparagus, cut into bite-sized pieces
- 2 medium-sized chopped tomatoes
- 1/4 cup of shredded Parmesan cheese
- 1/2 teaspoon of celery salt
- 1 teaspoon of garlic powder
- 3/4 teaspoon of rosemary leaves dried

Instructions:

- Combine vegetable stock, green beans, carrots, Great Northern beans, tomatoes, and rosemary in a Crock-Pot.
- Cook for around 3 hours, covered, with the asparagus pieces added in the last 30 minutes.
- Toss with spaghetti & Parmesan cheese after seasoning using celery salt, onion powder, & garlic powder. Enjoy!

18. Spicy Green Beans

(Preparation time: 20 minutes | Cooking time: 4 hours | Servings: 4)
Per serving: Calories 54, Total fat 4g, Protein 2g, Carbs 6g

Ingredients:

- 1 teaspoon of celery seeds
- 1 pound of green beans
- 1 teaspoon of sea salt
- 1 can (28-ounces) of petite diced tomatoes
- 1/4 teaspoon of crushed red pepper flakes
- 1 large-sized chopped red onion
- 1 teaspoon of dried oregano
- 4 cloves of minced garlic
- 1/4 teaspoon of ground black pepper
- 1 teaspoon of dried basil

Instructions:

- Inside a Crock-Pot, combine all of the ingredients.

- Cook for around 4 hours on high, covered, or till green beans are cooked.
- Season using salt & pepper to taste, then divide into serving bowls. Serve alongside boiled potatoes and your favorite seasonal salad for a quick and healthy dinner!

19. Spiced Mashed Beans

(Preparation time: 20 minutes | Cooking time: 8 hours | Servings: 10)
Per serving: Calories 275, Total fat 7g, Protein 13g, Carbs 39g

Ingredients:

- 1 yellow onion, cut into wedges
- 9 cups of water
- 1 tablespoon of Cajun seasoning
- 3 cups of canned pinto beans, rinsed
- 1 teaspoon of ground black pepper
- 1/2 poblano pepper, seeded & minced
- 1 teaspoon of cayenne pepper
- 2 minced cloves of garlic
- 1 teaspoon of fine sea salt

Instructions:

- Inside a Crock-Pot, combine all of the ingredients.
- Cook for around 8 hours on a high.
- Remove the liquid from the strainer and set it aside.
- As needed, add the conserved liquid to the beans to mash them.
- Serve with your favorite salad and sausage.

20. Vegetarian Style Sloppy Joes

(Preparation time: 20 minutes | Cooking time: 9 hours | Servings: 6)

Per serving: Calories 384, Total fat 20g, Protein 18g, Carbs 37g

Ingredients:

- 2 tablespoons of Balsamic vinegar
- 1 -1/2 tablespoons of olive oil
- 1 large chopped red bell pepper
- 2 cloves of peeled and minced garlic
- 1 tablespoon of brown sugar
- 1 cup of frozen corn kernels
- 1 large white onion, peeled & sliced thinly
- 1/2 cup of water
- 2 medium-sized carrots, peeled & sliced thinly
- 2 tablespoons of soy sauce
- 2 tablespoons of chili powder
- 1 cup of dry pinto beans, soaked in enough water to cover, overnight
- 1 chopped zucchini
- 1 – 8 ounces can of tomato sauce
- 2 tablespoons of tomato paste
- 1 teaspoon of salt
- 4 cups of cabbage, thinly sliced
- 8 to 10 hamburger buns (whole wheat preferred)
- 2 tablespoons of honey mustard
- 1 teaspoon of salt

Instructions:

- Inside a medium-sized skillet, heat the olive oil & add the garlic, onion, & carrot.
- Sauté for around 3 to 6 minutes, or till the onion is soft.
- Remove from flame and mix in the vinegar, scraping up all of the brown pieces from the bottom of the pan.
- Add the chili powder and mix well. Spray the inside of the Crock-Pot using nonstick cooking spray.
- Place the beans inside the Crock-Pot after draining and rinsing them.
- Stir in the bell pepper, water, tomato sauce, and paste.
- On top, put the onion carrot mixture. This will maintain the beans moist during cooking, ensuring that they are soft and not dried out.
- Cook on high for around 5 hours and low for around 9 hours, covered.
- Combine the zucchini, cabbage, and thawed & drained corn kernels.

- Cook for around 30 minutes on high, stirring in the honey mustard brown sugar & salt.
- Put the mixture on buns once ready to serve.

21. Vegetarian Stew

(Preparation time: 20 minutes | Cooking time: 4 hours | Servings: 4)
Per serving: Calories 429, Total fat 9g, Protein 20g, Carbs 49g

Ingredients:

- 1 cup of new potatoes
- 1 ½ cups of vegetable stock
- 4 green onions, sliced
- 1 cup of green beans
- 1 cup of Brussels sprouts
- 1/2 cup of carrots, chopped
- 1/4 cup of cold water
- 1/2 chopped turnips
- 1/4 teaspoon of paprika
- 2 medium-sized plum tomatoes, chopped
- 2 tablespoons of cornstarch
- 1/2 teaspoon of dried marjoram leaves
- 4 slices of vegetarian bacon, fried crisp, crumbled
- Salt, to taste
- 10 asparagus spears, cut into small chunks
- 3 cups of cooked brown rice, warm
- 1/4 teaspoon of ground black pepper

Instructions:

- Place vegetable stock, carrots, green beans, potatoes, onion, turnips, tomatoes, and marjoram leaves in a Crock-Pot.
- Cook for around 4 hours on high, covered.
- During the last 30 minutes of cooking time, add the additional ingredients, excluding the cooked rice.
- Enjoy over a bed of brown rice!

22. Vegetarian Creamed Corn Soup

(Preparation time: 20 minutes | Cooking time: 5 hours | Servings: 4)
Per serving: Calories 362, Total fat 28g, Protein 5g, Carbs 27g

Ingredients:

- 1 large-sized carrot, chopped
- 3 ½ cups of vegetable stock
- 2 tablespoons of cornstarch
- 1/2 cup of chopped scallions
- White pepper, to taste
- 1 clove of minced garlic
- 2 medium-sized potatoes, peeled & cubed
- Sour cream, as the garnish
- 1 can (151/2 ounces) of whole kernel corn, drained
- Paprika, as the garnish
- 1 cup of reduced-fat milk
- Celery salt, to taste

Instructions:

- Combine the vegetable stock, potato, scallions, carrots, and garlic inside a large-sized mixing bowl.
- Cook for around 4 hours on high, covered. Return the soup to the Crock-Pot after puréeing it in a food processor till creamy & smooth.
- Cook for another 30 minutes on high with the kernel corn. After that, add the reduced-fat milk & cornstarch mixture and stir consistently for 3 minutes. Stir in the celery salt & white pepper once more.

Serve with paprika & sour cream on the side.

23. Vegetable Curry

(Preparation time: 20 minutes | Cooking time: 9 hours | Servings: 4)
Per serving: Calories 245, Total fat 6g, Protein 8g, Carbs 32g

Ingredients:

- 2 tablespoons of quick-cooking tapioca
- 4 medium carrots, sliced into 1/2-inch slices
- 1/2 teaspoon of crushed red pepper
- 2 medium potatoes, cut into 1/2-inch cubes
- 1 cup of coarsely chopped onion
- 1 1/2 cups of vegetable broth
- 1 can (15 ounces) of garbanzo beans, drained
- 2 teaspoons of curry powder
- 1/2 pound of green beans, cut into 1-inch pieces, around 1 1/2 cups
- 1/8 teaspoon of ground cinnamon
- 3 to 4 cloves of garlic, minced
- 1 teaspoon of ground coriander
- 2 cups of hot cooked rice
- 1/4 teaspoon of salt
- 1 can (14.5 ounces) of diced tomatoes with juice

Instructions:

- Combine potatoes, carrots, garbanzo beans, curry powder, green beans, onion, garlic, tapioca, salt, coriander, red pepper, and cinnamon inside a 3 1/2- to 5-quart Crock-Pot. Pour the broth over everything. Cook on LOW for around 7–9 hours or HIGH for around 3 1/2–4 1/2 hours, covered. Toss in the tomatoes. Cook for another 5 minutes, covered.
- Serve with steaming rice.

24. Wild Rice Casserole

(Preparation time: 10 minutes | Cooking time: 3 hours | Servings: 4)
Per serving: Calories 267, Total fat 7g, Protein 6g, Carbs 47g

Ingredients:

- 1 envelope of dry onion soup mix
- 4 cups of water
- 1 1/2 cups of uncooked long-grained rice
- 8 oz. sliced fresh or canned mushrooms
- 1/2 cup of uncooked wild rice
- 1/4 cup of butter, melted
- 1 teaspoon of dried parsley flakes
- 1 bunch of green onions, chopped, around 8 green onions

Instructions:

- Combine all ingredients inside a mixing bowl. Pour into a Crock-Pot that has been lightly oiled.
- Cook, covered, for around 2 1/2 hours on HIGH, stirring periodically.

25. Wheat Berry and Lentil Stew

(Preparation time: 20 minutes | Cooking time: 8 hours | Servings: 8)
Per serving: Calories 167, Total fat 4g, Protein 5g, Carbs 30g

Ingredients:

- 1 cup of wheat berries
- 3 cups of vegetable broth
- 1 chopped carrot
- 1/2 cup of dried lentils
- 3 cloves of minced garlic
- 1 ½ pounds of potatoes, cubed
- Black pepper, to taste
- 1 cup of chopped leeks
- 1 chopped stalk of celery
- Celery salt, to taste

Instructions:

- Place all of the ingredients inside your Crock-Pot, cover with a lid, and cook on low for around 8 hours.
- Serve with cornbread of your choice & enjoy!

Chapter 8:
Crock-Pot Appetizer and
Snack Recipes

1. Appetizer Meatballs with Barbecue Sauce

(Preparation time: 10 minutes | Cooking time: 4 hours | Servings: 12)
Per serving: Calories 536, Total fat 18g, Protein 26g, Carbs 34g

Ingredients:

- 1 pound of lean ground beef
- 1 large-sized egg
- 1/2 pound of ground pork
- 1/2 teaspoon of red pepper flakes, crushed
- 1 finely chopped small-sized onion
- 2 cloves of minced garlic
- 2 cups of barbecue sauce
- 1/3 cup of dry bread crumbs
- 1 cup of orange marmalade
- 1/2 teaspoon of seasoned salt
- 1/2 teaspoon of ground black pepper

Instructions:

- Pork, beef, red pepper, onion, garlic, salt, egg, bread crumbs, & black pepper are combined inside a mixing bowl. To make the meatballs, put all of the ingredients in a mixing bowl and form them into 24 meatballs.
- Fill the Crock-Pot halfway with meatballs. Add the barbeque sauce & orange marmalade after that.

- Cook for around 4 hours, covered. Serve with cocktail sticks while still heated!

2. Curry Spiced Nuts

(Preparation time: 20 minutes | Cooking time: 2 hours | Servings: 4)
Per serving: Calories 180, Total fat 16g, Protein 5g, Carbs 6g

Ingredients:

- 1 teaspoon of curry powder
- Dash of cayenne
- 4 tablespoons of raw almonds
- Kosher salt
- Garlic powder
- 1/2 teaspoon of honey
- 1 3/4 teaspoon of coconut oil, melted
- 4 tablespoons of raw cashews
- 4 tablespoons of raw pecan halves

Instructions:

- Inside a 6-quart crockpot, combine all of the ingredients and whisk to combine. Cook, covered, on high till brown and crisp, around 15 minutes. Stir occasionally; this should take anywhere from 1 1/2 to 2 hours.
- Place the mixture on a baking sheet lined using parchment paper and set aside to cool and dry.
- When finished, transfer to an airtight container & store till ready to serve.

3. Crockpot Brownie Bites

(Preparation time: 20 minutes | Cooking time: 5 hours | Servings: 4)
Per serving: Calories 326, Total fat 24g, Protein 7g, Carbs 28g

Ingredients:

- 1 teaspoon of baking soda
- 2 tablespoons of brewed coffee or water
- 6 1/2 tablespoons of sugar
- 1 teaspoon of pure vanilla extract

- 4 ¾ tablespoons of cocoa powder
- 1/2 cup of coconut oil melted
- 3 ¼ tablespoons of milk
- 1 teaspoon of baking powder
- 1 egg
- 12 ¾ tablespoons of flour
- 1/2 teaspoon of salt

Instructions:

- To begin, grease the Crock-Pot with coconut oil.
- Then combine all of the ingredients and equally distribute them on the pot.
- Cook the mixture for around 4 to 5 hours, or till it is thoroughly cooked.
- Allow 30 minutes for cooling before scooping out with a large spoon or cookie scoop. Make balls out of it.
- If desired, drizzle the snack with the caramel glaze.

4. Crock-Pot Stuffed Peppers

(Preparation time: 20 minutes | Cooking time: 8 hours | Servings: 4)
Per serving: Calories 233, Total fat 11g, Protein 15g, Carbs 18g

Ingredients:

- 6 ounces of tomato paste
- 1/4 cup of beef stock
- 1 diced onion
- Salt & pepper to taste
- 1 lb. of ground meat
- 1/4 cup of Italian seasoning blend
- 4 cloves of garlic, minced
- 4 bell peppers
- 1 diced radish
- 1/2 head of cauliflower

Instructions:

- Pulse garlic, onion, carrots, and cauliflower till fine inside a food processor. Then take off the tops of the peppers but leave them whole. Remove the seeds as well.
- Combine the peppers, salt, seasonings, meat, tomato paste, and veggies inside a mixing dish, then spoon the combination into the peppers.
- To place the peppers inside the Crock-Pot, try to level them off at the top. Place the pepper tops on top of them now. Pour the liquid into the Crock-Pot's bottom, then simmer the mixture on low for around 6-8 hours.
- Serve with your choice of toppings.

5. Cereal Mix with Peanuts

(Preparation time: 20 minutes | Cooking time: 3 hours | Servings: 12)
Per serving: Calories 101, Total fat 6g, Protein 2g, Carbs 11g

Ingredients:

- 4 cups of rice cereal
- 1 cup of peanuts
- 5 cups of corn cereal
- A pinch of black pepper
- 2 cups of pretzels
- 1/2 teaspoon of allspice
- 1 cup of breakfast cereal of choice
- 1/4 cup of Worcestershire sauce
- 1 teaspoon of garlic powder
- 1/3 cup of melted butter
- 1 tablespoon of seasoned salt

Instructions:

- Place corn cereal, breakfast cereal, rice cereal, pretzels, & peanuts inside the Crock-Pot.
- To prepare the sauce, whisk together the remaining ingredients inside a medium-sized mixing bowl or measuring cup. To blend, whisk everything together thoroughly.
- Pour the sauce over the cereal-nut mixture & stir well. Toss everything together.
- Cover and simmer on low heat for around 3 hours, stirring once an hour. You can keep this delicious snack for up to around 3 weeks in an airtight container.

6. Crispy Hot Chicken Taquitos

(Preparation time: 20 minutes | Cooking time: 8 hours | Servings: 8)

Per serving: Calories 227, Total fat 14g, Protein 11g, Carbs 15g

Ingredients:

3 roughly chopped jalapeños
- 1 ½ cups of cream cheese
- 16 taco-sized flour tortillas
- 1/2 cup of water
- 1/2 teaspoon of garlic powder
- 4 medium-sized chicken breasts
- 1/2 cup of Mexican blend cheese
- 1/2 teaspoon of onion powder
- Green goddess dressing to taste
- 1 teaspoon of salt
- 1 ½ cups of Monterey Jack, shredded

Instructions:

- Inside a Crock-Pot, combine chicken, cream cheese, water, garlic powder, jalapenos, onion powder, and salt. Cook on low for around 8 hours, covered.
- Preheat your oven at 425°F and spray a cookie sheet using nonstick cooking spray in the meantime.
- Using shredder claws or 2 forks, shred cooked chicken. Remove from a Crock-Pot. To blend, stir everything together.
- After that, soften the flour tortillas in the microwave.
- Top each tortilla with a slice of cheese. Place 3 tablespoons chicken mixture on top.
- Taquitos are made by rolling packed tortillas into logs. Taquitos should be baked for around 15 minutes inside a preheated oven.
- Enjoy with a side of green goddess dressing!

7. Cinnamon Vanilla Walnuts

(Preparation time: 10 minutes | Cooking time: 3 hours | Servings: 16)

Per serving: Calories 216, Total fat 16g, Protein 4g, Carbs 16g

Ingredients:

- 1 pound of walnut halves
- 2/3 cup of powdered sugar
- 1 stick of butter, melted
- A pinch of salt
- 1 teaspoon of cinnamon
- 1 teaspoon of vanilla

Instructions:

- Inside your Crock-Pot, mix all of the ingredients.
- Cook for around 15 minutes on high with the lid on.
- After that, reduce the flame to low and cook for around 2 hours, stirring occasionally.
- Allow for complete cooling before serving & storing.

8. Chicken Pita Bites

(Preparation time: 10 minutes | Cooking time: 7 hours | Servings: 6)

Per serving: Calories 487, Total fat 19g, Protein 35g, Carbs 46g

Ingredients:

- 2 cloves of garlic, minced
- 1/2 teaspoon of cinnamon
- 1 pound of chicken, cubed
- 3 tablespoons of olive oil
- 1 tablespoon of apple cider vinegar
- 1 chopped large-sized onion
- 1 ½ cups of chicken stock
- 1 teaspoon of celery seeds
- 6 pita bread
- 1 teaspoon of allspice
- 1 teaspoon of paprika
- Salt, to taste

Instructions:

- Heat the olive oil inside a heavy skillet and sauté the garlic and onions till the onion is barely soft.
- Combine the cinnamon, celery seeds, allspice, and paprika. Cook, stirring often, for a few minutes.
- Cook for a few minutes longer, stirring constantly.
- Place the chicken inside the Crock-Pot. Over it, pour the spicy onion mixture.
- Pour in the chicken stock and season using salt & vinegar. Cover using the lid & cook on low for around 7 hours.
- Pitas should be toasted for around 10 minutes or till crispy. Pitas should be cut into small wedges. Serve with chicken that has been cooked.

9. Grandma's Blackberry Compote

(Preparation time: 10 minutes | Cooking time: 7 hours | Servings: 6)
Per serving: Calories 120, Total fat 1g, Protein 1g, Carbs 15g

Ingredients:

- 1/4 cup of brown sugar
- 1/4 cup of lukewarm water
- 2 cups of blackberries
- 1 cinnamon stick
- 6 English muffins or your favorite waffles, as the garnish
- 1 vanilla bean

Instructions:

- Inside a Crock-Pot, combine all of the ingredients.

- Turn your Crock-Pot to low at the start. Cook the compote for around 3 hours, covered.
- Remove the lid, turn to high, and cook for another 4 hours.
- Serve warm alongside English muffins or waffles of your choice. Take pleasure in this delicious old-fashioned snack!

10. Hummus with Carrot Sticks

(Preparation time: 10 minutes | Cooking time: 8 hours | Servings: 20)
Per serving: Calories 199, Total fat 14g, Protein 5g, Carbs 18g

Ingredients:

- 3 tablespoons of tahini (sesame seed paste)
- Water
- 1/2 teaspoon of salt
- 1 lb. of chickpeas, dried
- 2 tablespoons of balsamic vinegar
- 10 large-sized carrots, cut into snack-friendly sizes
- 2 to 3 cloves of garlic

Instructions:

- Fill your Crock-Pot halfway with water. Toss in the chickpeas and leave them to soak overnight.
- Cook for around 8 hours on low the next morning; drain but save the liquid.
- Inside a food processor, combine the cooked chickpeas with the tahini, garlic, balsamic vinegar, and salt. Pulse till creamy & smooth, scraping down the sides as needed.
- Enjoy with carrot sticks on the side!

11. Honey Party Wings

(Preparation time: 10 minutes | Cooking time: 7 hours | Servings: 10)
Per serving: Calories 354, Total fat 22g, Protein 20g, Carbs 20g

Ingredients:

- 1/4 cup of tamari sauce
- 1/2 teaspoon of onion powder
- 3 pounds of chicken wings
- 1/2 teaspoon of ground black pepper
- 1/4 cup of honey
- 1/2 teaspoon of garlic powder
- 1/2 teaspoon of celery salt
- 2 tablespoons of chili sauce

Instructions:

- Position the wings inside a Crock-Pot. Whisk together the remaining ingredients inside a small-sized mixing dish. Toss the wings in the sauce to thoroughly coat them.
- Cook on low for around 7 hours.

12. Juicy Orange Chicken Wings

(Preparation time: 10 minutes | Cooking time: 7 hours | Servings: 8)
Per serving: Calories 561, Total fat 43g, Protein 35g, Carbs 7g

Ingredients:

- 3 tablespoons of molasses
- 1/4 cup of fruit vinegar
- 3 tablespoons of orange juice
- 1/4 cup of tamari sauce
- 4 teaspoons of corn flour
- 2 tablespoons of chopped fresh parsley
- 1 clove of garlic, minced
- 1 tablespoon of water
- 1 teaspoon of ground ginger
- 2 lbs. of chicken wings

Instructions:

- Whisk together the fruit vinegar, ginger, tamari sauce, molasses, garlic, and orange juice inside a measuring cup or mixing bowl. Place the wings inside a Crock-Pot. Pour the orange sauce over the wings and toss to mix. Cook for around 6 to 7 hours on a low setting.

- Combine corn flour and water in a small mixing bowl. In the Crock-Pot, mix the corn flour mixture.
- Cook, covered, till the sauce has thickened. Serve hot or at room temperature, garnished with fresh parsley.

13. Kielbasa Bites with Tomato-Mustard Sauce

(Preparation time: 10 minutes | Cooking time: 5 hours | Servings: 6)
Per serving: Calories 400, Total fat 28g, Protein 13g, Carbs 29g

Ingredients:

- 1 tablespoon of soy sauce
- 2 cups of tomato paste
- 1 chili pepper, minced
- 2 tablespoons of tomato ketchup
- 1/2 cup of honey
- 1/2 cup of bourbon
- 1 tablespoon of orange juice
- 2 pounds of kielbasa, cut into 1/2-inch-thick rounds
- 1 teaspoon of mustard
- 1 cup of finely chopped shallots

Instructions:

- Inside the Crock-Pot, combine all of the ingredients.
- Cook on low for around 5 hours, covered with the lid.
- Serve with cocktail sticks & additional mustard.

14. Mexican Queso Fundido

(Preparation time: 20 minutes | Cooking time: 2 hours | Servings: 16)
Per serving: Calories 241, Total fat 19g, Protein 15g, Carbs 3g

Ingredients:

- 1/2 chopped roasted red pepper
- 1 ½ cups of sharp cheese shredded

- 16 corn tortillas, warm
- 2 teaspoons of pickled jalapeño chilies
- 1 cup of reduced-fat processed cheese, cubed
- Chopped chives as the garnish
- 2/3 cup of milk
- Chopped cilantro as the garnish
- 1 cup of chopped chorizo sausage

Instructions:

- Inside a Crock-Pot, combine the cheeses & simmer on high for around 30 minutes, or till melted.
- Cover & cook for around 1 1/2 hours, or till tortillas, cilantro, & chives are soft.
- To make the tortillas, divide the prepared mixture among them. Roll up with cilantro & chives sprinkled on top. Enjoy!

15. Mexican-Style Appetizer

(Preparation time: 10 minutes | Cooking time: 6 hours | Servings: 24)
Per serving: Calories 239, Total fat 18g, Protein 13g, Carbs 6g

Ingredients:

- 2-3 minced cloves of garlic
- 1/2 cup of tomato juice
- 3 pounds of lean ground beef, cooked & drained
- Salt to taste
- 1 medium-sized sliced yellow onion
- 2 pounds of cream cheese, cut into cubes
- 1 (15-ounces) can of refried beans
- 1 cup of tomato paste
- 1 cup of salsa
- 1 teaspoon of cayenne peppers

Instructions:

- Brown ground beef inside a large skillet on a medium flame for around 10 minutes. Place inside the Crock-Pot.
- Stir in the other ingredients till well combined.
- Cook for around 4 to 6 hours on low, stirring every 30 minutes.

- Season to taste, and if necessary, add more spices.

16. Old-Fashion Chicken Liver Pâté

(Preparation time: 10 minutes | Cooking time: 3 hours | Servings: 16)
Per serving: Calories 66, Total fat 5g, Protein 3g, Carbs 2g

Ingredients:

- 1 apple, peeled, cored & chopped
- 1 pound of chicken livers
- 1/2 teaspoon of paprika
- 1/4 cup of finely chopped red onion
- Salt, to taste
- 1/2 cup of butter, at room temperature
- 1/2 teaspoon of ground black pepper

Instructions:

- Inside a Crock-Pot, cook all of the ingredients for around 3 hours.
- Place the mixture inside a food processor. Puree till thick and creamy.
- With crackers, serve cold.

17. Saucy Cocktail Franks

(Preparation time: 10 minutes | Cooking time: 4 hours | Servings: 8)
Per serving: Calories 151, Total fat 11g, Protein 5g, Carbs 10g

Ingredients:

- 2 tablespoons of apple juice
- 3 cloves of minced garlic
- 1/4 cup of tomato sauce
- 2 tablespoons of soy sauce
- 2/3 cup of apricot preserves
- 1/4 teaspoon of black pepper
- 2 tablespoons of apple cider vinegar
- 1 shallot, chopped
- 2 pounds of mini cocktail frankfurters
- 1/3 cup of chicken stock
- 1/4 teaspoon of cayenne pepper

Instructions:

- Incorporate all ingredients inside a Crock-Pot, except for the franks, and stir well to combine.
- After that, throw in some franks.
- Cook on high for around 3 to 4 hours, covered.
- Serve with toothpicks and mustard on the side.

18. Sweet Hot Bites

(Preparation time: 10 minutes | Cooking time: 4 hours | Servings: 8)
Per serving: Calories 233, Total fat 13g, Protein 9g, Carbs 18g

Ingredients:

- 1 teaspoon of mustard
- 1 ½ pounds of Mennonite sausage, cut into rounds
- 2 bay leaves
- 1 cup of apricot jam
- 2 teaspoons of Sriracha Hot Sauce

Instructions:

- Inside the Crock-Pot, arrange the sausage. After that, add the bay leaves. Combine the remaining ingredients inside a measuring cup. Whisk everything together till it is completely smooth. Add to the Crock-Pot. Cover and cook for around 4 hours on high. Place each sausage round on a serving tray and secure it with a toothpick.

19. Three-Cheese Bean Appetizer

(Preparation time: 20 minutes | Cooking time: 2 hours | Servings: 16)
Per serving: Calories 323, Total fat 17g, Protein 12g, Carbs 32g

Ingredients:

- 1/2 cup of grated sharp blue cheese
- 1 cup of cubed Provolone cheese
- 1 can of diced green chilies

- 1 cup of cream cheese, at room temperature
- 2-3 cloves of garlic, minced
- 1/2 cup of mayonnaise
- 1 teaspoon of Tabasco sauce
- 1 cup of canned kidney beans, drained & rinsed

Instructions:

- Inside your Crock-Pot, combine all of the ingredients.
- Cover & cook on high for around 1 to 12 hours.
- Serve with your preferred dips & have fun!

20. Zesty Chicken Drumettes

(Preparation time: 10 minutes | Cooking time: 7 hours | Servings: 6)
Per serving: Calories 308, Total fat 6g, Protein 11g, Carbs 25g

Ingredients:

- 1 teaspoon of Creole mustard
- 1 cup of apples, cubed
- 1 teaspoon of lemon rind
- 1/2 teaspoon of ground black pepper
- 1/2 cup of honey
- Salt, to taste
- 10-12 chicken drumettes
- 1 tablespoon of lemon juice
- 1/4 teaspoon of grated ginger
- 1/2 cup of soy sauce
- 1 minced garlic clove

Instructions:

- To make the sauce, combine all ingredients, except for the chicken drumettes, in a medium-sized mixing bowl. To blend, whisk everything together thoroughly.
- After that, rinse and drain the chicken drumettes underneath cold running water.
- Place the chicken drumettes inside the Crock-Pot and pour the sauce over them.
- Cook on low for around 7 hours, covered. Warm it up and enjoy it!

Chapter 9:
Crock-Pot Dessert Recipes

1. Apricot-Peach Crisp with Walnuts

(Preparation time: 20 minutes | Cooking time: 2 hours | Servings: 4)
Per serving: Calories 412, Total fat 16g, Protein 6g, Carbs 50g

Ingredients:

- 6 peaches, pitted & sliced
- 1 teaspoon of ground cinnamon
- 6 apricots, halved
- 3/4 cup of rolled oats
- 1 teaspoon of ground cloves
- 6 tablespoons of margarine, softened
- 1/2 teaspoon of grated ginger
- 1/2 cup of packed light brown sugar
- 1/4 cup of granulated sugar
- 1 cup of walnuts
- Non-stick spray
- 1/2 cup of whole wheat pastry flour

Instructions:

- Place the apricots & peaches inside a dish. Combine the cinnamon, cloves, ginger, and sugar.
- Use nonstick cooking spray to coat your Crock-Pot. Arrange the apricots & peaches inside the Crock-Pot's bottom.
- Inside a food processor, combine the remaining ingredients, except for the walnuts, to make the topping. Pulse the mixture a few times till it is homogenous. The walnuts should then be roughly chopped and added to the prepared topping.
- Inside the Crock-Pot, evenly distribute the topping over the apricots & peaches. Cook for around 2 hours on high, covered. With a dollop of whipped cream, serve warm or cooled.

2. Apple and Almond Sweet Delight

(Preparation time: 20 minutes | Cooking time: 4 hours | Servings: 8)
Per serving: Calories 354, Total fat 13g, Protein 2g, Carbs 49g

Ingredients:

- 1 tablespoon of lemon juice
- Non-stick spray cooking spray
- 1/4 cup of melted butter
- 8 medium-sized apples, cored & sliced
- 1/2 teaspoon cinnamon
- 4 tablespoons of water
- Whipped cream for the serving
- 1/2 cup of chopped almonds
- 1/2 teaspoon of grated nutmeg
- 1/3 cup of sugar

Instructions:

- Using nonstick cooking spray, coat the Crock-Pot. Arrange the apples inside the Crock-Pot's bottom.
- Toss in the remaining ingredients inside the Crock-Pot.
- Cook for around 4 hours on low with the lid on. Serve cold with whipped cream on top.

3. Apple Brown Betty

(Preparation time: 20 minutes | Cooking time: 3 hours | Servings: 6)
Per serving: Calories 317, Total fat 15g, Protein 2g, Carbs 44g

Ingredients:

- 1 tablespoon of fresh orange juice
- 1/4 teaspoon of allspice

- 1 tablespoon of margarine, melted
- 1/2 teaspoon of cinnamon
- 6 apples, peeled, cored & cubed
- 1 tablespoon of maple syrup
- 1 ¾ cups of bread cubes
- 1/2 teaspoon of grated nutmeg
- 1/4 teaspoon of ground mace

Instructions:

- First, rub melted margarine all over the inside of the Crock-Pot. Combine the apples, maple syrup, orange juice, and spices. To incorporate the ingredients, stir them thoroughly. Cook for around 2 hours on high.
- Preheat your oven at 250°F. Spread the bread cubes out onto a baking sheet & bake for around 10 minutes, or till golden.

- Arrange the toasted bread cubes on top of the Crock-Pot mixture. Cook for another 10 minutes on high.

4. Banana Butter Cake with Coconut and Almonds

(Preparation time: 20 minutes | Cooking time: 4 hours | Servings: 8)
Per serving: Calories 444, Total fat 31g, Protein 11g, Carbs 37g

Ingredients:

- 1 cup of granulated white sugar
- 1 stick of butter
- 1/2 cup of half-and-half
- 1 cup of softened cream cheese
- A dash of cinnamon
- 1 1/3 cups of cake flour
- 1 tablespoon of molasses
- 3 medium-sized eggs
- 1/2 cup of chopped almonds
- 1 tablespoon of orange juice
- 1/2 teaspoon of baking powder
- 2 ripe bananas, sliced
- 1/2 cup of unsweetened grated coconut
- A dash of cardamom

- 1 teaspoon of baking soda
- A pinch of salt

Instructions:

- Inside a food processor, combine the half-and-half butter, orange juice, cheese, sugar, molasses, eggs, and bananas. Combine all ingredients inside a food processor and process till smooth. Combine the cake flour, baking soda, cinnamon, baking powder, salt, and cardamom inside a separate mixing bowl. Stir everything together thoroughly.
- Scrape the creamy banana mixture. Stir once more. Combine the almonds & coconut. Using parchment paper, line the bottom of your Crock-Pot and pour in the prepared batter.
- Cook on low for around 4 hours, covered.

5. Brownies with Hazelnut Ice Cream

(Preparation time: 20 minutes | Cooking time: 3 hours | Servings: 6)
Per serving: Calories 734, Total fat 59g, Protein 14g, Carbs 47g

Ingredients:

- 3 eggs, beaten
- 1 stick of melted butter
- 1/2 teaspoon of grated nutmeg
- 1 ½ cups of sugar
- 1/2 cup of chocolate chunks
- 2/3 cup of cocoa powder, unsweetened
- 1/2 teaspoon of ground cinnamon
- 1/3 cup of cake flour
- Hazelnut ice cream, as the garnish
- 1 teaspoon of pure hazelnut extract
- A pinch of kosher salt

Instructions:

- Using a large piece of foil, line a Crock-Pot & grease it thoroughly.
- Melted butter, sugar, eggs, cocoa, cake flour, and hazelnut essence are whisked together. Sprinkle with nutmeg, cinnamon,

and salt to taste. Mix in the chocolate chunks last.

- Scrape the batter into the Crock-Pot. Cover and cook on low for around 3 hours, or till the cake is gooey in the middle.
- Serve the cake with the hazelnut ice cream while it is still warm.

6. Baked Stuffed Apples with Currants

(Preparation time: 20 minutes | Cooking time: 3 hours | Servings: 4)
Per serving: Calories 362, Total fat 18g, Protein 3g, Carbs 53g

Ingredients:

- 1/4 cup of Zante currants
- 4 Jonathan apples, cored
- 1/4 teaspoon of ground cloves
- 1/4 cup of rolled oats
- 1/2 teaspoon of grated nutmeg
- 2 tablespoons of brown sugar
- 1/2 cup of orange juice
- 1/2 teaspoon of ground cinnamon
- 1 tablespoon of margarine

Instructions:

- Use a Crock-Pot liner to line your Crock-Pot. Arrange the apples in the Crock-Pot that has been prepped. Combine the remaining ingredients, except for the orange juice, inside a medium-sized mixing dish.
- Using a metal spatula, spoon the oat mixture into the middle of each apple. Inside the Crock-Pot, pour orange juice all around apples. Cook for around 3 hours on low with the lid on. Serve cooked apples in attractive serving bowls.

7. Country Apple Cake with Walnuts

(Preparation time: 20 minutes | Cooking time: 4 hours | Servings: 8)
Per serving: Calories 572, Total fat 28g, Protein 8g, Carbs 45g

Ingredients:

- 1 cup of granulated white sugar
- 1⁄2 cup of buttermilk
- 1 teaspoon of baking powder
- 1 cup of cream cheese, softened
- 1/4 teaspoon of allspice
- 1 stick of butter
- 2 tart apples, sliced
- 3 lightly beaten eggs
- 1/4 teaspoon of ground mace
- 1 1/3 cups of fine pastry flour
- 1 cup of chopped walnuts
- Sea salt, taste

Instructions:

- Inside a food processor, combine butter, cream cheese, buttermilk, sugar, eggs, and apples. Blend till the ingredients are thoroughly combined.
- Next, add your fine pastry flour, mace, baking powder, sea salt, and allspice in a separate mixing dish. To blend, stir everything together.
- Scrape the apple mixture into the pan. To blend, stir everything together. Combine the walnuts & fold them in.
- Cover the bottom of the Crock-Pot using parchment paper before pouring the batter in.
- Cook on low for around 4 hours, covered.

8. Chocolate and Peach Bread Pudding

(Preparation time: 20 minutes | Cooking time: 4 hours | Servings: 8)

Per serving: Calories 324, Total fat 15g, Protein 9g, Carbs 41g

Ingredients:

- 1 ½ cups of canned peaches, drained
- Non-stick cooking spray (butter flavor)
- 1 cup of cocoa
- 5 ½ cups of whole-wheat bread, cubed
- 1/4 teaspoon of allspice
- 1 ½ cups of reduced-fat evaporated milk
- A pinch of salt
- 1/4 cups of honey
- 1/2 teaspoon of grated ginger
- 1 cup of brown sugar
- 2 eggs

Instructions:

- Using cooking spray, coat the inside of a Crock-Pot. Inside a Crock-Pot, combine bread cubes and peaches.
- Heat the sugar, milk, honey, and cocoa inside a large, deep saucepan on medium flame, often stirring, for around 5 minutes.
- 1/2 of the mixture should be whisked into the eggs; season using salt, allspice, & grated ginger; return egg mixture to saucepan. Inside the Crock-Pot, pour this mixture over the bread & peaches.
- Cook for around 4 hours on high, or till the pudding is set. Serve warm and enjoy it!

9. Coconut Bananas Foster

(Preparation time: 20 minutes | Cooking time: 2 hours | Servings: 4)

Per serving: Calories 355, Total fat 12g, Protein 1g, Carbs 41g

Ingredients:

- 1 tablespoon of maple syrup
- Non-stick cooking spray (butter flavor)
- 1/2 teaspoon of grated ginger
- 4 ripe bananas, halved
- 1 teaspoon of almond extract
- 1 cup of granulated sugar
- 1/4 teaspoon of ground cloves
- 3 tablespoons of melted butter
- 1/4 cup of shredded coconut
- 1/4 cup of water
- 1/2 teaspoon of ground cinnamon

Instructions:

- Using cooking spray, coat the interior of your Crock-Pot.
- In the bottom of the Crock-Pot, place bananas.
- Combine the remaining ingredients, except for the coconut, in a mixing dish; pour on banana slices. Cook for around 2 hours on low with the cover on. Serve warm with shredded coconut on top.

10. Chocolate Pecan Cheesecake

(Preparation time: 20 minutes | Cooking time: 3 hours | Servings: 8)

Per serving: Calories 493, Total fat 33g, Protein 7g, Carbs 42g

Ingredients:

- 2 large-sized whole eggs
- 1/4 cup of toasted pecans, ground
- 1/2 cup of sugar
- 1 teaspoon of almond extract
- 3 tablespoons of honey
- 1 cup of vanilla wafer cookie crumbs
- 1/3 cup of mini chocolate morsels
- 2 tablespoons of melted butter
- A pinch of salt
- 1 lb. of crumbled cream cheese
- Cocoa powder for the garnish
- 1/2 cup of toasted pecans, chopped
- 1 tablespoon of corn flour
- 3/4 cup of sour cream

Instructions:

- To prepare the crust, inside a spring form pan, combine vanilla wafer cookie crumbs, pecans, honey, and butter; pat mixture evenly on the bottom of the pan.

- Combine sugar & cream cheese inside a mixing bowl and beat till frothy and homogeneous.
- Combine the eggs, corn flour, pecans, small chocolate morsels, and salt. Pour in the sour cream & pure almond essence into the prepared pie crust.
- In your Crock-Pot, place the pan on a rack, cover using the lid, & cook on high for around 3 hours.
- Refrigerate for at least one night. Serve chilled, dusted with the chocolate powder.

11. Country Honey-Sauced Pears

(Preparation time: 20 minutes | Cooking time: 3 hours | Servings: 6)

Per serving: Calories 425, Total fat 15g, Protein 3g, Carbs 51g

Ingredients:

- 1/2 cup of brown sugar
- 6 pears, peeled & cored
- 1/2 teaspoon of ground mace
- 1/4 cup of honey
- 1 tablespoon of corn flour
- 1 tablespoon of butter, melted
- 2 tablespoons of lemon juice
- 1 teaspoon of lemon zest
- 1/4 teaspoon of ground ginger

Instructions:

- Inside a Crock-Pot, arrange the pears upright.
- Combine all remaining ingredients in a bowl, except for the corn flour and lemon juice, and pour over pears.
- Cover and cook on high for around 2 1/2 hours, or till the pears are soft.
- Transfer the pears to the dessert bowls after removing them from the Crock-Pot.

- Blend corn flour with lemon juice inside a mixing bowl; stir to mix; pour into the Crock-Pot. Cover & cook on high for around 10 minutes, or till sauce has thickened.
- Turn your Crock-Pot off. Serve with a dollop of sauce on top of the pears.

12. Hot Chocolate Fondue

(Preparation time: 20 minutes | Cooking time: 2 hours | Servings: 12)

Per serving: Calories 103, Total fat 6g, Protein 2g, Carbs 11g

Ingredients:

- 1 cup of heavy cream
- 1/2 teaspoon of ground cinnamon
- 2 sticks of butter
- 2 cups of semisweet chocolate chips
- 1/2 cup of corn syrup
- 1 tablespoon of vanilla
- Pinch of salt
- 1/4 teaspoon of grated nutmeg

Instructions:

- Inside the Crock-Pot, combine the butter, salt, heavy cream, cinnamon, corn syrup, and nutmeg.
- Cook on low for around 1 hour, covered with the lid.
- Then, using a heatproof spatula, whisk in the other ingredients, cover, & cook for another 1 hour.
- Combine the chocolate chips & vanilla extract. Whisk till all the chocolate has melted.

13. Orange Tapioca Pudding

(Preparation time: 20 minutes | Cooking time: 3 hours | Servings: 8)

Per serving: Calories 190, Total fat 6g, Protein 5g, Carbs 30g

Ingredients:

- 2 teaspoons of orange extract
- 1/2 cup of sugar
- 3 egg yolks
- 4 cups of milk
- 1/2 teaspoon of allspice
- A pinch of salt
- Oranges, sectioned
- 1/2 cup of small tapioca pearls

Instructions:

- Inside a Crock-Pot, combine the sugar, allspice, milk, orange extract, salt, and tapioca pearls. Whisk till the sugar is completely dissolved.
- Cook for around 2 hours on high in the Crock-Pot, covered.
- Whisk the egg yolks inside a small-sized mixing dish till foamy. Pour one tablespoon of the hot tapioca pudding from Crock-Pot into the egg yolks & mix well.
- Then add the hot pudding to the egg yolks in a steady stream till you have roughly 2 cups of pudding-yolk combination.
- Slowly add this mixture into the remaining tapioca pudding inside the Crock-Pot; mix for around 4 to 5 minutes, or till everything is completely integrated. Cook for another hour on low. Enjoy when it is still warm, with oranges.

14. Orange-Glazed Chocolate Cake

(Preparation time: 20 minutes | Cooking time: 4 hours | Servings: 8)

Per serving: Calories 410, Total fat 14g, Protein 5g, Carbs 48g

Ingredients:

- A dash of grated nutmeg
- 3/4 cup of low-fat buttermilk
- 1 teaspoon of orange extract
- 1/4 cup of semisweet chocolate, melted
- 1/2 teaspoon of baking soda
- 1/2 cup of orange juice
- 1/2 teaspoon of baking powder

- 1 cup of sugar, granulated
- 6 tablespoons of butter, at room temperature
- A pinch of salt
- 1 egg
- 1 ½ cups of the cake flour
- 3/4 cup of powdered sugar
- A dash of ground cinnamon

Instructions:

- Combine the baking soda, buttermilk, & baking powder. Inside a large-sized mixing dish, cream together the butter, orange extract, & granulated sugar till light and fluffy.
- Then, while still combining, add the whole egg. Combine nutmeg, flour, cinnamon, and salt. Combine together the egg & buttermilk mixtures. About 1 1/2 cups of the prepared batter should be set aside; the remaining batter should be mixed with the melted chocolate. Next, alternately spoon batters into a greased & floured cake pan, swirling gently using a knife. Place the cake pan on the rack in the Crock-Pot, cover, and cook on high for around 4 hours. In the meantime, create orange syrup according to the instructions below. Heat three powdered sugar & orange juice inside a small-sized saucepan, stirring constantly. Cook till the sugar is completely dissolved.
- Pour the orange syrup over the prepared cake and set it aside for cooling before serving.

15. Peanut Butter Pudding Cake

(Preparation time: 20 minutes | Cooking time: 2 hours | Servings: 12)

Per serving: Calories 327, Total fat 17g, Protein 8g, Carbs 38g

Ingredients:

- 1 cup of peanut butter
- Non-stick cooking spray
- 2 tablespoons of boiling water

- 1/2 cup of sugar
- 2 cups of boiling water
- 1 ½ cups of whole wheat pastry flour
- 6 tablespoons of cocoa powder
- 3/4 cup of fat-free sour cream
- 1 teaspoon of baking powder
- 3 tablespoons of margarine, melted
- 2 tablespoons of chocolate syrup
- 3/4 cup of sugar

Instructions:

- Spray the inside of a Crock-Pot using nonstick cooking spray before starting. Combine the flour, sugar, & baking powder inside a mixing dish. Combine peanut butter, melted margarine, sour cream, & 2 tablespoons of boiling water in a separate bowl. To produce the batter, combine the wet & creamy peanut butter combination with the dry sugar-flour mixture. Fill the oiled Crock-Pot halfway using batter.
- Combine 3/4 cup of sugar, cocoa, with 2 cups of boiling water inside a mixing dish. In the Crock-Pot, pour the cocoa mixture over the batter.
- Set your Crock-Pot on high and simmer for around 1 1/2 hours, covered. Allow 20 minutes for the pudding to cool before drizzling using the chocolate syrup and serve.

16. Peach Hazelnut Cobbler

(Preparation time: 20 minutes | Cooking time: 2 hours | Servings: 8)
Per serving: Calories 182, Total fat 8g, Protein 2g, Carbs 26g

Ingredients:

- 1 (18-ounces) package of yellow cake mix
- 2 (21-ounces) cans of peach pie filling
- Whipped cream, as the garnish
- 1 stick of butter, melted
- 1/3 cup of hazelnuts

Instructions:

- Fill the Crock-Pot halfway with peach pie filling.
- Crumble the butter into the cake mix. In the crock cooker, evenly spread the pie filling.
- Finish with a sprinkling of hazelnuts. Cook for around 2 hours on high. Warm whipped cream is served on top. Enjoy!

17. Pear Honey Crumble

(Preparation time: 20 minutes | Cooking time: 4 hours | Servings: 6)
Per serving: Calories 366, Total fat 16g, Protein 4g, Carbs 45g

Ingredients:

- 2 tablespoons of brown sugar
- Non-stick cooking spray
- 1/8 cup of all-purpose flour
- 1 cup of cherries
- 3 sliced red pears
- 1/2 teaspoon of grated ginger
- 1 tablespoon of honey
- 1 teaspoon of cinnamon
- 2 tablespoons of unsalted butter, melted
- 1/4 teaspoon of ground cloves
- 1/2 cup oats

Instructions:

- Spray the inside of your Crock-Pot using nonstick cooking spray. Combine the cherries, pears, and brown sugar. Cook on high for around 3 hours. Combine the honey, butter, ginger, oats, flour, cloves, and cinnamon inside a medium-sized mixing dish.
- Cook on high for around 40 minutes after sprinkling the mixture over the fruit inside the Crock-Pot.

18. Rice Pudding with Blueberries and Almonds

(Preparation time: 20 minutes | Cooking time: 2 hours | Servings: 6)
Per serving: Calories 364, Total fat 19g, Protein 6g, Carbs 41g

Ingredients:

- 1 tablespoon of molasses
- 2 cups of water
- 1/2 teaspoon of ground cloves
- 1 cup of milk
- 1 cup of buttermilk
- 1/2 cup of sugar
- 1 cup of blueberries for serving
- 3/4 cup of brown rice, cooked
- 1/2 cup of slivered almonds
- 1/2 teaspoon of ground cinnamon

Instructions:

- In your Crock-Pot, combine all of the ingredients except for the almonds and raspberries.
- Slowly cook for around 1 1/2 to 2 hours on high.
- Serve with blueberries & slivered almonds on top. Enjoy!

19. Vanilla Strawberry Cobbler

(Preparation time: 20 minutes | Cooking time: 2 hours | Servings: 6)
Per serving: Calories 353, Total fat 20g, Protein 4g, Carbs 42g

Ingredients:

- 1 cup of whole wheat pastry flour
- Cooking spray
- 1/4 cup of melted butter
- 1 (21-ounces) can of strawberry pie filling
- 1/2 teaspoon of vanilla extract
- 1/4 cup of sugar

- Mixed berries for the garnish
- 1 teaspoon of baking powder
- 1/2 cup of milk

Instructions:

- Use cooking spray to coat the interior of your Crock-Pot.
- Inside the bottom of the Crock-Pot, spread the strawberry pie filling. Combine the remaining ingredients, except for the mixed berries, inside a medium-sized mixing bowl. Spread the strawberry pie filling evenly with the mixture.
- Cook for roughly around 2 hours on high, covered. Enjoy with a garnish of mixed berries!

20. White Chocolate and Strawberry Pie

(Preparation time: 20 minutes | Cooking time: 3 hours | Servings: 10)
Per serving: Calories 396, Total fat 28g, Protein 4g, Carbs 34g

Ingredients:

- 1 (18.25-ounces) package of cake mix
- 1/2 cup of white chocolate, broken into tiny pieces
- 21 ounces of strawberry pie filling
- 1/2 cup of margarine, melted

Instructions:

- Inside the bottom of a Crock-Pot, layer strawberry pie filling.
- Combine the remainder of the ingredients inside a large mixing dish. Over the strawberry pie filling, spread the mixture.
- Cook on low for around 3 hours, covered with the lid.
- Serve warm with a sprinkling of chocolate chunks on top.

Table of Tool Usage

Below is the list of tools used in the recipes.

1. Crock-Pot (all sizes or your preferred size)

2. Mixing dishes (small, medium and large)

3. Kitchen paper, parchment paper and aluminum foil

4. Blender

5. Food processor

6. Measuring cups and spoons

7. Skillet (small, medium and large)

8. Serving dishes/bowls/platters

9. Baking pans/sheets

10. Cake pan/Loaf pan

11. Chopping board

12. Mortar and pestle

13. Slotted spoon

14. Oven

15. Microwave

16. Saucepan and frying pan

17. Kitchen knives

18. Kitchen fork and spoons

19. Crockery liner

20. Dutch oven

21. Crock-Pot's rack

22. Strainer and sieve

23. Whisk

24. Electric beater

25. Roasting pan

26. Spatulas

27. Apron

28. Spring form pan

29. Oven-safe bowls

30. Heatproof spatula

31. Disposable Crock-Pot liner

Conclusion

We hope after reading this book, you have been inspired to use that Crock-Pot that has been gathering dust in your closet. Crock-Pots are a must-have kitchen appliance. You may use them to produce everything from main courses to appetizers and desserts. They are quite adaptable.

It is difficult to burn anything in them, and the recipes almost always turn out well. The nicest part is that there is almost never any fuss. You just pour the stuff in and let them go for a bit. You can even use a Crock-Pot for cooking while you are at work and enjoy it within minutes of getting home.

For family meals or parties, use your crock cooker. For a potluck supper, you can even serve your food straight from the Crock-Pot put on the table. Slow cooking has the advantage of retaining flavor & moisture in a recipe much better than baking, which causes liquids and flavors to evaporate. I guarantee that a Swiss steak cooked in a Dutch oven on the stove will never be as tasty as one cooked in a Crock-Pot.

A Crock-Pot is essential, especially if you are short on time. Simply combine all of the ingredients and cook your dinner during the night or while you are at work, and you will wake up or return home to a delicious meal. Is not that incredible?

Hopefully, pages of this book will help you create one of the most delicious recipes with easy-to-follow instructions for yourself, your family and friends. Good luck!

Made in the USA
Monee, IL
07 September 2022